HEIDEGGER AND THE DESTRUCTION OF ARISTOTLE

Northwestern University
Studies in Phenomenology
and
Existential Philosophy

General Editor   Anthony J. Steinbock

HEIDEGGER AND THE DESTRUCTION OF ARISTOTLE

On How to Read the Tradition

Sean D. Kirkland

Northwestern University Press
Evanston, Illinois

Northwestern University Press
www.nupress.northwestern.edu

Copyright © 2023 by Northwestern University. Published 2023 by Northwestern University Press. All rights reserved.

10 9 8 7 6 5 4 3 2 1

Library of Congress Cataloging-in-Publication Data

Names: Kirkland, Sean D., author.

Title: Heidegger and the destruction of Aristotle : on how to read the tradition / Sean D Kirkland.

Other titles: Northwestern University studies in phenomenology & existential philosophy.

Description: Evanston, Illinois : Northwestern University Press, 2023. | Series: Northwestern University studies in phenomenology and existential philosophy | Includes bibliographical references and index.

Identifiers: LCCN 2023007866 | ISBN 9780810146181 (paperback) | ISBN 9780810146198 (cloth) | ISBN 9780810146204 (ebook)

Subjects: LCSH: Heidegger, Martin, 1889–1976. | Aristotle. | Hermeneutics. | BISAC: PHILOSOPHY / Movements / Phenomenology | PHILOSOPHY / History & Surveys / Ancient & Classical

Classification: LCC B3279.H49 K529 2023 | DDC 193—dc23/eng/20230221

LC record available at https://lccn.loc.gov/2023007866

Contents

	Preface	vii
	List of Abbreviations	xv
	Introduction	3
1	The Experiential and the Conceptual in the Aristotelian Text	30
2	The Ground of Metaphysics and the *Krisis* in the Aristotelian Text	50
3	Three Aristotelian Concepts Destroyed	80
	Conclusion: The Turn and a "More Faithful Adherence to the Principle" of Destruction	108
	Acknowledgments	119
	Notes	121
	Bibliography	155
	Index	165

concepts, terminology, and philosophical positions—I became increasingly fascinated by the sophisticated and, to my mind, quite original and powerful *method* that Heidegger was introducing and employing there for interpreting traditionary or tradition-bearing texts.[3] In the lecture courses, papers, and other texts of this period, from 1919 to 1927, the year of *Being and Time*'s publication, Heidegger sometimes discusses this method, which he provocatively calls *Destruktion* or "destruction," in considerable depth and detail before applying it to whatever text he has before him. It is this interpretive approach, taken strictly on its own terms *as a hermeneutic*, that I strive to bring to light in the present volume—the specific steps or elements that are involved when Heidegger employs the method, its organizing aim, and even briefly, perhaps only suggestively, what I perceive to be its potential benefit for us in our present historical moment.

This book does not, therefore, aspire to present a comprehensive scholarly treatment of Heidegger's philosophy of history over the course of his career. Nor does it hope to present a thoroughgoing account of Heidegger's thinking during the decade with which it is concerned—indeed, there are a whole host of themes that are vital to Heidegger's early thought and development, about which I will have little or nothing to say. Insofar as this book aspires to present destruction *as an interpretive method*, it might best be understood ultimately as a sort of manual or a handbook for that method's employment. Other studies have taken up the theme of destruction in the context of the early Heidegger's philosophical project; these have sometimes focused on whether Heidegger's readings of this or that thinker perpetrate a kind of interpretive violence and, if so, whether the violence is defensible or not. They have sometimes focused on his transformation of Husserlian phenomenology, and some of them have even focused on Heidegger's analysis of how one might live "authentically" by interrupting traditional influences and experiencing more thoughtfully and more immediately our defining human finitude. The present study will, to be sure, have ample occasion to address these other scholarly approaches. In any case, what specifically intrigued me when I returned to Heidegger's early lecture courses, and what I will focus on primarily in the following pages, goes largely unaddressed in these various studies—namely, again, the specific steps or moves involved in Heideggerian destruction, or the interpretive technique, in a sense, that distinguishes it from other ways reading a text thoughtfully or critically.

In addition to this limitation in the scope of the project, there is also a certain limitation as regards its audience. At various points, I will refer to "the tradition" or "our tradition," intending specifically the tradition that was inaugurated by ancient Greek thinking, extending from

Preface

In the years since I began working on this project, I have had the opportunity to present the material to several audiences. In light of the ensuing conversations, it has become clear that a preliminary discussion of a few important elements will facilitate the reader's smooth and undistracted movement through the text's central argument. To that end, I would like to address here in a preface some issues relating to this book's limitations, translations, and citations.

First, with respect to its limitations, it may help to tell the story of how this book came to be. I had for several years been researching and writing a monograph on Aristotle and tragic temporality (specifically focused on the *Poetics* and the *Nicomachean Ethics* and Aristotle's presentation of our complex human relation to the past and the future). As I neared the completion of that manuscript, I had occasion to think back to my doctoral studies under Professor Klaus Held at the University of Wuppertal in Nordrhein-Westfalen, Germany. Though I was there to write a dissertation on Plato's early dialogues,[1] I attended as many seminars and participated in as many reading groups as I could during my years there, and because Wuppertal at that time was arguably the foremost department in the entire world for the study of Heidegger,[2] many of those seminars and reading groups focused on the Heideggerian corpus. Indeed, these many years later, I recalled reading for the first time with Wuppertal faculty two of Heidegger's early lecture courses on Aristotle and being fascinated by Heidegger's unorthodox, brilliant, close readings of the Aristotelian text. With this in mind, I decided that I should return briefly to those volumes to investigate whether Heidegger's early engagements with Aristotle might not enter into some fruitful conversation with my own interpretations, especially given that I follow Heidegger in approaching Aristotle as a sort of proto-phenomenologist. That was a little over five years ago now.

What I found when I returned to Heidegger's early lecture courses was quite unexpected. In addition to what had drawn me back to them—the challenging and compelling readings of specific passages in Aristotle and the often profound revelations concerning central Aristotelian

PREFACE

Aristotle down through the ages, and which provides us with many of the fundamental concepts still operative in our way of experiencing and thinking about our world and ourselves. I am well aware that there are many other rich cultural traditions operative in our world today, but the one that links us today back to Aristotle and the Greeks is the focus here. This book begins from the position that this particular traditional inheritance appears today to those of us who count ourselves as its inheritors as in need of, at the very least, questioning and deep examination, and it hopes to show that the destructive mode of interpretation described by the early Heidegger is a peculiarly potent tool for carrying out that urgent task.

The reader will rightly wonder which texts belong to the canon that gathers this "tradition" around itself (as well as which texts do not), and who exactly numbers among this often invoked "we" (and who does not). I am cognizant of the suspect rhetorical ends that the plural first-person pronoun sometimes serves. In response to such questions and concerns, however, I would plea for a stay of determination.[4] Perhaps in the wake of Western colonialism and imperialism, and in the ever more exhaustively globalized and media-saturated world in which we find ourselves today, these questions cannot be resolved *prior to* initiating a thoughtful conversation together about the works and figures that belong to this tradition that we might possibly consider "our own." There are surely some who feel so completely at home in the Western tradition that they are tempted to view it as utterly transparent to them and manipulable by them. Others will feel only lightly touched by it, and others still desperately entangled in it, even captured by it. Preliminarily, I would suggest that it is perhaps the *feeling*, after serious engagement with historical works or figures, of having to *either incorporate or overcome* them, which suggests what belongs to one's tradition and whether one numbers as an inheritor of that tradition. Only if it were *not ours* could we turn away in indifference and simply let it be.

Certainly, the tradition of European thought presents itself to many of us today as eminently question-worthy, ripe for critique or even renunciation. Already in the nineteenth and early twentieth centuries, the thinkers of what Paul Ricoeur refers to as the "school of suspicion,"[5] Marx, Nietzsche, and Freud, were observing their late modern European context and identifying there an economic, cultural, political, religious, and philosophical system that necessarily produced alienation and oppression, suffering and violence, neurosis and self-deception for the human beings in its throes. And even beyond the compelling insights of these critics of late European modernity, the prevalence and evident irrationality of Eurocentric thinking today and the demonstrably catastrophic effects of European colonialism and imperialism must surely provoke deep reservations about its philosophical foundations. Finally, there is the way in which twentieth- and twenty-first-century theorists, focused on issues relating to class, race, gender, sexuality, and other aspects of embodiment and identity, have found ample reason to push the criticism of the Western tradition even further. These critical theorists find that this tradition has not only applied its concepts and values improperly, inconsistently, and unjustly; even more radically, they see certain tendencies toward exclusion, bias, marginalization, and even violence as woven into the fabric of those concepts and values themselves.

In short, even setting aside the philosophical case Heidegger makes for the destructive project in part 1 of *Being and Time* (which we will rehearse in detail in the "Introduction"), there are many reasons today to see the European tradition as nearly everywhere still deeply at work and nearly everywhere urgently in need of critique. And no matter what the provocation, this study suggests, if one finds oneself confronting the problematic character of the European philosophical tradition and if one suspects that this tradition may exert some abiding influence on the way one thinks, experiences, and lives in one's world, the destructive method of approaching traditionary texts identified by the early Heidegger represents an extraordinarily powerful and productive mode of responding.[6] Only time will tell if readers agree. If a reader should find that they confront no such self-critical conundrum in relating to the tradition they inherit, well, there are other books.

It is necessary to address a final limitation, as it were, on the general willingness today to accept Heidegger as the source of a purportedly liberatory and vital critical method for taking up our tradition and thinking in relation to it. And surely there is good reason for this resistance, grounded perhaps in an awareness of Heidegger's condemnable actions before and during World War II, of his subsequent reticence after the war about his own complicity and about the horrors perpetrated under National Socialism, and now, with the rollout of the *Black Notebooks* since 2014, of just how deeply entrenched and how philosophically motivating his antisemitism and reactionary traditionalism ultimately might have been.[7] Nevertheless, I would suggest that the method Heidegger frames in the 1920s for engaging critically with one's tradition is worthy of our interest, because I do not find that method on its own terms to be in any way implicated in the odious ethno-nationalist project that some claim to find in the philosophy of the later Heidegger.

Indeed, this method is fundamentally a way of critiquing and complicating one's traditional inheritance, whatever it is. To be sure, Heidegger did not invent the notion of a historically affected, even determined, consciousness, but inherited this insight from the post-

PREFACE

Enlightenment historicism that runs through the work of Hegel, Herder, Marx, and Nietzsche into those thinkers with whom Heidegger engages directly on this issue.[8] Having inherited that historicist perspective, Heidegger articulates an original method for taking up and working through traditional philosophical texts, which I hope to show, through close readings of the texts of the 1920s, allows one perhaps to suspend the regrettable biases that can accompany any individual's historical perspectival constraints.[9] Would that the later Heidegger had availed himself of his own early method more deeply and more consistently.

Indeed, the method of destructive reading can be employed upon Heidegger's own texts. At one point, we will find Heidegger reading Plato destructively and observing there how the latter "had been caught up fantastically in λόγος and thus, consequently and in a Greek manner, went astray [*dabei, griechisch, konsequent verfährt*]," so that, in Plato's thinking, "the immediate, what is known, is the *average* and in this way *general*. In it everything is seen, addressed, and interpreted on its basis" (*BCArP* 238/352, translation modified). Might we not find, reading the texts of Heidegger destructively, those moments in which Heidegger himself was "caught up fantastically in" the rhetoric of German exceptionalism of his time and that he "went astray" in a manner peculiar to that period in German history, interpreting what he experienced in terms of what was then and there immediate, average, and general?

Second, a couple of notes on translation. Between 1919 and 1928, Heidegger uses the German noun *Destruktion* and the verb *destruieren* frequently and centrally, though not exclusively, to refer to the method of engaging with the works of the Western philosophical tradition, of which he considers himself an inheritor. These terms, as we shall see, are for Heidegger profoundly ambivalent, and for this reason they have confronted thoughtful translators with some resistance. There is a perceived need to indicate *both* a critical, questioning, destabilizing moment *and* a positive, rehabilitating, rejuvenating moment in a single English term. Some translators have suggested "deconstruction," "destructuring," or "dismantling," sometimes introducing a hyphen after the prefix, all in the attempt to fend off any implication of complete annihilation, laying waste, getting rid of, or setting aside. I propose here to render the Heideggerian term with its English cognate "destruction," and even to speak of "destroying" the tradition for the German *destruieren*. Is there a risk of misunderstanding? To be sure. My justification for preferring this translation, with this preliminary discussion as a clarifying caveat, is that Heidegger's original German term is presented again and again *with the very same caveat.* That is, I ask of my English readers no more than what Heidegger asks of his German readers—in what follows, do not hear "destruction" or "destroying" as entailing anything like a simple demolition or annihilation. Rather, try to understand these terms as indicating a complex critical, destabilizing interpretation of the texts of the tradition, which itself in the work of reading also uncovers and accesses previously hidden sources for renewed thinking today.[10]

The period in which we are interested ends with the dramatic raising of "the question of the meaning of Being" (*BT* 19/1) in 1927's *Being and Time*, a question that will remain at the center of Heidegger's thinking over the course of his long subsequent career. For this reason, the translation of terms relating to *Sein* must be discussed. It seems to me that it is important to maintain in English, if possible, the shared root of the gerund *Sein*, the verb *sein* (in its various conjugations), the present participle or verbal adjective *seind*, and the substantive form of that participle, *ein Seiendes* or *das Seinde*. I aspire to translate all of these consistently as, respectively, "Being," "to be" (in its various conjugations), "being," and "a being," "the being," or sometimes, "beings."

One complication that we must recognize from the outset, however, is that for Heidegger in the years leading up to 1927, *Sein* or "Being" comes to have two overlapping but ultimately different referents. On the one hand, Being is what the Western tradition of metaphysics from Plato and Aristotle through to Hegel and Nietzsche, according to Heidegger, has thought as the whole of "what is," as well as the property, determination, or condition that belongs by definition to every member of the class of "beings" or "things that are." On the other hand, Heidegger also wants Being to encompass something in excess of this totality of beings, including something like the ground for or the condition of these beings' being at all, as well as their being recognized and understood by us as beings. Indeed, he will in the years after *Being and Time* attempt to capture this excess to the sum totality of beings with terms like *Ereignis* or "event, eventuation, event of appropriation," *Seyn*, an attested archaic spelling of the gerund, or even the term with a line through it, as ~~Sein~~. Indeed, this latter aspect of Being, its grounding all beings but itself not being a being and thus being somehow in excess of the totality of beings, is what has been forgotten by the Western tradition according to Heidegger and, more importantly, this is precisely what we contact when we subject the traditionary texts of Western metaphysics to destructive reading. In light of this, perhaps the best preliminary definition of "Being" for us now, which might encompass both its metaphysical and, as it were, extra-metaphysical senses, would be something like "the all-encompassing whole that emerges into appearance in our experience and calls forth our questioning and thinking." In the texts we will be taking up, even quite early on as Heidegger's thinking of Being develops, the term can refer *both* to the sum of beings that present themselves to us and their beingness (metaphysical Being) *and* to the sum total of present beings along with the condition for or event of their emergence, which necessarily withdraws itself behind them and has thus traditionally remained utterly hidden and unthought (extra-metaphysical Being).[11] As we shall see, through the destructive reading of Aristotle, we begin by destabilizing the fundamental and all-determining Greek understanding of Being, which Heidegger insists still fundamentally orders the way we relate to our world today, and we end with the possibility of experiencing and thinking Being in a way which includes the source of that originating Greek experience, from within the Aristotelian text, in spite of its having remained hidden for that text's author. (Note that the capitalizing of the term "Being" should suggest something in excess of a being or of all beings, but it should not be taken as substantializing its referent, suggesting some sort of "Super Thing or transcendent being."[12] Not at all. As we shall see, for the early Heidegger, the word "Being" is an arrow pointing to the whole of what is thought by traditional metaphysics, but suggesting ultimately that there is more there at the site of the appearing of beings than metaphysical thinking could recognize; not another as yet non-appearing being standing behind those, but an excess to appearing as such.)

Finally, third, a brief word on citation. All references to Heidegger here are provided in interlinear citations, using abbreviations for the titles and English page numbers (where a translation exists) preceding the original German page numbers. References to Aristotle and Plato are also given interlinear citations in the same way, with the universal Bekker and Stephanus page and section numbering, respectively. See the "List of Abbreviations" for the titles that correspond to these, and the "Bibliography" for full bibliographic information. All references to secondary sources, however, are provided in endnotes after the book's conclusion. I have consigned most discussions of scholarly issues to the notes, excepting a few instances in which it seemed to me that a more extensive engagement with a given interpreter was especially helpful for understanding the Heideggerian text. In the notes, I will sometimes appeal to other scholars for support, sometimes respectfully disagree with them, and sometimes even introduce a topic that I take to be germane to or associated with the trajectory of the discussion in the main text, though not strictly speaking required for following the interpretive argument and evaluating its strength.

It is my hope that this book might appeal not only to specialists working on Heidegger, but to a broader audience as well. As already indicated, it will interest the former because destruction as a technical hermeneutic or interpretive method has not been a focus of much previous scholarly attention. And it will interest the latter, specifically those who wish to take up their own inherited tradition and engage with it critically in order to think more deeply into it, through it, and even beyond it, because the early Heidegger's method of destruction provides a uniquely powerful tool for undertaking that task. The citational measures just described are meant to reduce clutter in the main text and thereby increase its readability for the latter audience. And the main text is intended to provide nothing more, and nothing less, than a very close reading of some rich and even thrilling (yes, thrilling!) passages in Heidegger's early works, which are central to understanding the method of destructive interpretation in all its richness and complexity.

Abbreviations

Works by Heidegger

AM	*Aristotle's Metaphysics Θ1–3: On the Essence and Actuality of Force* (1981), GA 33
BCAncP	*Basic Concepts of Ancient Philosophy* (1926), GA 22
BCArP	*Basic Concepts of Aristotelian Philosophy* (1924), GA 18
BPP	*Basic Problems of Phenomenology* (1927), GA 24
BT	*Being and Time* (1927), GA 2
"BTBT"	"Being-There and Being-True According to Aristotle" (1924), in Kisiel and Sheehan, *Becoming Heidegger*
"Comm."	"Critical Comments on Karl Jaspers' *Psychology of Worldviews*" (1919), in Kisiel and Sheehan, *Becoming Heidegger*
CP	*Contributions to Philosophy* (1936–38), GA 65
"CT"	"The Concept of Time (Lecture)" (1924), GA 64
CT2	*Concept of Time* (Dilthey Draft), 1924, GA 64
"EPTT"	"The End of Philosophy and the Task of Thinking" (1964), GA 14
FCM	*Fundamental Concepts of Metaphysics: World, Finitude, Solitude* (1929/1930), GA 29/30
FS	*Four Seminars* (1973), GA 15
H	*Holzwege* (1950), GA 5
IPR	*Introduction to Phenomenological Research* (1923), GA 17
KPM	*Kant and the Problem of Metaphysics* (1929), GA 3
"LH"	"Letter on Humanism" (1946), GA 9
MLS	*Mein liebes Seelchen! Briefe Martin Heideggers an seine Frau Elfride, 1915–1970* (2005)
"MPSF"	"My Path So Far" (1937/38), in *Besinnung*, GA 66

"MWP"	"My Way into Phenomenology" (1963), in *Zur Sache des Denkens*, GA 14
OWL	*On the Way to Language* (1959), GA 12
"PIA"	"Phenomenological Interpretations with Respect to Aristotle: Indication of the Hermeneutical Situation" (1922), in Kisiel and Sheehan, *Becoming Heidegger*
PIAIPR	*Phenomenological Interpretations of Aristotle: Initiation into Phenomenological Research* (1921–22), GA 61
PIE	*Phenomenology of Intuition and Expression* (1920), GA 59
PISPA	*Phenomenological Interpretations of Select Passages in Aristotle on Ontology and Logik* (1922), GA 62
"Pref."	preface (1963) to Richardson, Heidegger: Through Phenomenology to Thought
PRL	*Phenomenology of Religious Life* (1920–21), GA 60
PS	*Plato's "Sophist"* (1924–25), GA 19
QCT	"Question concerning Technology" (1949), in GA 7
"WDR"	"Wilhelm Dilthey's Research and the Current Struggle for a Historical Worldview" (1925), in Kisiel and Sheehan, Becoming Heidegger
"WM"	"What Is Metaphysics?" (1929), GA 9
"WP"	"What Is Philosophy?" (1955), GA 11
WT	*What Is Called Thinking?* (1951–52), GA 8
WTKLG	*What Is a Thing?* (1935–36), GA 41

Works by Aristotle

Cat.	*Categories*
De int.	*De interpretatione*
Meta.	*Metaphysics*
NE	*Nicomachean Ethics*
Phys.	*Physics*
Pol.	*Politics*
Post. An.	*Posterior Analytics*
Top.	*Topics*

Works by Plato

L	*Laws*
Phdr.	*Phaedrus*
R	*Republic*
Soph.	*Sophist*
Th.	*Theaetetus*

All translations of passages from Aristotle and Plato are my own, from the Oxford Classical Texts critical editions of the Greek, unless otherwise noted.

HEIDEGGER AND THE DESTRUCTION OF ARISTOTLE

Introduction

Being and Time and the Need for Destruction

Before becoming one of the most original and influential thinkers of the twentieth century, Martin Heidegger began his philosophical career, it could be argued, as an interpreter of Aristotle. To be sure, a host of other influences and touchstones played important roles, but in the lecture courses and papers leading up to and just after the 1927 publication of *Being and Time*, Heidegger again and again turns to Aristotle, ultimately producing several lengthy investigations of the works of the ancient Stagirite.[1]

Moreover, beyond the frequency and extent of these early engagements, there is the undeniably central role that Aristotle played in Heidegger's own retrospective estimation of his philosophical development. In a short unpublished piece from 1937–38 called "My Path So Far ("Mein bisheriger Weg"), Heidegger looks back on his transformation from an aspiring student of theology into a young philosopher of evident originality and promise. He tells us that, after completing his habilitation in 1916, on the medieval thinking of the categories in Dun Scotus and Thomas of Erfuhrt, his philosophical path unfolded in "two directions," one phenomenological and the other historical. On the one hand, there was a "genuine training in the procedure of Husserl's 'phenomenology'" and, on the other hand, there was a "resolute return to Greek philosophy in the figure of its first essential culmination—Aristotle" ("MPSF," 412).[2] As one scholar puts it, "it was his reading of Aristotle that made it possible for him to redefine for himself the task of phenomenology."[3] That is to say, in initiating the radical,[4] ontologically focused study of everyday life that marked his first original philosophical contribution and his break from his mentor, Edmund Husserl, Heidegger found it necessary to go deeply and carefully and repeatedly *through* Aristotle.

Why? Why would the project that begins with *Being and Time*'s phenomenological analysis of lived human experience *necessitate* an elaborate historical detour through the work of this ancient Greek philosopher? This is a question that must confront any reader of the early Heidegger.

More vital still is the question that confronts anyone at all who is trying to think philosophically today: do *we* still feel the need for any such historical diversion? Whether or not we are interested in Heidegger and his development, do we see the value in thinking our way through, or even out of, the ancient Greeks, as in some sense the inaugurators of the Western philosophical tradition? Must we really "take on" Aristotle in order to philosophize genuinely at present, or might we be better served by declaring him "ancient history" and turning to fresh contemporary approaches that promise to be unimplicated in problematic historical dynamics and uncompromised by systemic exclusions, marginalizations, and biases?[5]

Here, by way of introduction, I will offer some of Heidegger's reasons for affirming this impulse and insisting on the value, indeed the necessity, of taking on our tradition and Aristotle in particular, as inhabitants of our late- or postmodern historical moment. In the rest of the book, turning from the question of *why* to the question of *how*, I present close readings of some, in my estimation, profound and fascinating passages in which the early Heidegger introduces and then employs a powerful method for approaching the traditionary texts of Western philosophy.

What we will come to see is that the result of taking up our history in this mode will be *neither* a positive appropriation of some timeless pearls of wisdom deposited in the texts of Aristotle, *nor* a negative purgation of that past presuming to liberate us from its noxious influence. No, both the method and its promised benefit for us will prove to be considerably more complex than either of these alternatives. Now, it is true that in the period with which we are concerned, when describing why and how we should approach the texts of the history we inherit, the term Heidegger uses more often than any other is "destruction [*Destruktion*]." From the winter semester of 1919–20, where the word in its technical sense makes its first appearance, through to 1928, when he begins phasing it out and replacing it with other vocabulary and other approaches, Heidegger calls on us to *destruieren* or "destroy" our received tradition.[6] As he cautions again and again throughout this period, however, this project of destruction is not to be taken as predominantly negative.[7] He states directly in *Being and Time* that "to bury the past in nullity is not the purpose of this destruction; its aim is *positive*" (*BT* 44/23). But what precisely would such a *positive destruction* entail?

In certain contexts, to clarify this ambivalence at the heart of the destructive method, Heidegger appeals to a distinction between the "past" and the "tradition" in referring to the interpretive method's proper objects, its material. The former, *die Vergangenheit*, refers to what *was* at a given historical moment and what unfolded there before and through human experience and thought. We relate to this past origin now primarily as what is gone, left behind, covered over. The latter, *die Tradition*, refers to a sum of original intellectual accomplishments of past thinkers, which, once torn from that originating context and inevitably stripped of their initial depth and richness, are then passed along as content through the millennia down to us. As Heidegger writes in 1925:

> Ruthlessness toward the tradition is reverence toward the past, and it is genuine only in an appropriation [*Aneignung*] of the latter (the past) out of a destruction of the former (the tradition). (*PS* 286/414)

Note here that being ruthless with respect to our traditionary texts *is itself* a way of revering the past, and is indeed an *Aneignung*, an "appropriating of" or better a "becoming proper relative to" that past. But one can only identify such ruthlessness with such reverence if there is a fundamentally occluding antagonism between the tradition and the past, such that a destruction of the former can *eo ipso* bring about a proper relation to the latter. What then, we must ask, is the nature of this occluding antagonism between the tradition and the past for Heidegger? To answer that question, let us turn to *Being and Time*.

Distress at the Present Historical Moment

In the "Introduction" to *Being and Time*, Heidegger provides a clear outline of what was to constitute the whole of this never-completed project. Part 1, of which Heidegger completed only the first two thirds, provides a phenomenological analysis of pre-reflective human experience, uncovering the fundamental temporality and, ultimately, historicality of our everyday way of life. That is, it uncovers our peculiar mode of existence, constitutively exposed to our past and our future and utterly immersed in history. According to the plan, part 1 was to be followed by part 2, a series of destructive readings of first Kant, then Descartes, and culminating with Aristotle.[8]

If we view the existing, published text of *Being and Time* in light of this plan, something peculiar suggests itself, something that readers of this masterwork of twentieth-century philosophy rarely perceive. The organizing and motivating aim of the published text of *Being and Time* is to bring the project of destruction to light as the urgent task of our historical moment (*BT* 41/19).[9] The book we call *"Being and Time"* is first and foremost *a call to destruction.*[10]

Let us take up our published version of *Being and Time* with precisely this in mind. The first thing to note is that, to accomplish this organizing aim, there is actually a necessary supplement to the phenomenological analysis of everyday experience and the uncovering of our essential temporality and historicality. That is, there is also a certain *Not* or "distress" and *Notwendigkeit* or "necessitation" (*BT* 22/3), which Heidegger sees as belonging to our present historical moment and which is to be provoked and amplified by the one-page preamble or prelude that appears before the book proper begins.[11] I say that the preamble does not technically belong to the book because, after all, it is not listed among the table of *Inhalt* or "Contents" which precedes it and which offers, it must be said, a peculiarly exhaustive and meticulous catalog of the book's elements. Indeed, *Being and Time*'s table of contents sets out everything in great detail—every part, division, chapter, numbered section, and lettered subsection, all with their respective titles. And yet, nowhere is the preamble mentioned here among the contents of the original German volume.

To be sure, the ultimate aspiration of Heidegger's project as a whole, parts 1 and 2 together, is summarily stated in the preamble—"our aim in the following treatise is to work out the question of the meaning of *Being*" (*BT* 19/1). However, much more vital than providing this one-line statement of the project's organizing aim, the preamble's true function, I would argue, is to provoke for the first time the ambient mood of distress within which part 1 is then to be situated, and indeed *must be situated*, in order to motivate the reader to undertake part 2, the destruction of the tradition. Let us take a close look, then, at this odd little exordium.

The preamble famously opens with a passage from Plato's *Sophist*, first in the original Greek and then in German translation. In this passage, which occurs just over halfway through the dialogue, the Eleatic Stranger looks back at the preceding attempts to define the essential character of the sophist and remarks on the fact that his uncertainty concerning what is signified by the participle *on* or "being" has only increased over the course of the discussion (*Soph*. 244a).

Having drawn attention to this moment of ancient philosophical self-doubt, Heidegger's own authorial voice is first heard posing a question. He asks, "Do we in our time have an answer to the question of what we really mean by the word 'being'?" The response is: "Not at all" (*BT* 19/1). Heidegger would seem to be wondering aloud: can it really be the case that we have no clear idea of what is meant when we say that something "is," or when we refer to something as a "being," much less when we gesture to the whole of "Being" itself? After nearly two and a half millennia of philosophizing in the West, are we really still without any

INTRODUCTION

clear answer to what seems, at least initially, the most elementary and fundamental of questions?

Heidegger proceeds. Clearly seeking to amplify the distress he hopes was provoked by this revelation, he asks, "Are we nowadays even perplexed at our inability to understand the expression 'being'?" The response is: "Not at all" (*BT* 19/1). That is, isn't it all the more troubling that, rather than being a source of consternation and energetic investigation, as it was for Plato apparently, the question of Being is seen for the most part as not even worth the posing? Even among philosophers and scientists, Heidegger will note, there is an indifference to and indeed an impatience with the question of Being. Quite evident here is Heidegger's purpose—to provoke and intensify an anxiety at this state of affairs, as an ambient mood within which part 1 will unfold.

In the face of this agitating and somewhat accusatory spur, the reader might wish to respond that it is precisely by setting aside the question of Being that we are often able to turn to more immediate, more urgent questions—what it means "to be human" rather than animal, "to be healthy" rather than sick, "to be an adult" rather than a child, "to be a citizen" rather than not. Or indeed what it is "to be just," "to be moral," "to be educated," "to be free," and so on. More often still, we turn away even from specific theoretical questions and toward immediate practical pursuits. We work to secure shelter, sustenance, health, safety, or comfort for ourselves and for those we hold dear. Perhaps we are also motivated to address broader social or political problems, working on behalf of others in our community, other human beings in the distant corners of the globe, other species, or even nature itself. In the course of living out our lives, questions at this supra-ontological level must be posed, undeniably pressing personal and communal needs and desires must be addressed straightaway, and actions must surely be taken swiftly. All this seems to require that we set aside the question of the meaning of Being, even if it remains unanswered, so as not to remain stupefied and paralyzed before it. Doubtlessly true.

And yet, Heidegger would respond, it must also be acknowledged that every theoretical or scientific contribution and every action taken, every policy initiative, every political movement, indeed everything we think and everything we do, will *always* be deeply determined by our unexamined presupposition of what it means "to be" anything at all, because all these endeavors unfold in a landscape exhaustively ordered by that presupposition. This is so, insofar as our pre-understanding of Being dictates what can appear on our horizon *as a being* at all; that is, what can emerge and present itself as "a thing that *is*" and thus as a thing to be asked about, investigated, understood, acted upon, or cared for. It also dictates what is relegated to ontologically secondary status, as dependent upon whatever we understand as legitimate, full-fledged "beings." Given the all-embracing significance of the answer, then, how can we afford not to know what it means "to be"? And again, more pressing still, how can we be so comfortable, so self-satisfied with our not knowing? What are the forces at work that maintain us in our complacent ignorance with respect to Being? This is the broadly discomforting worry that the preamble is specifically crafted to cultivate.

As we shall see, then, the existing text of *Being and Time* seems to present what we might recognize as a sort of Kantian hypothetical imperative: if Distress and Historicality, then Destruction. That is, *if* we find ourselves experiencing this anxiety at neither knowing nor even being curious about the meaning of Being, provoked by the preamble, and *if* both our historically embedded way of being in the world and the fundamentally problematic character of the specific tradition in which we find ourselves immersed have been compellingly revealed to us in part 1 of *Being and Time*, *then* we will feel compelled to take up the destructive interrogation of that tradition's canonical texts that was to be part 2.

Being and Dasein

If the ultimate aim of Heidegger's project was "to work out the question of the meaning of *being*" (*BT* 19/1), it should already be clear why that could not have proceeded simply by assembling and evaluating various possible answers to the question. Being does not yet appear before us with sufficient distinctness even to be the object of rigorous and focused investigation, thus leaving "the question itself obscure and without direction" (*BT* 24/4). Heidegger suggests nevertheless that it might be possible to reflect back upon the experience of even vague and open questioning, that is, the unfocused anxious wondering we now find ourselves undeniably involved in, thanks to the preamble.

In this reflection, we come before ourselves as beings asking after Being, even if in a preliminary and ill-defined way, and after all,

> *this vague average understanding of Being is still a Fact.* However much this understanding of Being (an understanding which is already available to us) may fluctuate and grow dim, and border on mere acquaintance with a word, its very indefiniteness is itself a positive phenomenon that needs to be clarified. (*BT* 25/5)

INTRODUCTION

Initially we can say that, negatively, "the Being of beings 'is' not itself a being" (*BT* 26/6). We sense, however indistinctly, that there is a vital difference introduced when we move from "the horse" to "the Being of the horse," from "beings" to "the Being of beings." Whatever else we may or may not be able to clarify about Being and how it relates to a particular being, we understand from the outset that there is an important distinction between Being and beings. This is what Heidegger calls in *Basic Problems of Phenomenology*, also from 1927, the "ontological difference" (*BPP* 17/23).[12] We may perhaps feel an impulse to initially reduce everything we experience here to the distinction between a particular being and its quality of being, or what in Latin we would refer to as the distinction between *ens* and *esse*. Or we may wish to reduce the experience to a distinction between a being and its Being in the specific sense of its essence, its *essentia*, what makes all x's what they are, their x-ness. But before we perpetrate any such reduction, Heidegger seems to want to pause in the initial moment of distinction—whatever it is, Being appears in this initial and only minimally directed inquiring as not simply identical to a particular being or to the totality of beings.

When we do pause with Heidegger here, we encounter ourselves as a kind of being that is "distinguished by the fact that, in its very Being, that Being is an *issue* for it," a being that "in its Being, has a relationship toward that Being" (*BT* 32/12). Let us unpack the significance of this observation a bit. Note first that Heidegger is not beginning his reflection upon "this being which each of us is" (*BT* 27/7) in the mode of a traditional philosophical anthropology or even a study of subjectivity, both of which would involve making some positive claims about the essential properties or nature of either the human or the experiencing subject. Instead, Heidegger begins with the observation of a fundamental indeterminacy, a question provoking distance between us and our Being. Inanimate beings seem at least to be what they are by simply holding themselves together and persisting as selfsame through time. Nonhuman living things have traditionally been seen to be what they are, not by this simple persisting, perhaps, but by living and moving in certain ways, and those activities have often been thought of as utterly determined by their nature, by their natural compulsions or instincts. When it comes to the kind of being that we are, however, "its essence lies rather in the fact that in each case it has its Being to be, and has it as its own" (*BT* 33/12). We have our Being neither as a *fait accompli* nor even, as it were, a *fait inévitable*; rather, we have "to be" as a possibility. In terms of eventually posing the question of the meaning of Being, this observation makes all the difference, because in our concernful dealings in the world, in our striving for this or planning on that or acting in the interest of the other, we are always directed *toward* accomplishing our Being. We thus have a prior relation to Being, our Being, which can provide a starting point for the investigation of the question of Being as such.

Next, Heidegger observes that we are also the kind of being to which "being-in-a-world belongs essentially" (*BT* 33/13, translation modified). That is, our way of being, which is the activity of accomplishing our Being and thus having our Being before us as a possibility, entails an environment, an encircling whole within which and in relation to which that possibility is realized or not. We do not appear to ourselves as discrete, atomistic things, possessed of and defined by a set of properties or an essential nature, where our relation to our surroundings would be something secondary and supplemental. Rather, our Being is accomplished through action in the world and as such we exist in essential constitutive relations to other beings. Beings present themselves to us in the context of this whole, they emerge and appear to us within the horizon of this world, and they do so in relation to *their own Being*. A horse presents itself *as* a horse, or as bearing a relation to the Being of a horse. Thus, our understanding of Being "pertains with equal primordiality both to an understanding of something like a 'world,' and to the understanding of the Being of the beings that become accessible within the world" (*BT* 33/13). We *have* the whole world, the whole of Being, already as the presupposed environing context of our every experience and every action, even if in a vague and unreflective way, and we also have both the beings with which we interact and the Being of beings, again even if that Being is understood only dimly and pre-conceptually.

This, our way of being, Heidegger refers to as *Existenz* or "existence," which he hears as an *ecstatic* mode of being, an *ek-sisting* or a "standing-out" beyond ourselves in being ourselves. We *are*, *not* by enclosing ourselves within a membrane and holding ourselves together, but precisely the opposite, by stretching out both spatially and temporally. That is, on the one hand, in our concerned way of going about, we *are* by stretching out into the world and entering into constitutive contact and interaction with other beings and Being. On the other hand, we *are* also by a stretching out in time in accomplishing our Being: by having emerged out of a given set of conditions (being stretched into the past) and projecting ourselves forward toward a possibility of our Being (being stretched into the future).[13]

All of this comes to light in *Being and Time* in great detail and depth, through a rigorous, precise, and clear phenomenological description of what is appearing to us in everyday human existence. Of course, Heidegger's language can often be disorienting and strange, but that is necessitated, as we shall see, insofar as the mode of being he is attempting

INTRODUCTION

to describe departs from the standard and unreflective way of conceiving of "what is" that we inherit from our tradition. It is necessary to push traditional language to its limits here, in order to trace the dimensions and features of this ecstatic mode of being. Indeed, because he conceives of our mode of being in this way, Heidegger refers to us not as "human beings" or "subjects" at all, but as *Dasein*, which literally translates as "being-there."[14]

And it is the essentially historical character of our ecstatic "being-there" that we must now consider. Heidegger writes:

> In its factual Being, any Dasein is as it already was, and it is "what" it already was. It *is* its past, whether explicitly or not. And this is so not only in that its past is, as it were, pushing itself along "behind" it, and that Dasein possesses what is past as a property which is still present-at-hand and which sometimes has after-effects upon it . . . [Rather,] Dasein has grown up both into and in a traditional way of interpreting itself: and it is in terms of this that it understands itself proximally and, within a certain range, constantly. By this understanding, the possibilities of its Being are disclosed and regulated. Its own past—and this always means the past of its "generation"—is not something that *follows along after Dasein*, but something which already goes ahead of it. (*BT* 41/20, translation modified)

We, as Dasein, as being-there in the world here and now, have our Being "to be," as we saw above. One might imagine, having heard this, that we are in a position of terrific freedom, standing perpetually before a manifold forking of our life's path, an open vista of possibilities. This turns out not to be the case, for most of us, most of the time. Rather, our tradition leaps out ahead of us, determining not just what has been, the past behind us, nor just what is, the present consequences of past events, but even the possibilities for being that might emerge before us, our future. Our historically ecstatic way of being is overwritten by our tradition.[15]

Indeed, from Heidegger's perspective, it is precisely our particular tradition at this moment in history, the European tradition at its most fundamental level, its basic all-embracing, all-determining conception of what it means "to be," that maintains us in both our ignorance of Being *and*, especially, in our ignorance of our own ignorance, the troubling indifference with respect to the question of Being that we became aware of in the preamble. Heidegger writes:

> This question [of Being] has been forgotten . . . . Yet the question we are touching upon is not just any question. It is one which provided a stimulus for the researches of Plato and Aristotle, only to subside

> from then on *as a theme for actual investigation* . . . Not only that. On the basis of the Greeks' initial contributions toward an interpretation of Being, a dogma has been developed which not only declares the question about the meaning of Being to be superfluous, but sanctions its complete neglect. . . . [And] the presuppositions and prejudices which are constantly reimplanting and fostering the belief that an inquiry into Being is unnecessary . . . are rooted in ancient ontology itself. (*BT* 21/2)

This should come as quite a revelation. Heidegger is declaring here that our ignorance concerning what "to be" even means *and* our general lack of concern about that ignorance are *both* rooted in "ancient ontology." After bringing to the surface and then intensifying our anxiety in the preamble, Heidegger now tells us that this situation is, in a sense, not our *fault*. Rather, it is the necessitated historical consequence of Plato and Aristotle's "interpretation of Being." Unlike us evidently, they were in a historical position to have their thinking coherently provoked by the question of Being, and they even came up with an answer to the question of what it means "to be." The answer they arrived at, however, resulted in the fact that no one all the way down through the tradition has ever even sought to make this question "a theme for actual investigation" again. That ancient Greek answer, for Heidegger, was the reduction of the meaning of Being to the presence of present beings.

Fallenness and the Metaphysics of Presence

Though Plato and Aristotle evidently confronted the question of Being (at least momentarily and in some fashion), the response they gave points to a certain condition already at work there in antiquity, a condition Heidegger refers to as *Verfallenheit*, "fallenness." That is, their response, as we shall see, arises from a site in which they find themselves already having fallen away from Being, as it were, in its excess with respect to all beings. Their response to the question of Being results from this falling. We, as the inheritors of that interpretation, have been doubly, continuously, and actively falling away from Being ever since.

Concerning this falling away from Being, Heidegger writes already in the 1924 lecture "The Concept of Time":

> Usually, the interpretation of Dasein is governed by everydayness, by what one says about Dasein and about human life in the way that is handed

down [*überlieferter Weise meint*], it is governed by the "they" [*das Man*], by tradition [*Tradition*]. ("CT" 9/114, translation modified)[16]

Our falling away from Being is the work of Being itself, as it was for the Greeks, but it is also the work of the tradition they inaugurated and our inheritance of it. For that tradition is always already there ordering the way beings appear to us at the most fundamental level, providing us with the terms, phrases, and even associations according to which we experience beings and bring them to light for ourselves and for one another. For Heidegger, we find ourselves initially capable of questioning and thinking only what our tradition gives us to question and think. And this is not some personal failing, some reproachable inclination toward conformity. Rather, it is a structural aspect of our very way of being, of the historicality of Dasein.[17] For this reason, it requires a radical intervention. We are not free to simply suspend this traditional influence and begin to think beings and Being anew. No, we must destroy it.[18]

This, our inherited interpretation of Being, is what Heidegger terms "metaphysical" thinking, which found its definitive initial formulation in the thought of Aristotle.[19] Having succeeded in posing the question of Being, the Greek and ultimately Aristotelian answer was that "to be" is nothing other than "to be present," Heidegger tells us. Being, that whole which first calls forth our questioning and thinking, was fatefully reduced to the sum total of present beings, for this Greek answer then determined the landscape within which all subsequent philosophy, science, and culture in the West have operated, directing their considerable intellectual energies to the more and more exhaustive comprehension and mastery of a world made up exclusively of present beings. And this *metaphysics of presence* reduces Being to "present" beings in two distinct senses:

1. On the one hand, the Greeks concluded that, in order to "be," "what is" must be *present in a temporal sense*. The only "things that are" are the things that are *now*. This "now" can be the now that is in time and bookended by past and future, or it can be the eternal now that is outside of time, the everlasting present of, say, Parmenides's Being or Plato's Ideas. In any case, only what is present *has being*, while non-present temporal dimensions or aspects have no *ontological legitimacy at all*. What is in the past simply *no longer is* and what is in the future *is not yet*. This will probably seem to us quite reasonable, indeed nearly tautological, because we are so thoroughly immersed in the tradition organized by the metaphysics of presence. As Heidegger shows in part 1 of *Being and Time*, however, through a careful analysis of everyday Dasein, the past out of which Dasein is emerging and the future into which it is projecting itself seem to have vital parts to play in Dasein's basic way of being. Our pastness and our futureness are features of what we *are*, such that, if we reduce Dasein

to what it is at present, to a mere slice of the movement of emergence and projection that defines it, we lose something that undeniably *is*. Nevertheless, since the Greeks, we have identified the whole of "what is" with the sum total of beings that exist *now*, insofar as they exist now.

2. On the other hand, for the Greeks, "what is" was taken to be *present in a quasi-spatial* or, better, *epistemological sense*. That is, "what is" is something in principle there before us, something that, because it is simply and utterly *there*, is also exhaustively available for our investigation, understanding, and eventual mastery. Everything in Being could be, again at least in principle, scrutinized, mapped out, and revealed without remainder. No doubt, there are many daunting practical obstacles to our coming to know certain regions or aspects of reality, e.g., the elemental makeup of a distant astral body, or the precise number of human beings living on earth at this moment, or the exact temperature of a tiger's beating heart. But nothing in Being is in itself unknowable or inaccessible to human thought and understanding. There is no part of Being, or aspect or moment in the life of Being, that is *as such* withdrawn or hidden from us, nothing in itself *irremediably* obscure. According to what Heidegger calls the tradition of metaphysical thinking inaugurated by the Greeks, concealment results entirely from shortcomings on the part of thinking or from obstacles in the medium that joins thought to Being.

If, then, as the analysis of Dasein in *Being and Time* seems to indicate, there may be ways in which non-presence at least seems to make a constitutive contribution to our being in the world—that is, ways in which past and future have a certain ontological legitimacy—and if there are perhaps even aspects of Being itself that are essentially not present and available for our investigation and cognizing, are we not compelled to try to think Being as otherwise than presence in both the above senses? Being as somehow in excess of the sum of present beings? Indeed, Heidegger is hoping so. The question that presents itself, however, in light of the historical embeddedness of Dasein, is how in the world we might begin to do so, if all we can think is what appears according to our tradition, a tradition exhaustively organized by the metaphysics of presence? This is where, Heidegger believes, destruction presents itself as a task necessitated of us in our present historical moment.[20] And in this mindset, he seems to imagine, every being we encounter, everything we experience, every thought we think, should have us grabbing for the texts of Aristotle with destruction on our minds.

To be sure, though our focus so far has been on *Being and Time*, the conviction that we need destruction is not something that bubbles to the surface only in 1927. At the very start of the period in which we are interested, Heidegger is already diagnosing our present age and calling for the destructive project, both in terms strongly foreshadowing those of his magnum opus. In a 1919 essay that was intended to be a book review of Karl Jaspers's *Psychology of Worldviews*, Heidegger writes:

> We are convinced that a sharpening of the *conscience* cannot be achieved in a genuine way by the "invention" of a "new" philosophical program. Rather, it has to be actualized quite concretely by way of *destruction* [Destruktion] aimed directly at what has been handed down to us in the tradition of intellectual history. . . . The very "representation" of the task of destruction is such that its sense and scope can hardly be overestimated. *If we restrict ourselves to this task of destruction* and consciously abandon traditional, still historically conditioned, aspirations to do "creative" philosophizing, we will quickly come to see "what needs to be done" concretely. ("Comm." 73/118)

As we shall see, throughout this early period, from 1919 to 1927, Heidegger again and again insists that the project of thinking philosophically today about the world and our place in it cannot proceed except by way of the project of destroying the tradition handed down to us, specifically as it traces itself back to Aristotle's initiating articulation.

The Abiding Relevance of Aristotelian Substance Ontology

Now, it is certainly the case that Heidegger directs his destructive interpretative method toward various figures and texts from the history of Western philosophy. Nevertheless, it is, I would suggest, at its most powerful and most dramatic when he brings it to bear on the texts in which he sees the tradition finding its definitive and fullest inaugurating expression—the Aristotelian corpus.

For even if Heidegger in other contexts implicates other Greek thinkers, for example, Thales, Anaximander, Heraclitus, Parmenides, or Plato, in the work of initiating Western ontology, it is principally Aristotle's critical response to and reformulation of his predecessors' thought that Heidegger sees unfurling into the Middle Ages, after which it is appropriated anew in the early modern period. Aristotle thus stands most illuminatingly, for Heidegger, at the threshold between the pre-traditional Greek experience of the world and the metaphysical tradition that derives so many of its most fundamental concepts from him.

Of course, Aristotle's teleological view of the natural world has now

INTRODUCTION

been definitively set aside with the dawning of modern science, and his insistence on the infinity of unfolding time has been rejected in favor of a "big bang" genesis and the eventual "heat death" of the universe. His faith in the perpetual sameness of natural species has, to be sure, been undermined by evolutionary biology. And even the Aristotelian theory of syllogistic reasoning was finally superseded at the end of the nineteenth century by modern mathematical logic. It might well seem that Aristotle has been left quite completely behind today.

In fact, this is not at all the case, for Aristotelian concepts continue to operate at the most basic pre-reflective, pre-scientific level. First and foremost, the fundamental realities that constitute the world *as we experience it* continue to be the basic units of Aristotle's metaphysics, or what he would have called *ousiai*. We will return to Aristotle's treatment of this term in depth in chapter 3, but for now we can simply note that the term in the singular, *ousia*, is most commonly translated as "substance" or "substantial individual," but that in terms of its etymology it would have been heard immediately as something like "beingness," and thus as "what *is* most of all." Aristotle accordingly makes the question of what qualifies as an *ousia* central to his studies in what will eventually be called his *Metaphysics*, for he assumes that whatever is properly referred to with that term will be "what *is*" in a paradigmatic or fundamental way (*Meta.* VII.1028a10–15).[21] In the *Categories*, the *Physics*, and at least initially the *Metaphysics*, Aristotle identifies *ousiai* as compellingly unified, persisting individuals, composites of some appropriate material and a definable and knowable form—for example, a particular human being or a particular horse (*Cat.* 2a10–12). The world that was presenting itself to Aristotle at that historical moment and which he theorized so powerfully and so influentially, he conceived of as fundamentally a collection of *ousiai*.[22]

And even today, in our late modern world, when I look out the window of my study, if I ask myself pre-scientifically and pre-philosophically, "What *is* out there?" or "What are the things that *are*?" or "What out there has *being*?," resisting the tendency to reflect and appeal to my philosophical or scientific commitments and trying instead to speak as directly from experience as possible, I am likely to list the human being doing the weeding in the garden, the tomato plants, the katsura tree, the wisteria bush, then the garden table at the edge of the patio, each of the four chairs around it, the basket holding cucumbers, each cucumber, and so on.

Could I perhaps see there before me a world composed according to a fundamentally different ontology? Perhaps. Could we, for instance, actually *experience* the world as made up fundamentally of atoms? Of energy? Could we experience a world that was first and foremost a com-

INTRODUCTION

plex of pre-substantial relations, or a snarl of burgeoning potencies, or a splatter of events of emergence? Perhaps. Indeed, are there peoples in the world belonging to different traditions who do experience their world in something like these ways? Again, perhaps, indeed almost certainly. But more important for us is the evident fact that, insofar as we are inheritors of the Western European tradition, we do not experience things pre-philosophically in those ways. The world we experience and from which we initially begin to think, whenever we do think, as inheritors of this tradition, is fundamentally an Aristotelian world, a world of Aristotelian *ousiai*. Not a Platonic, Cartesian, Lockean, Spinozist, Leibnizean, Kantian, Hegelian, Newtonian, or Einsteinian world. No, it is rather an Aristotelian world, for anyone touched deeply by this tradition, I would wager, just as it is for me. And this in spite of all the ways in which Aristotle's thinking seems to have been eclipsed in the millennia since he lived and thought.[23]

It is for precisely this reason that Heidegger can remark in a 1924 talk presented to the Kant Society at the University of Cologne:[24]

> The foundations of contemporary science as well as of philosophy are rooted in the investigations carried out by the Greek philosophers—ultimately and especially those of Aristotle. ("BTBT" 219)

This is so insofar as the scientist and the philosopher must always begin their work from out of their lived experience of the world. Even if their modern physical theories and their ultimate philosophical commitments, indeed the very logic by which they argue, are expressly non- or even anti-Aristotelian, Heidegger is suggesting that the practice and the work of scientists and philosophers remain nonetheless determined by the Aristotelian concepts that persist in organizing their everyday experience.[25] This is especially true of that most fundamental Greek philosophical concept, the notion of Being according to which it is identified with the sum total of Aristotelian substances, understood as temporally and epistemologically present beings.

For this reason, in what follows, of all the figures of Western philosophy who have participated in the generation and transmission of the traditional concepts we now inherit, I focus here on the destruction of Aristotle in particular. If Aristotle's conception of substance ontology persists in and fundamentally still organizes our own pre-reflective experience, as Heidegger insists, then a destruction of the Aristotelian text will be more than a historical detour. It will be a journey of self-discovery or even, given the peculiar power of this method, a project of self-recovery.[26]

From Husserl's Phenomenology of Transcendental Subjectivity to Heidegger's Phenomenology of Being

In *Being and Time*'s description of Dasein's everyday experience, Heidegger is overtly building upon what he learned from Husserlian phenomenology. However, in order to attend purely and scientifically to the structures and essential elements of what appears to consciousness, Husserl saw the need to disrupt our "natural attitude," our ordinary mode of experiencing things, with the performance of what he calls an *"epoché,"* a "suspension" of any judgment concerning the actual external or real-world existence of what is currently appearing to us—that is, phenomena. When proceeding philosophically with Husserl, I take up the phenomena that are presenting themselves to me, but instead of assuming that these are the appearances of something beyond the phenomena, some real being out there in the world, I attempt to describe the phenomena themselves exclusively, identifying distinctions, defining essences, tracing relations among them, and so on.

As Heidegger views it, this suspension of judgment entails that Husserl has shifted his philosophical gaze *away from* "what *is*," and thus away from Being. Opposing himself to this aspect of Husserlian phenomenology then,[27] Heidegger insists in *Being and Time* that when we move from pre-reflective experience to phenomenological reflection, although we are analyzing the content of what is appearing to us, we are nonetheless able to uncover not merely the constituting structures imposed by consciousness, but "what *is*," beings and even Being itself.[28] For Being is approached by Heidegger as what has already shown itself to us in those pre-reflective appearances of beings. As Samuel IJsseling observes, describing Heidegger's appropriation of and departure from Husserlian phenomenology, "for Husserl, the *wonder of wonders* was transcendental subjectivity, 'behind which it would be nonsensical to want to investigate further'; for Heidegger, the *wonder of wonders* is that beings are."[29] Indeed, the aim of phenomenology was for Heidegger, as he states it already in his 1920 Freiburg lecture course *Phenomenology of Intuition and Expression*, the "immanent illumination of life experience itself that remains in this experience and does not step out and turn it into objectivity" (*PIE* 131/171).

With this proposed transformation of the Husserlian phenomenological project, Heidegger effectively sets aside the basic way in which the relationship between Being and appearance has been understood throughout all of modern philosophy from Descartes onward, arguably up to and including Kant and Husserl. For Heidegger, Descartes's introduction of the method of hyperbolic doubt was a watershed moment in the history of Western philosophy, for it demanded that all unverified appearances, everything in ordinary experience, be treated as suspect, not in the sense of requiring clarification, investigation, and interpretation, but in the sense of possibly having *nothing at all to do with reality*. Since then, philosophy has been trying by various means to bridge the gap that opened up there between a subject's pre-reflective unverified experience (appearance) and "what is," understood as what exists in objective reality independent of the subject (Being). To be clear, I am not using the vocabulary of "object" or "objective" here in the technical senses these have for either Descartes or Kant.[30] Rather, I mean the term in its common, nontechnical sense, a sense one can hear in the etymology of the Latin *objectum*, from *jacere*, "to throw," and *ob-*, "in the way of, against," thus initially signifying "something set over against," and existing independently of, the experiencing subject.

The world that modern philosophy has been investigating for centuries, then, is emphatically not the initially appearing world, the world as it has always already given itself to Dasein in everyday pre-philosophical experience. That appearing world, again at least since Descartes, has been treated as a potentially *merely* appearing world, potentially severed from whatever might really exist and consequently as something that must be left behind at the threshold of legitimate philosophical investigation. Indeed, even after Kant's "Copernican revolution" and Husserl's phenomenological *epochê*, Heidegger would argue, their thinking continues to be negatively organized by the Cartesian cleft that had opened up between subject and object, insofar as both Kant (at least under a common interpretation)[31] and Husserl seem to abandon any aspiration to grasp that external reality existing independently of its appearing to consciousness, and instead attempt to ground knowledge through a precise and methodologically secured mapping of the structures of the subject's experience.

Heidegger's radical innovation here is that he accepts no such Cartesian pre-division, no such severance between subject and object, phenomenal and noumenal, interior and exterior, thing-for-us and thing-in-itself,[32] appearance and Being. Where Husserl, following Brentano, saw the intentionality of consciousness as providing a necessary link to some mental content, Heidegger sees it establishing a necessary link between beings (and Being for that matter) and the Dasein to whom beings are presenting themselves.[33] For Heidegger, the world that philosophy investigates is, as we have seen, precisely that which has appeared in pre-philosophical everyday life, provoking our wonder, questioning, and investigation.[34] Now, those initial appearances may well be and usually are received as inadequate, unclear, partial, oblique, and conflicting. They are generally in need of a great deal of clarification, analysis, and interpretation.

Even so, because Heidegger is investigating the phenomenal or appearing world as itself entailing an always already established connection between Being and Dasein,[35] the *task* of philosophizing for him is fundamentally different from that of modern philosophy. It is neither an attempt to bridge the gap and access objective reality (e.g., rationalism, empiricism), nor is it a rigorous mapping or diagramming of the a priori structures of intelligibility (forms, concepts, ideas, essences) at work within the experiencing subject (e.g., transcendental idealism, Husserlian phenomenology). Rather, Heidegger sets out to clarify or at least properly mark the initially obscure way in which the world is appearing to us, and analyze the fundamental structures of that appearing as belonging to Being, in order to determine when we are proceeding in an authentic or proper manner in receiving this appearing and when we are not. What Heidegger believes he can show is that most of us most of the time have fallen away from and obscured our own Dasein, our being-there in the world, and thus our relation to Being itself.

And arguably, with respect specifically to the project of phenomenology, Heidegger's greatest advance over Husserl is his recognition of the central role of *Stimmung* or "mood, attunement," in human experience and cognition. Husserl had of course posited the importance of context in any act of consciousness—specifically that whenever we perceive, experience, or think about anything at all, the intended object of consciousness is always situated for us in an all-encompassing, meaning-conveying, referential context, the ordinary term for which would be a "world." Whatever appears to us always implies a world within which it appears, a complex of other beings all gathered together into a whole within an encompassing horizon. Beginning from this groundbreaking Husserlian insight, Heidegger observes that this all-encompassing world is first opened up for us in everyday experience by what he calls *Grundstimmungen* or "fundamental moods, attunements." The world, as the totality of all beings and the whole environing context for my consciousness of any given object or being, is given to me, as Dasein, always already, in the grounding mood in which I find myself. And that whole is also the encompassing openness in which my possibilities for being are spread out before me—I choose to act and pursue this or that aim always within the encompassing whole world that my mood opens up for me. Vitally, for Heidegger, these fundamental moods are not merely subjective. They are not mere feelings about the whole, but rather as *Stimmungen* or "attunements," they are ways of being *gestimmt* or *bestimmt*, "attuned to" or "determined by" the way the totality of beings gives itself to us in our historical context.[36]

In the unpublished manuscript that is sometimes thought of as his late-period masterwork, *Contributions to Philosophy (of the Event)* (1936–38), Heidegger suggests that thought must situate itself in the fundamental mood of its historical moment. He suggests that when we look back at the Greeks, we see that they found themselves disposed toward the totality of beings, as the Western tradition was first blossoming into view, in the fundamental attunement of *thaumazein* or "wondering," with both Plato and Aristotle indicating, of course, that *philosophia* arises essentially out of an initial wonder at the self-presentation of beings (*Th.* 155d; *Meta.* I.982b12–22). But in his late historical moment, Heidegger observes, as the tradition of Western metaphysics draws to a close and seems ripe for a transition to an utterly unanticipatable way of being in and thinking about the world, the totality of beings is opened up, by contrast, in something like the mood of *Er-ahnen* or "foreboding" (*CP* 18/21). And this fundamental mood seems to have as it were three different aspects: *Erschrecken* or "shock, fear," *Verhaltenheit* or "restraint," and *Scheu* or "diffidence, awe" (*CP* 14/14), between which thinking would oscillate. To be sure, in *Being and Time*, Heidegger is not yet speaking in these terms when evoking and identifying the fundamental historical mood in which thinking must situate itself in its world. However, in the preamble we certainly did see Heidegger attempting to provoke and then intensify a kind of *Not* arising from *Notlosigkeit*—that is, a "need" arising from a "needlessness," a distress at our own lack of distress, with respect to the question of Being. This could be understood as a certain anxiety at the general withdrawal of Being, at the forgetting of Being, but even more so at the forgetting of the forgetting of Being, which the epigraph from Plato already seems to indicate must have occurred at some point either with or just subsequent to the Greek raising of the question of Being. This historically situated fundamental mood does indeed then seem to open up the totality of beings for us, the whole of "what is," as well as placing us in relation to the withdrawal of Being.

It is important here to recognize and note, however, that these fundamental moods for Heidegger are essentially *ambivalent* with respect to the response they might provoke. The anxiety with which *Being and Time* opens may well, on the one hand, allow us to experience for the first time the world that is the totality of present entities in relation to Being as their abyssally self-withdrawing and self-occluding, long-forgotten ground. Or it may, on the other hand, motivate a frenzied investigation and mapping of those beings, an energetic revealing of everything about present entities experienced exclusively in their presence and their availability for investigation, knowledge, and mastery, which would entail a vigorous avoidance of the experience of the withdrawal of Being. Fundamental moods are not yet either the metaphysical or the extra-metaphysical *experience* of the totality of beings—they are rather the potential for either. Heidegger is hoping that, with the revelation of our fundamental historicity as Dasein, this anxiety might motivate the destructive engagement with our inherited tradition, as the tradition of the forgetting of Being.

Between Nietzschean Genealogy and Derridean Deconstruction

Perhaps there are those today who feel themselves compelled to take on the tradition of Western thought out of which, to some significant extent and for better or worse, they see their own worldview as having emerged. It matters not whether our direct provocation for this comes from the anxiety provoked and the historicity revealed by part 1 of *Being and Time*. It might well come directly from our experience of life on earth at this historical moment. Perhaps we perceive systemic and long-standing injustices, myopias, and exclusions that plague contemporary social-political relations, or the seemingly irresistible power of dehumanizing economic forces at work today, or the catastrophic idiocy of our indifference to the needs of our planet, or the consuming and ubiquitous technological frenzy that, maybe more than anything else, organizes contemporary life. Wherever it comes from, it seems that we may feel welling up within us a certain elemental critical urge vis-à-vis the Western tradition extending back to Aristotle and the Greeks.

If so, I would suggest that Heideggerian destruction merits serious consideration as the method to be employed in this endeavor. Positioned as he is in the lineage of Continental philosophy between Friedrich Nietzsche and Jacques Derrida, one might begin to see the potential power of Heidegger's destructive method as emerging out of the former's project of "genealogy" even as it issues forth into the latter's "deconstruction." And indeed, I would argue, Heideggerian destruction enjoys the cardinal virtues of both.

Already early on in his career, in 1874's "On the Utility and Liability of History for Life," Friedrich Nietzsche calls for an explicitly "critical" approach to history. This approach was to be deployed in concert with "monumental" and "antiquarian" modes, each providing something vital for our healthy relation to history *and* each acting as the antidote to a certain threat posed by one of the other modes, if taken too far. Nietzsche declares that learning this complex relation to our past is necessary for anyone in what he saw as his past-saturated late-modern historical moment, for "those who are oppressed by a present need [*Noth*] and who wish to throw off this burden [of the past] at all costs."³⁷ In *Being and Time*, we find an affirmative remark about this threefold Nietzschean approach to history as anticipating what Heidegger sketches as the authentic way for Dasein to take up its own past (*BT* 448/396).

This three-pronged critical-monumental-antiquarian mode of relating to history seems to be what the middle-period Nietzsche will develop into the "genealogical" method and put to such brilliant use, for example, in the attack on a morality of self-sacrifice in the first essay in the *Genealogy of Morals*. There Nietzsche calls into question the real benefit or health of some of Western society's most treasured moral principles, tracing these back to their messy and problematic sites of historical emergence through genealogical analysis.³⁸

Let us not forget that the ultimate aim of this genealogical critique is not destructive or critical in a simple sense, but *positive* and even *productive*. As Nietzsche had written in "On the Utility and Liability of History for Life":

> When the past speaks it always speaks as an oracle: only if you are an architect of the future and know the present will you understand it.³⁹

That is, throughout his career Nietzsche hoped by means of a highly critical and disruptive interpretation of our inherited past to free up or even activate a natural creative power, that very power which originally in an earlier age funded the invention of the principles and concepts that we now passively receive as reified absolutes. In *The Birth of Tragedy*, Nietzsche saw this now squandered subterranean force in the play of the Dionysian and Apollonian drives that had produced Greek tragedy. In *Philosophy in the Tragic Age of the Greeks*, he saw it as the *phusis* or "nature" conceptualized in the maverick inventions of the pre-Platonic philosophers. And later on, he will think its intricate dynamics under the title of the "will to power." In any case, from his early to his middle to his late period, it is only by critically destabilizing our reified inherited system of values and concepts that we can rediscover the creative power that was once at work at the distant site of their historical emergence, access that power once again, and undertake a revaluation and reinvention of all contemporary values and concepts, in a mode that incorporates an awareness of their unfolding from out of that very source. And it is in this respect that we can see here a very clear predecessor to Heideggerian destruction.⁴⁰

For Jacques Derrida, *déconstruction* names a method of interpretation that is in the end not a method at all, insofar as it emphatically does not operate according to a set of predetermined rules or principles. Whatever it is, Derrida himself traces the neologism he uses to indicate this non-method back to Heidegger.

In his essay "Letter to a Japanese Friend," Derrida first cautions us that

> the word "deconstruction," like all other words, acquires its value only from its inscription in a chain of possible substitutions, in what is too blithely called a "context."[41]

And just as the word "deconstruction" acquires its signifying value from its relations (opposition, equivalence, inclusion, exclusion, etc.) to other words in the context in which it appears, this always intensely immanent approach to reading the texts of our tradition receives its specific character and takes its logic and its strategies for intervention entirely from whatever text is being read. Thus, each time it appears, it occurs in a new and context-specific form.

In a 1971 interview, however, Derrida does describe deconstruction generally as involving a "double gesture": a "phase of overturning" and a phase of the "irruptive emergence of a new concept."[42] In this early description of the project at least, the deconstructive reader would seem to proceed by identifying one or more of "the binary oppositions of metaphysics"[43]—presence/absence, essence/appearance, speech/writing, reason/passion, interior/exterior, male/female, and so on—which are found to be operative in a given canonical (or at least representatively traditional) philosophical or literary text, such that one of the opposed terms is valued over the other. Once the binary has been thoroughly mapped in the text, some technique or intervention is brought to bear, with the result that the logic by which that hierarchy is justified and put in place breaks down, since the purported superiority of the one is often dependent upon the unjustified and problematic demotion or devaluation of the other. This overturning of the traditional evaluation then gives way to a reintroduction of the previously maligned term as the origin and ground of the field within which the opposition is situated, thereby producing a wholly new concept. However, these new concepts Derrida refers to as "undecidables," because they

> can no longer be included within the philosophical (binary) opposition, resisting and disorganizing it, *without ever* constituting a third term, without ever leaving room for a solution in the form of speculative dialectics (the *pharmakon* is neither remedy nor poison, neither good nor evil, neither the inside nor the outside, neither speech nor writing; the *supplement* is neither a plus nor a minus . . . etc.).[44]

INTRODUCTION

In completely inhabiting historical texts, revealing unremarked complications and unworking illicitly engineered grounds and values, and ultimately generating "undecidable" concepts, deconstruction brings us, its readers, to suffer a profound *aporia* or "waylessness, frustration," and it invites us to incorporate that undecidability into thinking itself. Indeed, this is the great gift of Derridean deconstruction.

Over a decade later, Derrida will say of the term "deconstruction":

> When I chose this word, or when it imposed itself upon me—I think it was in *Of Grammatology*—I little thought it would be credited with such a central role in the discourse that interested me at the time. Among other things, I wished to translate and adapt to my own ends the Heideggerian word *Destruktion* or *Abbau*.[45]

Precisely, then, as a bridge between these two powerful approaches to our tradition, between Nietzschean genealogy and Derridean deconstruction, Heidegger's peculiar method of addressing oneself to one's inherited past may just succeed in drawing together their respective strengths. This is to say, it presents a critical assessment of our present concepts and values by tracing them back to their problematic moments of historical emergence, so that we, à la Derrida, suffer the complications that discomfort any presumed moral or epistemological certainty or authority and generate concepts that must be thought as incorporating into themselves their abyssal origins; even as we also, à la Nietzsche, find ourselves perhaps liberated and energized by the possibility, even the necessity and inevitability, of creating concepts and values in the face of those very discomforting complications, powered by a renewed contact with the original sources out of which the traditional concepts we are critiquing first unfolded. This is precisely what has been neglected, I would argue, even by serious and sympathetic readers of the early Heidegger—the character of Heideggerian destruction *as an interpretive or hermeneutic method*, as an approach to reading traditionary philosophical texts.[46]

The fact that, in spite of its power and promise, Heidegger's early method of destructive reading has been understudied and underappreciated in the secondary literature surely results in part from its *locus classicus* being §6 of *Being and Time*. For there appears in that section only a summary statement of the method and not its actual application. But if we focus our attention instead on the lecture courses and other papers leading up to *Being and Time*, especially those focused on Aristotle, we find a number of astonishingly rich discussions of precisely how and to what end historical texts are to be read today in the destructive mode, as well as numerous actual destructive interpretations.

In what follows, we will proceed simply by moving from one very close reading of a passage to the next and making our way through the central moments of those texts from the 1920s. We will ask in chapter 1, what are the concrete tropes, the specific tactics or strategies involved in taking up a given historical text and approaching it "destructively"? In other words, what precisely distinguishes reading a text destructively, in the technical Heideggerian sense, from simply reading a text carefully or critically? In chapter 2, our question will be: if our historical moment does in fact urgently call for "a destruction, i.e., a critical de-constructing of traditional concepts . . . down to the sources out of which they were created" (*BPP* 22–23/32), what exactly are these "sources," how do we access them, and what is to be gained by entering into a new relation with them? Finally, in chapter 3, we will take up Heidegger's treatments of three fundamental Aristotelian concepts—*ousia* or "substance," the "human being" as *zôon logon echon* or "animal having *logos*," and finally *dunamis* or "potency." These serve as case studies, as it were, for how to employ Heidegger's destructive hermeneutic of traditional texts.

§6 of *Being and Time*

Before closing this introduction, however, I would like to take a moment to identify some initial paths of inquiry suggested by that sketch of the destructive method in *Being and Time*. For, though short on detail and offering no application of the method, that discussion does indicate in a preliminary way, on the one hand, the basic *mode* in which texts are to be read and, on the other hand, the *ultimate aim* of the destructive reading—on which we will focus in chapter 1 and chapter 2, respectively.

Heidegger writes in *Being and Time*:

> In thus demonstrating the origin of our basic ontological concepts by an investigation in which their "birth certificate" is displayed, we have nothing to do with a vicious relativizing of ontological standpoints. For this "destruction" is just as far from having the *negative* sense of a shaking off [*Abschüttelung*] of the ontological tradition. To the contrary, it should mark it out in its positive possibilities [*in ihren positiven Möglichkeiten*], which is to say, within its *limits* [Grenzen]; these in turn are given factically with the posing of the question each time [*mit der jeweiligen Fragestellung*] and with the consequently prescribed delimitation of the field of investigation [*der aus dieser vorgezeichneten Umgrenzung des möglichen Feldes der Untersuchung*]. (*BT* 44/22)

Let us attend to this passage in detail. In a description surely intended to invoke genealogy in its more usual sense, Heidegger tells us that our own most fundamental concepts, ontological concepts, will by way of destruction come forth and present their "birth certificates." That is, they will be traced back to some specific site of historical origination, some moment in which the concept emerged and was first articulated by a thinker, before then being passed down through the ages to be inherited by us.

And yet, identifying an idea's historically and culturally situated moment of generation does not amount to a "relativizing" of the idea, Heidegger insists. How so? Does not revealing a given concept as a product of a given philosopher's response to a specific environment necessarily entail that its value and its significance are now viewed only relative to that individual and their context? Apparently not. Heidegger can make such a claim because, as we saw above, he does not presuppose the existence of a subject-object gap, neither when he engages in a phenomenological analysis of Dasein, nor when he reads the history of philosophy. He does not approach past philosophers as subjects striving to bridge a gap between their own internal impressions and an external or objective reality. They are, thus, not subjects who *may or may not* have succeeded in securing in their arguments and analyses a philosophically established and thus secured connection to "what *is*" and, thereby, to Being itself. Heidegger simply rejects the existence of any gap or severance between pre-philosophical experience and what *is*.

Rather, as suggested above, by Heidegger's lights, thinkers of every era enjoy an inviolable contact with Being. For him, historically vital works of philosophy *all* manifest a substantive reception of and connection to beings and Being, even if sometimes in a deficient mode. And it is for just this reason that, though *Being and Time*'s planned destructive reading of our inherited tradition amounts to the most fundamental possible critique, one that will break our concepts down and reveal their moment of historically situated invention, this does not "relativize" their value, significance, or truth. Destruction may well expose a source that exceeds those concepts, a source which they in some complex sense fail to accommodate fully, but this is anything but a "shaking off" of the past that formed and unfolded into those concepts.

Indeed, read with sufficient care, the passage just cited offers a three-step précis of how we should read historical texts in order to accomplish this; that is, the method of textual interpretation or reading to be employed in destruction:

1. We must see the "positive possibilities" in the traditional text, for instance Aristotle's. I take this to mean that we must read the text and mark its *positively bringing something to light*, something Aristotle does

capture of the unfolding of beings into appearance before him and succeeds in conceptualizing.

2. However, this attentiveness to the positive insights must also be integrated with an attentiveness to the way in which the Aristotelian text operates "within its *limits*." This entails that we endeavor to experience the limit in the text as a limit, which is to say, we must reveal destructively an indication or a pointing in the text to what is beyond that which is successfully brought to light there; that is, to what remains concealed in that unfolding.

3. Finally, this holding-together of the positive possibilities and the concomitant limitation in a text will be accomplished, Heidegger tells us here, only if our hermeneutic has a somewhat unorthodox focus. That is, we should train our gaze on the concrete "posing of the question each time" and thereby on the "prescribed delimitation of the field of investigation." Importantly, the destructive method of reading the texts of the history of philosophy does not apparently focus its attentions on a given thinker's ultimate claims, conclusions, positions, or systematic philosophical *results*. Much more, the destructive interpretive eye must be trained on that moment in the text at which philosophical questioning is first opening up, when it is first decided where, how, and in what direction the questioning is to proceed. This is a remarkable and unorthodox hermeneutic principle. We must endeavor to understand the significance of it in the following pages, for, it will be precisely in the *initiating provocation* to think Being that Being's abidingly hidden and ultimately withdrawn, non-present face will show itself in the Aristotelian text, so to speak, as non-presence.[47]

We seem to have arrived, then, at a preliminary indication here of the *ultimate aim* of destruction. As to its *basic mode*, Heidegger goes on to say:

> [This] task we understand as one in which, taking *the question of Being as our clue*, a destruction [*Destruktion*] of the transmitted content [*des überlieferten Bestandes*] of ancient ontology is accomplished until we arrive at those originary experiences [*die ursprünglichen Erfahrungen*], in which the first and leading determinations of Being were first won [*in denen die ersten und leitenden Bestimmungen des Seins gewonnen wurden*]. (*BT* 44/22)

In reading the "ancient ontology" preeminently articulated by Aristotle, it would seem that we must strive to identify two registers in the text. On the one hand, there is the "transmitted content," the philosophical determinations and concepts that emerged there and which were subsequently passed along to and refined by later thinkers in the tradition.

On the other hand, there will also apparently be some record or some mark in the text of the "original, originating experiences [*ursprüngliche Erfahrungen*]" from which that content was first "won" through the work of philosophizing.⁴⁸ This suggests precisely that concrete method of reading destructively that is the focus of chapter 1.

1

The Experiential and the Conceptual in the Aristotelian Text

And before *Being and Time* became *Being and Time*, it was a book on how to read Aristotle.¹

After some reluctance to publish, having spent a good while, in the words of his mentor Husserl, "struggling, searching for himself and laboriously shaping his own unique style," 33-year-old Martin Heidegger set aside a stretch of time in the fall of 1922 to plan out what would be his first book. In so doing, he "labored over the manuscripts of his Aristotle courses to extract from them an introduction serving to found and develop the 'hermeneutical situation' in which Aristotle's works were to be interpreted."² After completing this introduction and a projected table of contents, Heidegger sent these off to Paul Natorp in Marburg, and it was on this basis that he received his first appointment and began teaching at that university in 1923. The prospectus bears the title "Phenomenological Interpretations with Respect to Aristotle: Indication of the Hermeneutical Situation."

And one hears throughout this 1922 sketch clear anticipations of the book Heidegger would eventually come to call *Being and Time*. He undertakes in the sketch a study of "human Dasein" with respect to the "basic movement of factic life," which is characterized by Dasein's "concrete temporalizing and maturation [*Zeitigung*]" and its being "concerned about its Being, even when it goes out of its way to avoid itself" ("PIA" 157). And in the context of that study, Heidegger insists on the need to take on Aristotle in order to think philosophically about the world we are experiencing today and our place in it. Vital is Heidegger's insistence, however, that

> the history of philosophy does not divert present understanding into merely seeking an expansion of knowledge, but rather it forces the present back on itself in order to magnify its questionability. ("PIA" 157)

In other words, engaging in a critical study of Aristotle *does not* entail a mere "expansion of knowledge," that is, a shift away from seeking to know present facts and toward seeking to know, in addition, past facts, such as what Aristotle thought about this or that, when and where precisely he thought it, and how his thinking related to the thinking of those who came before and after him. Rather than addressing the past as a formerly present but now long-gone reality, we address it as participating in our present, shaping it, originating it. And we read and interpret Aristotle, then, only insofar as he is *already* influencing and even determining our way of living and thinking. We are focused on *our own* received set of originally Aristotelian concepts and on making them for the first time non-self-evident for ourselves. As Heidegger remarks, "critique of history is always only critique of the present" ("PIA" 157). Here in chapter 1, we wish to plot out the precise steps involved in this method of critique, and for that we will focus in on one early lecture course in particular, which Heidegger delivered in the summer semester of his first year at Marburg.

Aristotelian Concepts "in Their Conceptuality": Going beyond Definition

Let's recall what we just heard from the brief sketch in *Being and Time* §6, where Heidegger suggests a methodological principle of reading traditionary texts in two registers and calls for "a destruction of the transmitted content of ancient ontology until we arrive at those primordial experiences in which the first and leading determinations of Being were accomplished" (*BT* 44/22). It is in his 1924 course on Aristotle, I would argue, that Heidegger provides his richest and most developed account of precisely how these two levels relate to one another, how we identify them in the text, and how we read the text of Aristotle as suspended between them. The title of the course is *Basic Concepts of Aristotelian Philosophy*.

This title would seem to offer a straightforward announcement of the course content. One expects a simple catalog of fundamental Aristotelian ideas and theories, and perhaps even just a reading of *Metaphysics* Book Delta, where Aristotle presents what amounts to a philosophical lexicon. However, while Heidegger does gesture to Delta in the very first lecture, he soon indicates to his students that he plans on frustrating this expectation. He declares that he and his students will be emphatically uninterested in the familiar project of identifying Aristotle's basic notions, determining their definitions, and then mastering their logical relations with one another.

Heidegger eschews that project, it would seem, because he wishes to introduce an essential redefinition of the "basic concept" itself. Indeed, he will go on to reassess, in vital and profound ways, how the concept is properly thought as concept, how it relates to that of which it is a concept, its ground, and, ultimately, what that ground itself is, out of which all concepts unfold. We might say that Heidegger wishes to draw his students' attention to the *Grundbegriffe* or "basic concepts" of Aristotelian philosophy, but in so doing so he will redefine both of the elements of that term, *Begriff* or "concept" and *Grund* or "ground, fundament."

He begins:

> We do not discover, fundamentally [*im Grunde*], what a concept is from the definition without something further [*ohne weiteres aus der Definition*]. (*BCArP* 9–10/10)[3]

This is a startling declaration indeed. "What a concept *is*" is not exhausted by, and remains only partly discovered in, even a perfectly correct and essential definition? How so? And what precisely is it that belongs to the concept and yet remains necessarily, in some sense, in excess of its definition?

To be sure, Heidegger does not say here that we can simply disregard the definitions of concepts, as though he were insisting instead on the possibility of engineering an immediate and intuitive intellectual perception of an idea. No, he simply says that in order to think a concept properly, as what it is, we must also experience it in relation to what extends somehow beyond its own definition. But we must ask then, how are we to think concepts properly, fundamentally, as they are, both by way of their definitions and then with reference to or as somehow invoking what constitutively exceeds that definition? And how are we to approach the Aristotelian text, according to Heidegger, in order to think his concepts with this double focus?

We can begin responding to these questions by noting that, in the first ten pages of text, when introducing the approach to the concept that he has in mind, Heidegger repeats an important qualifying phrase no fewer than seven times. To cite just one of these occurrences:

> This course will concern the understanding of fundamental concepts *in their conceptuality* [in ihrer Begrifflichkeit]. (*BCArP* 4/4, my emphasis; see also another instance further down on 4/4, and then 5/6, 10/11, 11/13, 13/15, 14/17, 15/18)

THE EXPERIENTIAL AND THE CONCEPTUAL IN THE
ARISTOTELIAN TEXT

What does this qualification intend to introduce exactly? How is understanding a concept *in its conceptuality* different from simply understanding a concept and, vitally, how might thinking concepts *in their conceptuality* promise to push our thinking beyond the concept's definition?

In other texts, when thematizing the notion of the "concept," Heidegger is fond of noting and playing upon the etymological link between *Begriff* and *greifen*, the noun "concept" and the verb meaning "to grasp, grab, take hold or possession of." And this etymology points us in the right direction in the 1924 course as well, though Heidegger does not explicitly appeal to it here.

Indeed, much later in his career, it will be precisely this implied grasping, controlling, and mastering aspect of conceptual thinking that Heidegger will see as its defining feature and indeed as cause for abandoning it in favor of a nonconceptual mode of thinking. That is, by reducing "what is" to what is graspable, and thus available and exchangeable, conceptual thinking will come to be identified by the later Heidegger with a calculative manipulation of re-presentations of present entities. As such, it seems entirely caught up within the metaphysics of presence and incapable of escaping it.

Consider the following especially rich and critical description of conceptual thought in *What Is Called Thinking?* a lecture course first delivered in the winter semester of 1951–52, noting the employment of various terms related to *greifen*. Heidegger writes:

> Thinking is . . . not a grasping [*Greifen*], neither a grasping up [*Zugriff*] of what lies before us nor an attack [*Angriff*] against it. What lies before us is not, in λέγειν and νοεῖν, worked over with a grasping. Thinking is not con-ceptualizing [*Denken is kein Be-greifen*]. In the high youth of its essential unfolding, thinking knows no concept [*Begriff*]. And this is in no way a matter of thinking's being undeveloped here. Rather, it is much more a case of self-unfolding thinking being not yet confined within limits [*noch nicht in Grenzen eingeschlossen*] that would limit it by setting up constraints to its essential unfolding . . . But all the great thinking of the Greek thinkers, including Aristotle, thinks non-conceptually [*begrifflos*]. (*WT* 211–12/128)[4]

Heidegger is concerned here, just as he is in our 1924 course, with the proper relationship between thinking and concepts, and with the real nature of the concept. However, in the 1950s he draws lines and oppositions in ways that differ substantially from our lecture course from the mid-1920s. We would do well, then, to mark the differences, even as we allow this much later discussion to provide us with some preliminary guidance in interpreting the earlier work's approach to the concept.

In the passage from 1951–52, Heidegger identifies genuine thinking as something *other than* the thinking of concepts. If our minds set out to grasp, to grab hold of and attack what lies before us, he reasons here, we will necessarily lose sight of anything that is essentially ungraspable and unavailable, if such exists, and precisely thereby we will go astray. Furthermore, when this later Heidegger argues here for the greatness of Aristotle and his privileged role in our tradition, he locates in Aristotle a thinking that is not yet limited in its "essential unfolding" in the way that subsequent conceptual thinking will be.

In the 1924 course, we find Heidegger less interested in rejecting conceptual thinking altogether. Rather, he is attempting to distinguish, we might say, two different modes of thinking concepts, a traditional or metaphysical mode and an extra-metaphysical mode. Heidegger will insist here that when it is genuine and true *to the nature of the concept itself*, conceptual thinking is *as such* required to go deeper and to encompass more than the familiar conceptual thinking of the metaphysical tradition. He can, thus, interpret Aristotle as very much a thinker of concepts, and nonetheless praise him for precisely this excess. Indeed, the Aristotelian *Grundbegriffe* or "basic concepts," when we impose our destructive method upon the text, will present themselves as indicating and relating to what is essentially out beyond their standard definitions, what exceeds their definitions necessarily. And thus, Aristotle's concepts come to be understood as they are *only in relation to what is not yet grasped, not yet seized upon and taken hold of,* indeed what only comes to be grasped, to whatever extent it does, through the work of that concept's emergence. Concepts "in their conceptuality" point to *a dynamic event of emerging into intelligibility, not the static and preexisting intelligible nature of the thing conceived.*

Concepts are addressed here, then, in a way that retains their originally verbal sense as *Begriffe*, from *greifen*, that is, as things "having been grasped," or even as things "being grasped." It is just this verbal and dynamic notion of the concept that the destructive method works with. By its lights, Aristotelian concepts do not present themselves as abstract forms with already established exhaustive definitions, linked together logically, and exchangeable one for the other in various combinations. Rather, precisely in being destroyed they show themselves first and foremost as indicating movements of emergence by way of which what exceeds our grasp becomes nevertheless to some extent clear, illuminated, understood.[5]

Heidegger remarks at one point, concerning the aim of his interpretation of Aristotle's texts: "It is the *soil* [Boden] that must be seen, that out of which these fundamental concepts grow forth [*aus dem diese Grundbegriffe erwachsen*]" (*BCArP* 4/4). And at another point in the discussion, he tells us that it is necessary to seek out the *Bodenständigkeit der Begrifflichkeit*, which is to say, conceptuality's "autochthony" or its own "rootedness," its "condition of being in touch with the *Boden* or soil" (*BCArP* 13/15). It is becoming clear how this understanding of the concept in relation to its source or ground might map onto the experiential and the conceptual levels we found suggested in *Being and Time*'s sketch of destruction.[6]

Kant and the Definition of the Concept

But what precisely is the relationship of the concept to this *Boden* or *Grund*, its "soil" or "ground"? How exactly, and to what extent, is that base taken up and incorporated into the concept? It is important at this stage, as Heidegger responds to these questions, to note the somewhat unexpected figure to whom he turns—Immanuel Kant.

Heidegger announces that he is making use of Kant's 1780 or 1781 *Vienna Logic* here. For Kant in those lectures, Heidegger writes,

> every intuition . . . is a *representatio singularis*, while the concept, which is also a *representatio*, a "self-presenting," is a *representatio per notas communes* . . . It is a "general representation." (*BCArP* 10/10)

Furthermore,

> The concept is, for Kant, distinguished from intuition insofar as intuition simply sees an individual in its being-there, while a concept sees the same object but, so to speak, understands it. (*BCArP* 11/12)

As we know from the *Critique of Pure Reason*, for the Kant of the critical period, categories of the understanding are pure (non-empirical) concepts, which are grasped a priori. They are not abstracted from intuitions of particulars but are rather to be thought of as the most basic structures of cognition (along with the forms of intuition or perception, time and space), which are imposed on the raw content of our experience and give it intelligible order. And this is precisely why this turn to Kant should be surprising, for it seems so obviously at odds with how concept formation is described by that thinker who is the focus of this course, Aristotle.

In *Posterior Analytics* II.19, Aristotle lays out in detail the steps in the process of "how perception engenders the universal [*hê aesthesis houtô to katholou empoiei*]" (*Post. An.* II.100b5). He describes there an ascent from an *aisthêsis* or "perception," many of which can be gathered together if the animal in question also has the power of *mnêmê* or "memory." These perceptions lodge themselves in memory, behaving as soldiers halting their own retreat and turning to resist an enemy surge, Aristotle tells us. One perception somehow musters the strength to take a stand and stick in the soul, presumably when it stops withdrawing from consciousness in the constant and obliterating rush and whirl of one perception's flowing and dissolving into the next. And then other perceptions subsequently gravitate toward it and take a stand alongside it, gathering themselves together *like to like* (*Post. An.* II.100a10–14). On the basis of these collected perceptions of like beings over time, grouping thusly together in memory, one can eventually claim to have *empeiria* or "experience," which is to say, the condition of being experienced, familiar, or competent in dealing with this or that type of thing. Indeed, at this point, even just in being experienced, Aristotle tells us that, in a certain sense, the "whole universal has settled in the soul" (*Post. An.* II.100a6–7).

We must remember here, however, that the Greek term for "universal" is *to katholou*, which literally translates as the thing taken in *kata* or "according to" the *holos* or "whole." For instance, having experience of many cases of scurvy, one would have the universal of scurvy in one's soul, some conception of the defining *eidos* or the "look, form" of scurvy that the whole of all those remembered scurvy sufferers exhibited. And just on the basis of that, when faced with a new case, one could presumably identify it as such and effectively prescribe a given remedy, say citrus fruit, knowing that this remedy had worked for others exhibiting that look or form, that particular set of symptoms.

However, as Aristotle makes clear when he maps some of the very same relations among the capacities of the soul in the *Metaphysics*, this level of experience is not yet the full and proper grasp of the universal concept, for the experienced individual only understands the "that," but not the "why," with respect to this form (*Meta.* I.980a28–981b8). To grasp the concept fully, in the mode of either *technê*, "craft," if it is to be put to use in production, or *epistêmê*, "scientific understanding," if it is out of purely theoretical interest, one must understand what constitutes this form as it is, its sources, causes, or elements. One's grasp of the concept or the form would only then be complete and proper, as technical or scientific.

In setting out these distinctions, Aristotle charts an ascension from *to kath' hekaston*, literally "the thing according to each" or "the thing taken individually," up to *to katholou*, literally "the thing according to the whole" (*Post. An.* II.99b35–100b6), which is to say from the "particular" to the "universal."[7] And in Aristotle's account of the emergence of the universal, the ground or soil of the concept would seem to be *nothing other than the intuitions, or more precisely, the perceptions of individual entities as such*. Given this emphasis, it begins to become clear why, when he wishes to trace the emergence of concepts from their ground, Heidegger might choose to clarify this dynamic by appealing to Kant, rather than to Aristotle's own account. Heidegger does so, I would suggest, in order to find *more* in the concept's grounding moment than merely the collected perceptions of like particulars.

After all, Heidegger trains his interpretive eye explicitly on this "more" and attempts to bring it to light, when he then introduces Kant's peculiar treatment of *definition* in the *Logic*, drawing out its relation to the concept. Heidegger says:

> Definition [for Kant in the *Logic*] is a *methodological* issue, designed to lend precision to knowledge. It is treated as the means for conveying [what Kant calls] the "precision of concepts *with regard to their content*." (*BCArP* 9/10)

What Heidegger seems to find here in Kant is definition being conceived of as more than a static equivalent of the concept, more than a unifying articulation that is interchangeable with the concept in logical relations. Instead, definition for Heidegger's Kant should be understood first and foremost in the context of a *truth-accomplishing activity*, a movement whereby a given being is described in such a way that it is brought to light, becomes visible, knowable to oneself and to others. Definition, *as methodological rather than logical*, is originally to be understood as a *defining* or a *delimiting*, and thus as relating a given concept *not to other concepts*, but back to that concept's ground. This is crucial.

Indeed, Kant identifies an important distinction between a "genuine" and a "nominal" (or non-genuine) definition, to which Heidegger appeals here. Citing from Kant throughout this passage, Heidegger writes:

> Conceptuality and the sense of the concept [*Die Begrifflichkeit und Sinn des Begriffs*] depend on how one understands, in general, the question concerning *what* something is, where this question originates. The concept yields, in the explicitness of the definition, *what* the object, the *res*, is. Thus, the genuine [*eigentliche*] definition is the so-called "real definition," which determines *what* the *res* in itself is . . . It is noteworthy that Kant now says, to be sure, the real definition has the task of determining the What of the matter from the "first ground" [*ersten Grunde*] of its "possibility," or [the task of] determining the matter [*Sache*] according to its "inner possibility." [But Kant also says] that the determination of the *definitio*, insofar as it occurs by way of the *genus proximum et differentiam*

specificam, only counts for the "nominal definition," which comes about by comparison [*durch Vergleichung*]. And it is precisely this way of determining that *does not come into play* [kommt nicht in Frage] with the definition of the *res*. (*BCArP* 10/11–12)

Kant can be heard here insisting that concepts be pushed beyond their nominal definitions in order to be understood properly and to be "genuinely" defined; that is, in order to appear as the concepts they are and do the work of conveying "what *is*" with respect to their subject matter, the *res* or the "thing," the "being" that they "mean," in terms of the "ground" of the being's "possibility." What Heidegger derives from his discussion of Kant, then, is the claim that the "genuine" definition of the concept is whatever *logos* or "account" brings the *being* of its subject matter to light by indicating all that contributes to making it possible for that being to be what it is.[8] But Kant says explicitly that this "genuine" or "real" definition is not, in the first instance, the classical determination by way of *genus* and *differentia,* or "genus" and "specific difference," for such a definition does not succeed in addressing the being from out of its "first ground" and according to its "inner possibility" as a being. Rather, nominal definition in this sense would seem to proceed "by comparison," which is to say, horizontally from one concept to another, linking the concept of the species form (human being) to the concept of the genus (animal) and the concept of the differentia (with *logos*), rather than proceeding vertically or down toward the concept's originating ground in experience.

Kant provides Heidegger, then, with the observation that the traditional way of defining concepts, by establishing a thing's proximal genus and its specific differentiating trait or feature within that genus, fails in its own proper task—to define the concept by bringing to light (in its way of being) that being to which the concept refers.

Aristotle and the Concept of Definition

But this traditional, nominal, and non-genuine notion of definition, Heidegger then proceeds to note, is an Aristotelian invention. It is Aristotle's own determination of what qualifies as a proper definition of a concept, which is to say, it is his *concept of definition.* Heidegger writes:

> We go back to Aristotle in order to show that what, in traditional logic, is treated as *definition* has a *fully determinate origin,* and that definition is a symptom of decline [*Verfallserscheinung*], a mere thought technique,

that was once the *basic possibility of human speech* [Grundmöglichkeit des Sprechens des Menschen]. In the definition [of the standard Aristotelian variety], the concept becomes explicit. Still, what the concept itself is in its conceptuality is not yet visible [*sichtbar*]. (*BCArP* 11/13)

This is a vital passage, and we must take our time in unpacking it. First, Heidegger traces back to Aristotle our current understanding of how concepts are defined (which thanks to Heidegger's reading of Kant we now see as impoverished). Heidegger is referencing here Aristotle's technical determination of *horismos* or "definition" as a *logos* or "account" of *ti estin* or "*what 'x' is*" (*Post. An.* II.93b29–30).[9] And what was with Aristotle an innovation of thought, a new technical way of bringing "what something is" to light, subsequently became the formulaic, shallow, and self-evident understanding of definition that has been passed down through the long intervening tradition to us.

Just prior to the passage cited above, Heidegger observes that, with Aristotle,

definitio is ὁρισμός, ὁρισμός is a λόγος, a "self-expression" about being-there as Being . . . The specific character of ὁρισμός ultimately arises from the fact that the being itself is determined in its being as circumscribed by the πέρας. Being means being-completed [*Sein heißt Fertigsein*]. (*BCArP* 11/12)

According to Heidegger, at the base of Aristotle's own concept of definition, we are able to identify in his own texts a certain Greek pre-philosophical experience of what counts as a being, as "what really is" most of all. Aristotle's concept of definition can be, through destruction, related properly back to the originary experience of beings from which it arises. And this is so, despite the fact that, on the basis of his experience of beings, Aristotle then generated and passed along a concept of definition that no longer insists that concepts be defined in this way, vertically digging down to their ground in experience, but instead allows and encourages us to define them horizontally, through their logical relations to other concepts.

And we come to realize that, according to the specific way in which "what *is*" shows itself always already to Aristotle and his contemporaries, what can qualify as a being or as "what is," pre-reflectively, is "what has a determining *finis* or *peras*," a "limit" or "boundary." Its fundamental way of being, then, is to be delimited or defined, and it is this way of being which ensures that we can, with the proper *logos* or "account," produce complete and exhaustive determinations of beings as they are. Even at the most fundamental experiential level, Being just is "being finished, complete, determined, defined," and thus, being perfectly present and available for human investigation and, in principle, understanding. Aristotle's thinking adheres to and unfolds within the metaphysics of presence, as it generates its concepts and arguments for the first time, because the world of the Greeks is experienced always already as a world of completed or finished, and thus definable, present beings.

Three Steps in the Destruction of the Concept

Recall that we read earlier, in *Being and Time*, that we should, as a general strategy, attend in the text to "the posing of the question each time and with the consequently prescribed delimitation of the field of investigation" (*BT* 44/22), rather than focusing on the conclusions or ultimate philosophical positions at which this thinking arrives. Here in 1924, Heidegger adheres to this strategy quite clearly, identifying three distinct steps or moments involved in this hermeneutic.

He writes, "We must ask what is meant by the concept [*das was in dem Begriff Gemeinte*] . . . in the sense of that which is *concretely experienced* in the concept as it is meant" (*BCArP* 12/13). Heidegger clarifies this; we must ask, for instance, "Which sense of being did he mean in speaking of 'moving being'?" and in doing so we proceed "not with the aim of gaining knowledge of conceptual content, but rather we ask how the matter meant [*die gemeinte Sache*] is experienced" (*BCArP* 12/13). Heidegger is focusing in here on a certain common feature of speech: that when we *meinen* or "mean" something, this may refer both to a concrete individual thing and occurrence or, just as easily, to the idea and concept that this thing instantiates.

Indeed, this is the very ambivalence that Socrates confronts again and again in the Platonic dialogues. He poses the quintessential Socratic question, "What is x?"—for example, "What is virtue?" or "What is the beautiful?"—and then receives as responses from the likes of Meno and Hippias a litany of particular instantiations of virtue or instantiations of beauty. In response, Socrates must again and again strive to make clear that, as the "being of virtue" or the "being of beauty," he is looking for the essential characteristics or form that all virtuous or beautiful things share, not the particular material instantiations of that form.

Heidegger is finding an ambivalence in speech parallel to that featured in Plato's early Socratic dialogues, and he is highlighting any term's capacity to point toward either a concept or the concretely experienced beings that the concept claims to stand for. And having done so, Heidegger insists that we search in the text for indications of the "*basic experience* [Grunderfahrung]" (*BCArP* 12/14) of a concrete particular being, which Aristotle would characterize, in terms of his basic concepts, as, for example, "substance," or the "human being," or "movement," or "potency." We should think here not of the elements that come together to constitute one of these concepts, but rather of the thing that one experiences, even before any reflection or definition, in its mode of being what it is, and in response to which one is provoked to say, "That is a substance," "That is a human," "That is a movement," or "That is a potency." This shifting of our focus from the conceptual level of meaning to the concrete individual level is the first step in the hermeneutic method of destruction.

The second step is this: having undertaken this shift, we must then ask, how "that which is originally seen is primarily addressed." That is,

> does [Aristotle] clarify . . . by way of concepts or theories that are already available, and that, perhaps, Platonistically, say that [e.g.] movement is a transition from nonbeing to being? Or is it that those determinations that arise for him lie in the phenomenon itself? In what way is a phenomenon . . . addressed so as to accord with the *leading demand* of the matter seen [führenden Anspruch *an die gesehende Sache*]? (*BCArP* 12/14, translation modified)

Here we are required to place Aristotle in his historical context, to think about the transmission of ideas and mechanisms of influence. Once we have uncovered the basic experience related to a given Aristotelian concept, then we can ask whether, in speaking about that phenomenon, the terms and concepts that Aristotle uses seem to be called forth by the being that is experienced in its Being or are imposed on it from the outside, a foreign importation from the conceptual apparatus of a previous thinker, for instance Aristotle's teacher Plato. If we attend closely enough to the being in question in its appearing in a basic experience, we will be able to note a *führenden Anspruch*, literally a "demand" or an "appeal" emanating from the thing itself that "leads" one toward how the being must be thought, conceptualized, explained. A thinker, like Aristotle, can in response be seen to either heed that appeal or override it on the basis of inherited and preestablished discursive categories.

Finally, third and explicitly in cooperation with the first two steps, Heidegger tells us we must ask, "How is the phenomenon thus seen *unfolded more precisely* . . . ? What *demand of intelligibility* [Verständlichkeit] is placed on that which is seen thusly?" (*BCArP* 12/14). We must ask after the "specific character of the intelligibility, the specific tendency toward intelligibility" (*BCArP* 12/14). In some being's question-worthy mode of appearing, that being nevertheless shows itself to us, even if as question-worthy, as not yet fully manifest. In doing so and provoking our inquiry, it leads or guides us by suggesting terms and concepts that bring it more to light, that serve in articulating it and making it more *verständlich* or "intelligible, understandable" as "what it *is*." And furthermore, in engaging in this pursuit, in trying to deploy language to bring a being more to light as it is, there are certain alterations in its appearing that will count as increases in intelligibility—for example, if we arrive at more descriptive detail, or at a more complete account, or at an explanation that points beyond features or characteristics to the causes or sources of the being in question, and so on. Heidegger sums up:

> We will interrogate Aristotle's basic concepts from these three points of view. We will see whether the matters meant by these basic concepts [*der in ihnen gemeinten Sachen*] are thereby genuinely understood. (*BCArP* 12/14)

In sum, the following are the concrete three steps or tactics that belong to the destructive method of reading the Aristotelian text:

1. We shift our focus from the static definitions of Aristotle's various concepts to the particular beings these concepts are understood to "mean" in their mode of being.
2. We take up the specific vocabulary Aristotle turns to in describing and thinking about that being and we ask, in Aristotle's intellectual milieu, whether those terminological choices are made more on the basis of the experience of the being in question or more on the basis of inherited categories and tendencies.
3. Finally, we attend to precisely what seems to count as clarifying a given concept or making a given concept more intelligible, and what does not.

And although it is quite compressed in the 1924 course, we quite clearly see Heidegger taking up the basic experience of beings as providing the guiding claim for how beings are to be defined, and thus how Aristotle must articulate his concept of "definition." Heidegger then identifies the terms such as *horismos*, *logos*, and *peras* which Aristotle brings to bear on that original experience of beings. And he lastly interprets "definition" for Aristotle as merely a technical mode of *legein*, "speaking," which is to say, as a certain modification and rigidification of the ordinary linguistic activity of speaking about beings and trying to let them appear as they are, both to oneself and to others. This amounts to identifying a tendency towards intelligibility—"making intelligible" means, initially, letting things show themselves (not, for instance, generating valid arguments, even if that might play a role).[10]

The Ambivalence at the Threshold of Conceptuality

The question of how Heidegger assesses Aristotle's concepts, and their adequacy with respect to the experiences by which they are provoked, is a complex one indeed. For in the end, generally speaking, Heidegger will insist *both* that Aristotle's concepts are genuine expressions of their originary experiences *and* that, by way of destruction, we can nonetheless find something there in the *Boden* or *Grund* of those concepts that failed to be recuperated in Aristotle's "concept creation" (*BCAncP* 10/11).[11] In the brief snapshot offered above of Heidegger's moving through the three steps involved in interpreting Aristotle's concept of "definition" in its conceptuality, the relationship between originary experiences and conceptual content is drawn into the foreground, in order for that relationship to be assessed. And here Heidegger seems to suggest that Aristotle's concept of "definition" genuinely arises from an originary experience of beings as delimited, present, and available for exhaustive elucidation.

On the other hand, Heidegger has also indicated above that there is something un-recuperated. Consider the passage cited above in which Heidegger declares Aristotle's concept of definition "a symptom of decline, a mere thought technique," as well as Heidegger's observation that in Aristotle's fundamental way of understanding the task of definition, the concept may "become explicit" in spite of the fact that "what the concept itself is in its conceptuality is not yet visible" (*BCArP* 11/13). Here, it would seem that although the Aristotelian concept of "definition" arises genuinely from his originary experience of beings, it nonetheless fails to do complete justice to beings in their way of being. It is, somehow, also *not* an entirely proper unfolding out of what emerges before it in originary experience.

How can Heidegger have it both ways? There is a radical ontological claim at work here, being gestured to already in Heidegger's earliest thinking, which has to do with the ontological difference, that is, the difference between beings and Being, and the dynamic according to which the proper mode of Being's participation in the self-showing or emergence of beings is withdrawal, non-appearance, and even, on the ontological level, nearly non-occurrence. But this must wait until chapter 2, where we will undertake our destructive excavation of the *Grund* of Aristotelian *Grundbegriffe*, or the ultimate "ground" out of which Aristotle's "basic concepts" arise.

Heidegger's Shifting Terminology for Destructive Thinking

Before we move on to chapter 2, just a word about the various and often conflicting ways in which Heidegger describes this project of destructive reading, for this shifting terminology could easily be a source of confusion. To be sure, Heidegger's thought is so experimental, so adamantly situated at the very limit of what is thinkable and sayable according to the metaphysical vocabulary that he inherits from the tradition, that his project must take place on the very threshold of incomprehensibility.[12]

Specifically with reference to our focus here, when Heidegger is searching for the proper technical terms to describe the mode of thinking that will be provoked by and indeed accompany a destruction of Aristotle, he uses a litany of terms with quite different associations and values, often clarifying these through their opposition to other more orthodox and familiar disciplines or modes of research. The problem we wish to address here is simply that, beyond the variety of terminology, it is the case that the meanings and the relative values of the terms used undergo dramatic reversals from one context to the next. A given term can assume a negative value in one discussion and be criticized as irremediably tradition-bound and metaphysical, while in another discussion one finds the very same term rehabilitated and now naming the mode of potentially extra-metaphysical destruction-supported inquiry that Heidegger himself champions and presents as worthy of pursuit and praise. Indeed, over the course of this period, Heidegger will refer to this radical destructive thinking as *scientific, phenomenological,* and *philosophical,* as *logic* itself, as the *history of philosophy,* and finally as emphatically *neither philosophical nor historiological,* but rather as *philological.* Clearly, this requires a bit of sorting out.

I would suggest that this is because Heidegger is always confronting a *context-specific* decision about how to radicalize his inherited metaphysical vocabulary and, consequently, he is forced to employ a host of tactics rather than a general strategy. Context-determined requirements dictate his terminological decisions at every turn. Rather than simply generating arbitrary neologisms in order to think in excess of the inherited metaphysical tradition, Heidegger feels compelled to take on the traditional vocabulary and press it into service, radicalizing it and amplifying some of its undeveloped tendencies. In many contexts, he will introduce a distinction within the semantic field of a traditional term, and then point to some of its tendencies or modes as potentially revealing and helpful, while criticizing others as irremediably metaphysical, attentive only to present beings in their presence. At other points, Heidegger recuperates a given term by placing it in an extreme, sometimes exaggerated, logical opposition with another term, even if their actual usage and associations do not support the rigidity or extremity of this oppositional definition. Finally, Heidegger sometimes takes a traditional term and distances it from its usual associations simply by unpacking its etymology.

Consider Heidegger's recuperation of the term *Wissenschaft* or "science, discipline, branch of knowledge" in his 1926 course, *Basic Concepts of Ancient Philosophy*. As is well known, later on in his career, Heidegger will often energetically oppose his own thinking, or the thinking he sees as demanded of us today, to the scientific mode. For example, in a somewhat infamous and intentionally provocative statement in the above-cited 1951–52 lecture course, *What Is Called Thinking?* Heidegger will declare simply and definitively, "Science does not think" (*WT* 4/8). However, in the 1926 lecture course, Heidegger embraces science and even identifies his own destructive project with one particular manifestation or mode of scientific thinking: destruction engages in "critical science," which is then opposed to "positive science" (*BCAncP* 4–5/5–6). We will return in chapter 2 to a deeper discussion of this particular distinction, but for our purposes here, we can just note the way in which critical science becomes essentially defined as marking and thinking a certain Aristotelian *krisis* or "separation" of Being from beings, while positive science is shown to think nothing but present beings already "posited" or "positioned" there and appearing in their simple presence before us.

In 1925, in a set of lectures he presented to the Kassel Society for Art and Science entitled "Wilhelm Dilthey's Research and the Current Struggle for a Historical Worldview," Heidegger describes this very same destructive project not as "critical science," but as emphatically "phenomenological" thinking, though here too he will need to introduce a distinction between different modes of phenomenology.[13] Indeed, he introduces destruction as a necessary extension of and a (perhaps not so friendly) amendment to what he sees as Husserl's ahistorical phenomenological project ("WDR" 273).[14] Heidegger writes near the end of this talk:

> To bring home the meaning of historical research and its possibilities we will choose as our example the history of philosophy. This example has not been chosen arbitrarily, but rather because phenomenology,

> a genuine and radical trend in [the recent history of] philosophy, is marked by a lack of history, even an animosity toward history. For it believes that it can dispense with all that has been as irrelevant and come to the matters themselves on its own. But here phenomenology remains suspended in traditional ways of raising questions. And yet it belongs to the very sense of phenomenological research to meditate time and time again upon its own sense and shake off all spurious traditions in order activate a genuine sense of the past. ("WDR" 273)

For Heidegger, here and elsewhere, Dilthey's central contribution is his insight into human Dasein as essentially historical. Dilthey thereby offers a response to what Heidegger sees as a contemporary "crisis of philosophy as a science," and brings about "a revolution in the very way philosophical questions are being raised" ("WDR" 242). The phenomenology of Husserl remained mired in this contemporary crisis precisely due to its ahistoricality, as well as its turning away from ontology, from the question of Being or "what is," in Heidegger's assessment. If thinking is fundamentally historical and if human experience and thought are *always already* of beings and Being, then Husserlian phenomenology must be rejected as not scientific and not philosophical enough, indeed not phenomenological enough.

Heidegger writes here, in an extremely rich passage that crystallizes much of the trajectory of his thinking during the rest of the 1920s and beyond:

> The question of historical inquiry in philosophy is referred back to the fundamental question of Being itself. This question of Being must be raised in a way that preserves its continuity with the first scientific formulation of the question of Being by the Greeks, in order to investigate the legitimacy and fundamental limits of this formulation. If we succeed in returning scientific philosophy to its real themes, we may be assured that this kind of research will once again be fruitful for the sciences. Logic will then not be a supplementary formulation after the fact of scientific procedures, but rather a basic guide that runs ahead of the sciences and discloses their fundamental concepts. For this, we need the history of philosophy, so that we may understand the ancients anew. We must press forward so that we may once again be equal to the questioning of the ancient Greeks. ("WDR" 274)

As we discussed in the "Introduction," the question of Being, which we neither ask today nor worry about in the least, but which is evidently fundamental to our understanding of our world and ourselves, is what sends us back into the history of philosophy and ultimately to Aristotle. For it is that history that transmits to us a preconception of what it means to be, such that we never manage to suffer this question as a question. By destructively tracing our own implicit notion of Being back to its origin among the Greeks, we can once again confront beings in their relation to Being. This would provide the sciences, and their studies of present beings, with the foundation they are at present only presuming to possess. And if we were to allow this historically destroyed and, thus, liberated confrontation with beings to dictate our logic, that is, the rules according to which beings demand to be thought, logic would cease to be a mere handmaiden to the sciences. It would be understood rather as what first gives science its subject matter.[15]

Finally, just a year prior, in the 1924 course we investigated earlier, destruction is rendered in yet again quite different terms. Heidegger insists here that the destructive reading of Aristotle

> has no philosophical aim at all [*keine philosophische Abzweckung*]; it is concerned with understanding basic concepts in their conceptuality. The aim is *philological* in that it intends to bring the *reading* of philosophers somewhat more into practice. (*BCArP* 4/5)

What exactly does Heidegger have in mind here? Destructively interpreting Aristotelian concepts is not philosophical, but rather philological?[16] It is philological, insofar as it engages in and hopes to model the actual "reading" of the Aristotelian text. He then explains:

> [In these lectures] we offer *no philosophy*, much less a history of philosophy. If *philology* means the *passion* [Leidenschaft] *for knowledge of what has been expressed*, then what we are doing is philology. (*BCArP* 4/5)

The task here is avowedly not "philosophical," *if this means* engaging in a quasi-scientific universalizing mode of thinking that would seek to define and make use of concepts abstracted from their origins. As we have heard, thinking concepts in their conceptuality requires the exact opposite of this, thinking them as not entirely abstractable. Insofar as these concepts are to be thought in their *Bodenständigkeit*, or in their arising out of and "standing" on a peculiar *Boden*, "soil," or "earth," they are not to be thought as "just any basic concepts, but *as Aristotle's*" (*BCArP* 13/15). We must think them in their emergence from the very peculiar set of originary experiences of the world in its unfolding at that historical moment, which is uncovered by the destructive method of reading. Anything else would be to misunderstand what makes a concept a concept, namely, its conceptuality, its dynamic confrontation with and emergence out of what is not yet grasped and mastered by thought.

However, this does not entail that destruction is engaged in studying the "history of philosophy" as it is usually carried out. As Heidegger writes in 1926,

> Our concern is philosophical understanding, not historiography [*keine Historie*] . . . [and] such understanding is not a matter of becoming informed about opinions, tenets, views. What *is* necessary is that we co-philosophize [*mitphilosophieren*]. (*BCAncP* 9/12–13)

In an orthodox or analytic mode, historiographers of philosophy tend to think of their subject matter as reducible to the positions of, or the ultimate claims of, and the arguments provided by a given philosopher. One speaks of the historical developments in philosophy in terms of "Cartesianism" or "Kantianism," of "rationalism" or "empiricism," of "idealism" or "realism," and one means thereby to refer to a certain established profile of this or that thinker, this or that school, or simply a basic tenet or set of tenets. The moment prior to the emergence of the concept, and *prior to the logic that this emergence generates,* is by definition illogical or at least extra-logical, and for precisely this reason has no value for orthodox historians of philosophy. They cannot possibly take a scholarly interest in being immersed in, much less co-philosophizing along with, what we find through destruction in the text of Aristotle, namely the dynamic activity of ushering concepts into existence from out of originating preconceptual experiences. From the Heideggerian perspective, the analytic historian of philosophy is like a cartographer studying all the world's rivers who decides, as a methodological principle, to stop in each case a kilometer short of the river's source, its spring. It might be possible in this way to chart the course of many rivers with great precision, but one will remain forever uncomprehending of where they come from and why they flow.

It is on these specific terms, then, that Heidegger renounces in 1924 both philosophy and the history of philosophy in favor of "philology," albeit in a form radicalized according to the third tactic mentioned above; that is, a philology that has been returned to the roots indicated by its etymology. This philology is a *philia* of *logos,* specifically a "desire" or "fondness" for Aristotle's gathering "discourse," his "text." Indeed, Heidegger emphasizes the element here of *Leidenschaft* or "passion," in order to point toward that ultimate source of Aristotle's originary experiences. We find ourselves related to that source not by cognizing it or grasping it clearly, but by *leiden* or "suffering," being "affected by" and thereby called back to his text and what gave itself to his thinking as he inaugurated the metaphysical tradition we inherit.

In sum, we must be prepared to take up the project of destruction in various contexts and understand how different aspects of it can be illuminated by describing it as critically scientific, philosophical, historical, phenomenological, philosophical, or philological and passionate, or even by opposing it in turn to any of these. All together, these help us understand precisely how the destructive method inhabits and operates within the Aristotelian text. In chapter 2, we must go deeper into the source or ground that gives itself, in its own proper manner, in the experiences out of which Aristotle generates his fundamental concepts.

2

The Ground of Metaphysics and the *Krisis* in the Aristotelian Text

Early on in *Basic Concepts of Aristotelian Philosophy*, the 1924 course that was our primary focus in chapter 1, Heidegger observes that the project on which he and his students are embarking, the destructive reading of the Aristotelian text, proceeds on the strength of a certain unexamined principle, a belief. He writes:

> A *methodological* presupposition [of this course is]: *a faith in history* [Glauben an die Geschichte], in the sense that *history and the historical past have the possibility, insofar as the way is made clear for them* [sofern ihn nur die Bahn frei gemacht wird], *of giving a jolt* [einen Stoß] *to the present or, better yet, to the future*. (*BCArP* 5/6, translation modified)

As we saw already in the "Introduction," beginning with a certain mood of dissatisfaction with our present, Heidegger sees us as being called upon to turn our attention to our past, to the distant Greek origin of philosophizing in the West and to Aristotle particularly. But this response to our present dissatisfaction only makes sense, Heidegger rightly observes here, if one possesses what he refers to as a "faith in history"—a belief that by way of a thoughtful engagement with the past we might both deliver and receive the *Stoß*, the "jolt, knock" that would help to liberate us from the constraints on thought and action under which we currently labor. Indeed, we must even believe that the past could go beyond just interrupting or disrupting the present. Perhaps it could, precisely as our past, send us somehow *toward* as-yet undetermined, even unimaginable, future ways of thinking and being in the world. In any case, if we turn to Aristotle and the tradition that unfolds after him at this moment with any such aspiration, we do so only in the belief that the past can somehow effect this urgently needed liberation of thought and action, if only "the way is made clear for it" to do so. And this "clearing the way for" such an alteration is precisely what is accomplished by the hermeneutic method Heidegger calls "destruction."

Neither Solicitation and Repetition nor Quarantine and Rejection

It is hard *not* to hear in the passage above a clear echo of Nietzsche's oft-cited remark from the second of his *Unfashionable Observations*. At the outset of "On the Utility and Liability of History for Life," Nietzsche proclaims:

> It is only to the extent that I am a student of more ancient times—above all, of ancient Greece—that I, as a child of our time, have had such unfashionable experiences [*unzeitgemässen Erfahrungen*]. But I have to concede this much to myself as someone who by occupation is a classical philologist, for I have no idea what the significance of classical philology would be in our age, if not to have an unfashionable effect—that is, to work against the time and thereby have an effect upon it, hopefully for the benefit of a future time [*das heisst gegen die Zeit und dadurch auf die Zeit und hoffentlich zu Gunsten einer kommenden Zeit—zu wirken*].[1]

In this essay, Nietzsche has set his critical sights on the powerful and ascendant surge of historicism in late modern thought, which he diagnoses as oppressive to creativity and to the lively exercise of human faculties. European culture had over the centuries seen the gradual undermining of long-trusted authoritative sources of value and meaning, such as the church or even worldly figures of authority, a complex historical process that Nietzsche will characterize in *The Gay Science* as the "death of God."[2] Buoyed by the manifest successes of modern natural science, the Enlightenment response to the decline of those past idols was the belief that Reason itself could provide every individual human being with their own sufficient internal ground for both moral conduct and an understanding of one's world. However, Reason proved itself capable not only of sustaining and justifying desirable moral conduct, political structures, and traditional wisdom about the world, but of interrogating and utterly destabilizing any and all of these as well.

As the Enlightenment thus lost momentum, historicism blossomed at the end of the eighteenth and early nineteenth centuries, suggesting that the exhaustive, scientific, and systematic study of the historical past, an accurate and detailed mapping of facts on the ground and the dynamics in play there, would allow us to thoroughly understand any historical event, and even perhaps our own present. All could in principle be illuminated by this historically contextualizing light. Thinking and value might well be irremediably historically constituted, never a purified and verified execution of divine will or Reason itself, but history itself could nonetheless be studied and thoroughly illuminated by the employment of historiological method, which holds exhaustive illumination as a regulative ideal, a guiding aspiration. This confidence unleashed a frenzy of historical studies in Europe, especially among the Germans. And it is the presumption of the absolute, unimpeachable, and all-justifying value of coming to know every single thing about our past that Nietzsche paints in the second of the *Unfashionable Observations* as toxic, as antagonistic to the creation of new values and to the articulation of new and unprecedented interpretations of the world in which we find ourselves. For Nietzsche, in late modernity, the present's fascination with the past eclipses its future.

And it is in opposition to this historicist tendency that Nietzsche proposes in the essay a certain valorization of the power of forgetting, after which he introduces that complex, threefold method by which we can both take up and leave behind our inherited tradition, as was briefly discussed earlier in the "Introduction." He maps out the complex combination of a certain mining of the past for moments of creative, energetic non-conformity that might serve to inspire and direct our own futural projects (*monumental history*), a passionate and devoted appreciation of and desire to preserve the past in all its complexity and detail (*antiquarian history*), and a probing and uncompromising critique of the past and its shortcomings or blind spots (*critical history*).[3] Nietzsche calls for this multifaceted serial approach, in which *life* is then allowed to act as the alchemist, determining how the three modes come together into a compound whole over time. This will allow us, Nietzsche hopes, to resist the stranglehold of scientific historiography, freeing contemporary culture from the past's constraints, while nonetheless providing it with a way of safely mining the past for the material out of which to create new and un-anticipatable values and concepts.

Is Heidegger not thinking along quite similar lines when he imagines a destructive reading of the Aristotelian text effecting a jolt or a knock to the present, indeed, in such a way that the present opens up into an as-yet undetermined future? If so, I suggest that we ask precisely how Heideggerian destruction presumes to bring about this liberation and this futurally directed impulse or push. Scholars have suggested two ways of explaining how the early Heidegger imagines the destruction of Aristotle providing such a push: either in the mode of *solicitation and repetition* or in the mode of *quarantine and rejection.*

On the one hand, some have seen destruction as capable of making an untimely and salubrious contribution to our present thinking about our world and our place in it insofar as this method excavates, calls forth, articulates, and then allows for the repetition of some positive insight or insights, some still-relevant wisdom, that is present in the Aristotelian text.[4] In this fundamentally nostalgic version of Heideggerian destruction, one would push back through the obscuring and reifying subsequent interpretations of classical sources to find certain experiential content at the base of Aristotelian conceptualizing, which we might then uncover and retrieve, in order to begin to think and conduct ourselves differently.

And admittedly, Heidegger does seem at times to suggest something along these lines, for instance when he observes in *Being and Time*:

> Tradition takes what has come down to us and delivers it over to self-evidence; it blocks our access to those primordial "sources" [*ursprüngliche "Quellen"*] from which the categories and concepts handed down to us have been in part genuinely created [*in echter Weise geschöpft*]. (*BT* 43/21)

Here, the *ursprüngliche Quellen*, or "originary sources" might seem to be present and then accessible there in the experience of Aristotle, and perhaps even more so in those who came before him and Plato, the pre-Socratics. We need only set aside the subsequent Romanizing then Christianizing and then modernizing reception of Aristotle's immediate and thoughtful response to his world, in order to gain access to that register of pre-metaphysical experience.[5]

On the other hand, and quite to the contrary, scholars have also seen the task of destruction as wholly negative, as an attempt to show the way in which the concepts of the Aristotelian tradition emerge out of and are grounded in an already metaphysically determined originary experience of beings. Under this interpretation, the task of destruction would be to disconnect from the tradition, from the concepts *and the originary experiences from which they are drawn*, by critically revealing first the myopia or at least metaphysically predetermined and reductive mode of experiencing beings that was already at work among even the ancient Greeks, as well as then also the ultimately unhealthy and dehumanizing consequences of the concepts that emerged there. We would thereby free ourselves from our inherited traditional conceptual constraints and become capable of encountering beings directly and thinking them otherwise.[6] Heidegger might be heard describing this more exclusively negative or critical project, also in *Being and Time*, when he writes:

> If the question of Being is to have its own history made transparent, then this hardened tradition must be loosened up [*Auflockerung*], and the concealments [*Verdeckungen*] it has brought about must be dissolved [*Ablösung*]. (*BT* 44/22)

I wish to insist here that Heidegger's destructive method of reading the texts of Aristotle amounts to neither a simple repetition nor a simple rejection of Aristotelian thought. It is not that these interpretations of destruction are simply wrong, so much as they are partial or incomplete, with each lacking the true insight of the other. Indeed, as we shall see, the destructive method resists being reduced to either of these interpretations because it presumes *a radical and complex ontology of the Aristotelian text*—Heidegger approaches the text *as being more than itself, as saying more than it says.* What is "in" the text includes its beyond, and thinking in relation to that excessive moment in the Aristotelian text is the ultimate positive accomplishment of destructive reading.

Gadamer and Arendt on the Ambivalence of Heidegger's Destruction of Aristotle

This fundamental ambivalence at the very heart of the project of destruction was noted by those in attendance at the talks and lecture courses in which Heidegger first introduced it. Hans-Georg Gadamer reports:

> Today no one would doubt that the basic purpose of Heidegger's preoccupation with Aristotle was a critical and destructive one. At that time [during the lecture courses of the early 1920s], however, this purpose was not so clear . . . Perhaps what happened then, not only to the students, but to Heidegger himself, was that the power of Aristotle, though an adversary, came to dominate him for a time.[7]

Looking back here in 1964, Gadamer claims that in the decades since the 1920s, among interpreters of Heidegger, the purely negative conception of destruction laid out above has largely won out over the positive or recuperative one. Most scholars, he seems to suggest, see Aristotle clearly and simply as Heidegger's "adversary" in the method of destructive reading. Perhaps Gadamer is right in his estimation of the scholarly state of the question, perhaps not. More interesting, in any case, is Gadamer's insistence that at the time the lecture courses were taking place, the students (and even Heidegger himself) seemed to experience a fundamental and unresolved ambivalence in the project of destruction. That is, Heidegger's students in the courses were often not certain whether, on the one hand, they were witnessing a deeply revealing and insightful new interpretation of Aristotle, that is, an excavation of what was right there in the text of Aristotle itself though previously unremarked by scholars; or, on the other hand, they were being confronted with Professor Heidegger's purely critical attack on and rejection of Aristotle, supplemented by and grounded in his own original and revolutionary insights into factical life.

And to be clear, this lack of clarity in no way hindered, but rather seemed to fuel the rise of Heidegger's reputation as a teacher. On the basis of these courses, among an entire generation of philosophy students all over Germany, either through direct experience or secondhand accounts, Heidegger's renown was spreading, in the oft-quoted phrase of Hannah Arendt, "like the rumor of a hidden king." And Arendt goes on to say:

> The rumor about Heidegger put it quite simply. Thinking has come to life again; the cultural treasures of the past, believed to be dead, are being made to speak, in the course of which it turns out that they propose things altogether different from the familiar, worn-out trivialities they had been presumed to say. There exists a teacher; one can perhaps learn to think.[8]

In her account of the reception of the destructive project being carried out in those courses, Arendt does nothing to mitigate that impression of deep ambivalence which Gadamer describes. Heidegger was indeed understood to be engaging with and mining the "cultural treasures of the past," but apparently not in order to repeat or get it right about what was said there, or at least not what had long been presumed to be said there. Nor was he aiming simply to critique and set those treasures aside. Rather, Heidegger was reading in such a way as to provoke these traditionary texts into saying something unheard of, unnoticed there, and, precisely thereby, something revolutionary. Most vitally, Arendt makes very clear that this way of engaging with the past was understood *as itself a new and revolutionary "thinking."* It was not a preparatory historical study on the way to our being able to think originally and philosophically. Rather, destruction was thinking itself now "come to life."

Werner Marx's *Heidegger and the Tradition*

Let us start off from that school of interpretation which Gadamer suggests had won the day, the conception of Heidegger's destructive project as primarily negative, a critical rejection of and departure from the tradition. We can find a rich, admirably clear, and influential articulation of this approach in Werner Marx's study, *Heidegger and the Tradition*.[9]

Indeed, one comes to understand very early in Marx's book that the "and" in its title is intended as emphatically *disjunctive*, a sort of *uncoupling*. It presents the traditional or metaphysical thinking concerning three concepts—Being, essence, and human being—and opposes these to Heidegger's completely distinct and alternative manner of thinking each concept. It is clear that, for Marx, Heidegger approaches the entire history of Western philosophy as a monolithic whole, finding "the same basic traits [*dieselben Grunzüge*]" in the thinking that extends from Aristotle's *ousia* to Hegel's *Sein*. Marx sums up this thought, saying:

> This is essentially why we regard ourselves as justified in terming the thinking from Plato and Aristotle to Hegel simply as "the tradition" and viewing, on the other hand, Heidegger's thinking as the attempt toward a "turning away" from this tradition. From this we derive the justification for the title of the present work [i.e., *Heidegger and the Tradition*].[10]

And there are numerous passages in which Marx repeats his fundamental characterization of the Heideggerian destructive project as a dismissal and a setting-aside of traditional Aristotelian thinking. He writes, for instance:

> The task of the present exposition will be to demonstrate how Heidegger's question as to Being and essence, turning away in another direction from the Aristotelian, gains access to another *region* [*in einen anderen Bereich*], attains another dimension [*in eine andere Dimension*].[11]

For Marx and other like-minded interpreters, Heidegger's thinking turns in "another direction" relative to that of Aristotle. And it would ultimately aim to establish itself even in "another region" or "another dimension" with respect to the territory mapped by the entire metaphysical tradition. As will become clear, I disagree fundamentally with this characterization of how Heidegger's thinking relates to the tradition in the mode of destruction.

Nonetheless, I do find in Marx's book many helpful and illuminating observations and I would like to begin with one of those. Marx observes that, for Heidegger, in order to bring his readers to think essence and Being wholly otherwise, which is to say, according to Marx, in order to access that entirely other region of thinking, it is not possible to simply present those readers with an alternative definition, explanation, or description of Being and its relation to beings. Any such effort would by its very form render its *definiendum* a present and available being, by treating it as definable, explainable, or describable in traditional terms. Thus, Marx rightly insists, Heidegger must proceed instead by asking his readers to *Mitfragen* or "question along with" him, immersing themselves in the activity of questioning what gives itself to us today as the urgently "to-be-thought [*das Zu-denkende*]" or as what is "worthy of thought [*denkwürdig*]," but what is nonetheless *not yet* seized upon and not yet mastered by thought in its traditional mode.[12] Marx writes:

> Only an attitude that *asks-along-with* [*eine* mitfragende *Einstellung*] has the prospect of understanding the meaning of Being and essence that departs from the tradition . . . Every asking-along, however, must attain to a *thinking-along-with* [Mitdenken] . . . [which] can succeed only if it holds itself open in a relationship of *krisis*, or separation, from its thought content, but of course in such a manner that it still remains close to it and does not sacrifice the purpose of a thinking-along-with.[13]

This is a vital point, for Marx has identified both the real challenge for Heidegger, thinking beings and Being in an altogether unprecedented way, and a central and powerful aspect of Heidegger's specific response to this challenge—namely, a certain way of marking and even maintaining *in thinking*, rather than bridging, the distance between questioning and the subject matter of questioning.[14]

According to Marx, Heidegger attempts to bring a certain feature of "questioning" into our substantive and truth-accomplishing "thinking" of Being. As Marx observes above, when we encounter a subject matter in the mode of authentic questioning and wondering, the *krisis*—Greek for "separation, division"—that separates us from what is being asked after and inquired into is explicitly and by definition experienced and acknowledged in our comportment toward our subject matter. The great challenge for Heidegger, in Marx's eyes, is how to move from a mode in which he is asking after Being and beings to a mode in which he thinks these, while nevertheless maintaining and incorporating the initial interrogative *krisis* into his thoughtful relation to his subject matter. This is an extremely helpful formulation of Heidegger's task, to my mind, which we will do well to keep in mind as we proceed to think through the ultimate aim of destruction.

Unfortunately, Marx himself sees the destructive reading of the metaphysical tradition as playing only a limited and preliminary role, critically insulating us from traditional ways of thinking and effecting a kind of transposition to a new region, a new extra-traditional and extra-metaphysical dimension. But destruction does not function in this purely critical and preparatory mode for Heidegger, I would suggest. Indeed, as we heard earlier in a remark from *Being and Time*, "to bury the past in nullity [*Nichtigkeit*] is not the purpose of destruction; its aim is *positive*" (*BT*

44/23). The question remains, however, how precisely does destruction, and its engagement with texts in the tradition of metaphysical thinking, accomplish something "positive" for the project of thinking in excess of metaphysics?

Philosophy as "Critical Science"

Contra Marx, and paradoxically, destruction will prove to make a positive contribution to thinking in excess of the tradition only through a complete descent into that very tradition, only through a radical immersion in the thinking of, for instance, Aristotle. Indeed, by way of a destructive descent or immersion, Heidegger (along with us, his readers) will encounter and hope to maintain that very *krisis* which Marx rightly identified as central to Heidegger's project. For, right at the heart of the most traditional of texts in the history of metaphysics, Heideggerian destruction locates the *krisis* that opens up between us and Being, which it is the task of the extra-metaphysical thinking of "what is" not to overcome, but to guard, acknowledge, and maintain.

Let us turn now to the 1926 lecture course, *Basic Concepts of Ancient Philosophy*, a set of sometimes quite elliptical lecture notes, in which Heidegger introduces his project in the following terms. He writes:

> Aim [*Absicht*]: Penetrating into the understanding [*Eindringen in das Verständnis*] of fundamental scientific concepts . . .
> Character: Introductory, i.e., pressing forward step by step toward what is meant in the concepts [*zu dem in den Begriffen Gemeinten*] and toward the manner of creating and grounding these concepts [Bildung *und* Bergündung *dieser Begriffe*]. (*BCAncP* 1/1)

This course will be "introductory," specifically in the sense that it is directed primarily toward accomplishing a certain *Eindringen*, literally a "pushing or pressing into," a "penetration" or a "permeation," of the grounding concepts of ancient Greek philosophy that we inherit today.

What precisely does this mean? According to Heidegger here, this requires moving forward "step by step." More specifically, we must not grasp the concept merely as a logical form, but rather we have to move through this and beyond it, seeing the concept in relation to "what is meant by the concept." We will then, along with Heidegger, trace the movement by which the ancients create or form their concepts in an attempt to do justice to what they "mean," that reality to which those concepts refer.

There is a deep resonance here with the method described and employed in the 1924 course on which we focused primarily in chapter 1, *Basic Concepts of Aristotelian Philosophy*. However, as we shall see, Heidegger here seems to be digging down not merely through the concepts into their subtending register of experience, but emphatically beyond this, beneath the register of experience. He will try to bring his students (and us) into contact with what is ultimately "meant" or "intended" by the concepts— not the pre-conceptual experiences, but the beings that emerged into view and showed themselves to the ancient thinker in those experiences, as well as the Being that is their source or ground.

Heidegger sets out pursuing a "preliminary orientation regarding the essence and task of philosophy" as such, and he suggests that one path by which we could uncover the task and essence of philosophy is by returning to its moment of origination, "tracing its original breakthrough, its first decisive formation" (*BCAncP* 4/5). However, for that we require some preparation. Thus, he writes:

> We will pursue another path preliminarily, the one that lies nearest: What is nearest is the sphere of the non-philosophical sciences. It is in distinguishing it [philosophy] from these [*In Unterscheidung gegen sie*] that we wish to [preliminarily] determine philosophy. (*BCAncP* 4/5, translation modified)

Before turning to the invention of philosophy with the Greeks in order to determine what is essential to philosophizing, Heidegger suggests that we begin instead by opposing philosophy as one branch of "science" to the other nonphilosophical "sciences," because these latter are "nearest" to us here at the outset, in the hermeneutical context from which we are initiating an interpretation of Aristotle and the other ancients. Presumably Heidegger means here that the nonphilosophical sciences are "nearest" insofar as they represent the determining and dominant way of engaging with the world for himself and for his students, as members of the university community at that late-modern historical moment and in this place in the world. If you wish to know "what is" in Germany in 1926, science is the first and obvious choice.

One is reminded here of what Heidegger will say in 1929, in the lecture "What Is Metaphysics?" There, as we have already noted in the "Introduction," Heidegger famously declares the necessity and the value of thinking nothing. Indeed, he intends to expose himself and his listeners in their thinking to the full sway of nothing, that is, to what is held quite distinct from any and all of the beings to which the sciences by definition generally limit their investigations. The sciences maintain their purity by rigorously insisting that they study this or that being, this or that region of beings, "and beyond that, nothing," to which Heidegger asks, "What about this nothing?" ("WM" 84/180). It is in launching this project that Heidegger observes at one point the hermeneutical situation in which he and his listeners are situated:

> We are questioning, here and now, for ourselves. Our Dasein—in the community of researchers, teachers, and students [i.e., immersed in the life of a European university]—is determined by science. ("WM" 82/178, translation modified)

Beginning apparently from this very same situation of inquiry in the 1926 course, Heidegger points out the striking fact that even in a world in which science seems to have a monopoly on truth, none of the other sciences at the university asks or thinks about what they themselves are.

> If the mathematician wished to say what mathematics is, not by presenting mathematical problems and proofs, but by talking *about* mathematics, its objects and method, then he could no longer employ mathematical proofs or concepts . . . When scientists try to answer such questions, they are beginning to philosophize. (*BCAncP* 4/5–6)

It is in light of this observation that philosophy first comes into view here. In this context, it presents itself accordingly not as a non-science, but as "the most radical science [*die radikalste Wissenschaft*]," in the sense of pressing down to the *radix* or the "root" of every science, and as "*quite simply* the *most original and proper science* [die ursprünglichste und eigentliche Wissenschaft schlechthin]" (*BCAncP* 3/3).

A vital distinction must be made here, for it is not simply the case that philosophy is a science just like all the others, with the additional feature of being more rigorous or more well-grounded (since one might insist, for instance, that philosophy alone has in principle no unexamined presuppositions). Not at all. Rather, there is a more profound difference here in play and, as was briefly mentioned at the end of chapter 1, Heidegger introduces two distinct species within the genus "science" in order to convey this difference. All other sciences are "*positive* sciences," whereas philosophy alone is the "*critical* science." He appeals to etymology to explain this:

Positive: *ponere*—"to posit," "to lay down"; *positum*—"what has been laid down," what already lies there before us [*was schon vorliegt*]. Numbers are already there, spatial relations exist, nature is at hand, language is present, and so is literature. All this is *positum*, it lies there. It is a being; everything uncovered in science is *a being*. *Positive sciences are sciences of beings.*
. . .
Critical: κρίνειν—"to separate [*scheiden*]," "to differentiate [*unterscheiden*]" . . . [but] every science is constantly differentiating and thus determining the differentiated [thing]. Thus, if philosophy . . . has a preeminently "critical" character, it must accomplish a preeminent differentiating . . . This differentiation concerns not beings and beings, but beings and Being. "Being"—under this term nothing is to be represented [*darunter ist nichts vorzustellen*] . . . In beings *to see and to lay hold of and distinguish Being from beings* [das Sein zu sehen und zu erfassen und gegen Seiendes zu unterscheiden], that is the task of the differentiating science, of philosophy. Its theme is Being and never beings. (*BCAncP* 5/6–7, translation modified)

This is an extremely rich passage, and the distinctions in play here will continue to be a salient feature of Heidegger's thinking over the course of his entire career, for we have Heidegger introducing very clearly nothing other than what he will later term "the ontological difference" (*BPP* 17/23),[15] the distinction between Being and beings. Let us thus take our time moving through this passage, appealing where necessary to a few other moments in the lecture course for clarification and expansion.

Heidegger will have us understand philosophy, at its moment of origination among the ancient Greeks, as "critical science," in the crucial sense that, unlike the "positive" sciences, its subject matter, Being, is not laying there before it when philosophy is initiated. Its subject matter is not *schon* or "already" there, present and available for scrutiny, offering itself for exhaustive knowing and mastering. Philosophy's subject matter, Being, is precisely what is not yet there to be thought or asked after as such; it must first be glimpsed so that it can be wondered at, questioned, and eventually perhaps thought.

Philosophy, Heidegger tells us, accomplished this by allowing a *krisis* or a "separation, differentiation" to present itself for the first time, and it is that separation which first relates philosophy to its subject matter, Being. Notice that we do not say that philosophy must itself introduce or engineer such a separation—it is not the case that the distinction between Being and beings is a philosophical construction. Rather, philosophy must initially question and then think in such a way that Being for the first time emerges in relation to, but also as distinguished from, the beings that are always already lying there before us in experience. Prior to philosophy's letting Being show itself as distinguished from beings, the distinction between these two is not there to be experienced, but there is nonetheless some potential for a distinction between Being and beings that philosophy allows to unfold.

Crucial for us is Heidegger's insistence here that, for the Greeks and for Aristotle in particular, Being, as the subject matter of this philosophical or critical scientific thinking, is confronted as

> what does not lie there [*was nicht vorliegt*] for natural experience, but is rather hidden [*verborgen*], what never lies before and is nevertheless already and indeed always understood [*nie vorliegt und doch schon und zwar immer verstanden*]. (*BCAncP* 6/7)

What precisely does this entail for the method of destruction? How are we to read the pre-Socratics, Plato, and especially Aristotle as, for Heidegger, engaging already in precisely this critical science?

As we learned earlier from *Being and Time*, we focus destructively on "the posing of the question each time [*die jeweilige Fragestellung*]" (*BT* 44/22). The Greek philosophers first confront Being in their texts as "initially unknown, closed off, inaccessible [*zunächst unbekannt, verschlossen, unzugänglich*]" (*BCAncP* 6/8), as withdrawn behind or within beings but somehow nevertheless already experienced in its non-presence—Being "never lies before" us and "is not given in experience," though it is in some oblique way "already and always understood" or, from another passage just a bit later, "*always*, though *implicitly, co-understood* [immer, *obzwar* unausdrücklich, *mitverstanden*]" (*BCAncP* 6–7/9). That is, in experiencing beings, in their presentation of themselves as beings, we in some sense "co-understand" the Being that supports them, that makes them all beings, but precisely in its receding behind them. And we use the terms "is," "are," and "being" according to this oblique presumed pre-understanding. Heidegger writes:

> Everyone understands when we say, the weather "is" dreary, the trees "are" in bloom ... [We have] Being-understanding [*Seinsverständis*], although no concept [of Being]. (*BCAncP* 7/9)

Greek philosophers, Heidegger insists in this course, up to and culminating in Aristotle, responded to precisely this condition—recognizing Being as not yet known, as unavailable, but as co-understood with the beings it allows to emerge. And this initial experience of Being *as question-*

worthy, despite the immediate availability and accessibility everywhere of beings, is what Heidegger sees as the real accomplishment of Aristotle's critical philosophy.

The Double *Krisis* in the Aristotelian Text

In spite of the fact that, due to the exigencies of everyday praxis, "all methods and concepts are tailored toward the laying hold of and determining of beings" (*BCAncP* 6/8), the Greeks nevertheless succeeded in separating off Being and asking about it as such, addressing themselves to it, *in their questioning*, as hidden and withdrawn behind the dizzying landscape of beings that are emerging before us in human experience. The Greeks realized that in order to proceed critically, differentiating Being as not yet accessible, philosophy "required its own ways and investigations [*eigene Wege und Forschungen*], in order to uncover it [Being] [*es zu entdecken*], i.e., to perform the differentiation [of Being from beings] [*den Unterschied zu vollziehen*]" (*BCAncP* 6/8).

This is the first *krisis* introduced by the critical science of philosophy itself, which achieved its full articulation in the *Metaphysics* of Aristotle—the distinguishing of Being from beings. Although the Greeks still experience and ultimately conceptualize Being only as the Being *of beings*, they nevertheless confronted Being first in the initial questioning moment *precisely as* "unknown, closed off, inaccessible [*unbekannt, verschlossen, unzugänglich*]" (*BCAncP* 6/8), and that questioning moment is, for Heidegger, more than the response that reduced Being to the presence of present beings. Indeed, the experience of that *krisis* in the questioning moment is the high-water mark of Greek philosophizing, as critical science.

It is important to note that for Heidegger, it is not the case that philosophy, as critical, separates off Being from beings and then investigates the former rather than the latter. No, the distinction between science and philosophy, or positive and critical science, is that the former investigates beings with no thought of Being at all, while the latter approaches beings *in their relation to Being*, which is to say, initially in relation to their Being as problematic and hidden. Beings appear to critical questioning as troubled by their relation to Being. Heidegger writes:

> Every critical [i.e., philosophical] investigation does look to beings, but in a different sense than do the positive sciences: it [philosophy as critical science] does not make beings its theme. Every one of the positive sciences co-understands [*versteht . . . mit*] Being in beings, but in a

different sense than does the critical science. They do not make Being a theme [*macht Sein nicht zum Thema*], the concept of Being and the structures of Being are not made problems; on the contrary the theme is the investigation of beings, such as those of nature or history. (*BCAncP* 7/9, translation modified)

This critical thinking of Being can be further illuminated by considering the peculiar way in which philosophy "deals with something '*universal*'" (*BCAncP* 7/9). Heidegger observes that

> Being is universal with regard to all beings; *every* being *is*, every being, *as* a being, has *Being*, and this universality of Being over against beings is a preeminent one, for there is also a universal that occurs in and among beings [*innerhalb des Seienden*]. (*BCAncP* 7/9)

Heidegger here is speaking of the way that, among a given class of beings, some feature or character can be universal, that is, possessed in general by every member of the class. Being a mammal is universal to all mammals, whether they are dogs, humans, or wallabies. And a feature of *this* kind of universality is that, if we were to draw together all the mammals, past, present, and future, the universal "mammal-ness" will be *exhaustively* present, distributed as it is throughout the entire set and being in effect *nowhere else outside the set.*

But this is what is different about the universality of Being. Although Being relates universally to all beings, giving each and every one of them their status as beings, it is not exhausted by the sum total of beings. It is not possessed by them in the way other universal features or essential characteristics are possessed by the class of beings to which they belong. Heidegger writes here:

> Being in general *lies out beyond* [liegt hinaus]. This lying beyond of Being and of the determinations of the Being of beings, over and above beings as such, is *transcendere*—"to surpass," transcendence. Not as supersensible, metaphysical in a bad sense, whereby what is meant is still a being. (*BCAncP* 7/10)

The early Heidegger's thinking is groping here toward a truly radical dimension of Being. And he is finding it exclusively in the first opening moments when Being is addressed in ancient thought as *question-worthy*. In that questioning of Being, before any concept is generated, he sees a hint, a trace of Being as essentially *hinaus liegend* or "lying out beyond" beings, as not exhausted by even the sum total of all beings. It is not a universal

THE GROUND OF METAPHYSICS AND THE *KRISIS* IN THE
ARISTOTELIAN TEXT

like other universals, but one that transcends its instantiations. However, this transcendence, this *übersteigen* or "surpassing, rising above," does not entail some supreme being situated somewhere else, some God or Nature or *Logos* or History controlling the unfolding of the whole sum of beings from an independent space.[16]

The trace in the Aristotelian text of this "surpassing" sense of Being only emerges into view through the destructive method of interpretation, in its co-philosophizing with Aristotle. The destructive interpreter does so, even if, in response to that initial and rich transcendence or withdrawal of Being, Aristotle will go on to reduce Being to the presence of present beings (to an ordinary universal) and let slip away that trace of Being in its question-worthiness, accomplishing its definitive eclipse for the entirety of the subsequent Western tradition. Nonetheless, destruction allows here a second *krisis* in the Aristotelian text to emerge.

In sum, Being is first distinguished from beings through philosophy's questioning in the mode of critical science—What does it mean *to be*? What is it precisely that we are saying when we say that a being *is*? In this moment of Aristotelian metaphysical questioning, Being recedes behind the things that populate the world of our everyday experience, giving itself to us initially *as what lies out beyond them* and thus beyond our experience and knowledge. First *krisis*.

Then Greek philosophy goes to work and, ultimately with Aristotle, arrives at the interpretation of Being as presence—"being" is nothing other than the presence and availability of present beings. With this, Being is reduced to its positive role in allowing beings to present themselves to us, and their problematic relation to Being is thereby overcome as they settle into an exhaustive and comforting intelligibility. Being is seen as a feature universally distributed over all present beings. Nothing else.

Destruction then takes up the Aristotelian text in this sense and attempts to activate the distinction or differentiation between that positive aspect of Being, as the presencing of present beings, and the negative aspect of Being, its withdrawal behind beings.[17] Being is recognized here as what is not experienced or thought properly by any of the means proper to the science of beings. Already here in 1926, at least at certain moments in this text, Heidegger approaches the task of thinking Being, first along with the Greeks and then against them, *as essentially and irremediably withdrawn, hidden, concealed*. And the means by which we do so is destruction, reading the Greek text and revivifying, that is, cooperating and co-philosophizing with, that *initial questioning moment* before the metaphysical interpretation of Being is articulated. Second *krisis*.

Importantly, philosophy's task, in the destructive mode of co-philosophizing, is not to then bridge this second *krisis*, the *krisis* within

Being between what it ultimately showed to Aristotle, the presencing of present beings, and what it initially showed in its question-provoking appearance, the dynamic of emergence that allows for and draws open a space for that presencing. Philosophy's task, already here with the early Heidegger, is to think along with Aristotle, but in relation to Being as he never thought it, never even positively experienced it.

This is why Heidegger will go on to insist that the project of philosophy is an activity carried out in recognition of an insuperable distance which, as Marx suggested, must nonetheless be taken up into thought. For Heidegger here, philosophy is the suffering of a sense of infinitely unresolvable responsibility, for it is tasked with finding a way to again and again uncover and attend to Being's unthinkability, its unrepresentability *as such*. Consider this passage, which summarily concludes the introduction to the 1926 course, in which Heidegger takes up the etymology of the term *philosophia*. He writes that philosophy, as the critical science,

> is not positive, because its object is not pre-given to it, but it must first be uncovered. Uncovering, opening up, determining, and questioning after Being [*Entdecken, Erschließen, Bestimmen und Fragen*] is σοφία. Σοφός— the one who has a taste and an instinct for that which remains hidden [*verborgen bleibt*] to the common understanding. Σοφός knows at the same time that this demands specially suited tasks and strenuous research. [The philosopher] is not simply in secure possession of that to which he is devoted, what he "loves"—φιλεῖν—but rather he searches and must constantly search [*sondern sucht und muß standig suchen*]. Σοφία, the opening up [*Erschließung*] of the Being of beings, is φιλοσοφία, a searching questioning after this, [a questioning] that as such places itself under the most radical critique. (*BCAncP* 8/11)

This is a thrilling passage, if we proceed patiently and take every step seriously. That is, if we refuse to let it recede into platitudes and empty gestures. First, *sophia* or "wisdom" is itself declared to be the moment of *Erschliessung* or "uncovering, opening up" the Being of beings. However, it turns out that this entails *not* an overcoming or setting aside of what is question-worthy in Being. Rather, wisdom emerges through destruction as the questioning itself. The wise individual is the one with a taste for what "remains hidden" to the common understanding entirely, but even to the philosophical understanding in some sense, so long as wisdom is itself questioning. Philosophy subjects itself to the "most radical critique" in that the *krisis* to which it attends is the most radical *krisis*, not merely the separation between the Being of beings and beings themselves, which can or even must be mapped and mastered. More profoundly, philosophy marks and suffers that deeper separation between beings and Being as transcendent and surpassing, between the thinkable and the unthinkable, or at least what is only otherwise and obliquely thinkable. This *krisis*, which opens up within the Aristotelian text only through destructive intervention, must be simultaneously acknowledged by thinking *and* granted its insuperability. And the task of attending to this *krisis* is endless, it must be infinitely repeated, constantly renewed, for it must never be anything more, and never anything less, than a loving of Being that renounces its possession. True *sophia* is only ever *philosophia*, the *philein* or "desiring" of and searching for a true thinking of Being.

The "Original Repetition" of Aristotle's Questioning

After this stunningly bold introduction—imagine just for a moment being a young philosophy student in that lecture hall in 1926—Heidegger goes on to see the pre-Socratics, Plato, and finally Aristotle as confronted with the philosophical task in precisely this sense, in response to which they uncovered Being as the presence, the now-ness and there-ness, the availability, of those beings that lie before us and offer themselves to the positive sciences. And our destructive task is not at all simply identifying the interpretation of Being at which the Greeks arrive in their texts, criticizing it, and setting it aside in favor of a new, extra-metaphysical thinking.

Rather, as we have seen, we must uncover and tarry with the moment in the text where Being is experienced in its question-worthiness. Only in doing so can the destructive reading accomplish something radical, once again, as a returning to the ultimate *radix* or "root" of ancient thought itself, a ground that, while somehow accessible in the text *for the destructive reader*, nevertheless was not positively experienced or thought by Aristotle. Heidegger writes that the aim and method of the course is to

> allow the differentiation to be seen . . . [insofar as] we participate in [*mitmachen*], or as it were *repeat* [wiederholen], the *first decisive beginning of scientific philosophy* [das erste entscheidende Anfangen]. We will repeat the path of the discovery of Being out of beings [*wiederholen den Gang der Entdeckung des Seins aus dem Seienden*]—it is the most radical and the most difficult task facing human knowledge, and it has not yet been purely accomplished. We are able, by this, to measure the meager steps that subsequent scientific philosophy has taken since [its beginning among the Greeks]. (*BCAncP* 8–9/11)

We mark the "meager steps" that have been taken in philosophy since the Greeks, insofar as their metaphysical interpretation of Being was simply passed along, passively taken on, all the way down to our present. But beyond this, Heideggerian destruction clearly requires a *mitmachen* or a "participating in," literally a "making along with," the original metaphysical thinking of Being, immersing ourselves in the text in order to *wiederholen* or "repeat" the movement by which the *krisis* or differentiation of Being and beings was accomplished, and ancient philosophical concepts were then formed. This radical immersion and repetition does not, however, entail that we thereby only succeed in thinking what Aristotle thought. As Heidegger remarks in the very last line of the 1926 course,[18] "We will understand the Greeks only . . . by vigorously countering their questioning with our own" (*BCAncP* 231/277). We participate in and repeat their questioning of Being, questioningly.

In the above-mentioned 1922 plan for Heidegger's Aristotle book, "Phenomenological Interpretations with Respect to Aristotle," Heidegger already has a very sophisticated conception of what this immersion in the text, and specifically in the questioning and searching moment of the text, can accomplish. In their introduction to this text, the editors, Theodore Kisiel and Thomas Sheehan, focus in on a certain issue relating to historical interpretation. They comment on the apparent obstacle presented by the fact that we cannot read and interpret Aristotle from within his own lived context but only ever from our own, writing:

> This temporal differentiation of hermeneutical situations each according to its time . . . does not prevent a present time from understanding, appropriating, and in fact "repeating" ("*wiederholen*") what a past philosophical inquiry took to be its basic concern and central question in its situation and for its time. This is not a rote repetition, a simple borrowing of its principles and basic concepts, but rather an original repetition of these questions and answers which are now understood in our own present situation and for that situation, such that these questions (and not just the resolutions) of the past are themselves the subject of a radical critique or "destruction." For a philosophical past has a future not in its results but in the originality of its interrogative thrust, which can later serve as a model evoking further and ever more original questions and thus "becomes a present in ever new forms."[19]

This is precisely what Heidegger emphasizes in the 1926 course. Inhabiting the moment in which Being remains a question in the Aristotelian text, the moment to which he is responding in interpreting Being as the presence of present beings, the destructive reader is capable of finding something more than what is "there" in the text of Aristotle. The aspect of Being that exceeds this interpretation can present itself as excessive, as only intimated by means of a trace or an indication, precisely there in the moment when the "philosophical inquiry" and "concern" point out to what lies beyond them, toward what they do not yet possess and yet what provokes them. What destructive interpretation insists on "repeating" is not the result of Aristotelian thinking and concept creation, but the still open "interrogative thrust" in the Aristotelian text that points to, and thereby allows the destructive reader to enter into a relationship with, Being as in excess of its metaphysical interpretation.

Kisiel and Sheehan describe what destruction accomplishes with the paradoxical phrase "original repetition," and this is to my mind quite apt. Destructively, Heidegger is telling us, we immerse ourselves in the Aristotelian text, at the moment when the question of Being is still open, not yet decided. At that moment, destruction has a twofold task. On the one hand, it must endeavor to trace the emergence of Aristotle's concept of Being, as the presence of present beings, out of his originary quintessentially Greek experience of beings as present and available before him. And on the other hand, destruction activates the interrogative, questioning, concerned comportment to point to what was not recuperated in the metaphysical interpretation of Being as the being of Beings—namely the *krisis*, the separation or differentiation, perhaps even the seam or fold, *within Being itself* as it brings forth beings in their presence and recedes behind them.

In other courses and papers from the 1920s, Heidegger employs various terminologies in order to capture the complex project of the destructive hermeneutic. It may well be helpful, here at the close of chapter 2, to turn briefly to two alternative vocabularies for describing how destruction registers the ambivalence it uncovers in the Aristotelian text.

Reading "What Is Not There" in the Aristotelian Text

First, in a text entitled "Being-There and Being-True According to Aristotle," we find an extraordinary passage. Here Heidegger observes:

> The aim of the present interpretation is to enable Aristotle to speak again, not in order to bring about a renewal of Aristotelianism, but rather in order to prepare the battleground for a radical engagement with Greek philosophy—the very philosophy in which we still stand. If

CHAPTER 2

> an examination of Aristotle's text should [subsequently] show that much of what we say here is not there in the text [*nicht dasteht*], that would not be an argument against our interpretation. For an interpretation is genuine [*eigentliche*] only when, in going through the whole text, it comes upon that which is not there [*nicht dasteht*] for a crude understanding, but which, although unspoken [*unausgesprochen*], nonetheless makes up the ground [*Boden*] and the genuine foundations of the kind of vision [*Art des Sehens*] from out of which the text itself was able to grow. ("BTBT" 58, translation modified)

We must take our time here, noting that this passage has been quite neglected in the scholarly discussion of destruction in the early Heidegger, tucked away as it is in this little-read stand-alone talk delivered to the Kant Society at the University of Cologne in December 1924.

Heidegger tells us first that destruction "enables Aristotle to speak" to us once again. In hearing him speak, however, what we gain is not simply a more accurate grasp of the transmitted content of his philosophy, such that we might then reproduce it today. Listening closely in the destructive mode, we enter a space within the Aristotelian text that serves as the "battleground" for a "radical engagement" with ancient thought, which is to say, with the ontological foundations of our own contemporary philosophical and scientific worldview.

Heidegger goes on to say, quite strikingly, that if destruction hears things addressing us in listening to Aristotle, things that are, in a technical sense, "not there" in the text, that is not a criticism of destructive interpretation. Indeed, he insists that an interpretation is *eigentlich*, "authentic, proper, or genuine," only insofar as it arrives at that which a simple or coarse approach to the text will never find there. And this is not only an insistence on the sophisticated insights that truly gifted interpreters provide, finding subtext in the text, where the dimwitted find nothing at all. No, the reason why destruction hears in the text what is "not there for a crude understanding" is that it is "unspoken" in the text itself, for it is the subtending ground and foundation for what emerges into view and is articulated by the Aristotle in the text. What is entailed here is a radical ontology of the text, indeed, and this is what subtends the hermeneutic approach of destruction. As we saw above, only because the text is approached as always already more than itself, bearing the traces and indications of what lies beyond it, of what exceeds it, is it possible for Heidegger to claim that a destructive interpretation will not take its measure from what is simply there, encounterable, available in the text for any perspective to see.

What precisely is this excess, this beyond that belongs to the tra-

THE GROUND OF METAPHYSICS AND THE *KRISIS* IN THE ARISTOTELIAN TEXT

ditionary text, and to the Aristotelian text most of all? It is Being itself, of course, but under a certain aspect. Just as we saw earlier in the 1926 course, Being is approached here not only as the presence of present beings, which Aristotle himself experiences, thinks, and passes along to the metaphysical tradition, but as the withdrawn source of that presencing, which strictly speaking is "not there" and remains "unspoken" in the Aristotelian text. By way of destruction, and the contestation that it stages by focusing on the moment of questioning when Being is emphatically differentiated from beings, we encounter the *Boden* or the "ground" for Aristotle's *Art des Sehens*, his "manner of seeing," which means his manner of experiencing beings as present and available.[20]

This is extraordinary indeed. Once again, Heidegger is suggesting that we might come to wonder about, question, and perhaps think Being otherwise than metaphysically, by destructively immersing ourselves in the Aristotelian text, and listening to its definitive metaphysical interpretation of Being even as we hear in the text something in excess of this.

Phenomenological Reduction, Construction, and Destruction

Second, in the 1927 lecture course *Basic Problems of Phenomenology*, Heidegger offers us another fascinating and quite differently contextualized discussion of the destructive interpretation of the tradition. Unlike the last text we read, this lecture course has rightfully garnered a good deal of scholarly attention. However, the specifics of the combination of *destruction* and *construction* that Heidegger insists here must belong to phenomenological philosophizing have not been a common focus for that scholarly work, as they will be in what follows.

Heidegger begins the course by dismissing an expectation which the course title might have aroused, namely, that he will be taking up as his subject matter "the circumstances of the modern movement in philosophy called phenomenology" (*BPP* 1/1). Of course not. Rather than turning, for instance, to the articulation or definition of the method of phenomenology presented in the work of Edmund Husserl, Heidegger suggests that they treat phenomenology, according to its etymology, as the *logos* of *phainomena*, the "study discourse" proper to "appearances," and specifically, appearances of "what *is*." As such, phenomenology would seem to be the quintessential philosophical method, insofar as philosophy is essentially identifiable with or at least grounded in ontology, as the study of Being as what belongs to all "things that *are*."

Heidegger then proceeds by distinguishing philosophy from all other sciences in a manner that should be familiar to us from our earlier discussion of the 1926 course. He writes:

> The method of ontology, that is, of philosophy in general, is distinguished by the fact that ontology has nothing in common with any method of any of the other sciences, all of which as positive sciences deal with beings. (*BPP* 19/26)

As we have already heard, philosophy is properly the study of Being, ontology, and in this it marks the *krisis* between Being and beings, and studies beings only with respect to Being. It does not properly or fundamentally, as philosophy, take up what makes this or that being the specific type of being it is, but focuses rather on what makes them be at all. The method of philosophy, thus, cannot be the method by which the positive sciences proceed.

Indeed, already insisting here on a shift in the notion of Being, and then a concomitant shift in the notion of truth itself, Heidegger will declare that the world that calls forth our thinking is in fact not a collection of objects, about which we may or may not have accurate subjective perceptions or representations. He writes:

> Being is given only if there is disclosure, that is to say, if there is truth. But there is truth only if a being exists which opens up, which discloses, and indeed in such a way that disclosing belongs itself to the mode of being of this being. We ourselves are such a being. Dasein itself exists in the truth. To Dasein there belongs essentially a disclosed world and with that the disclosedness of Dasein itself. Dasein, by the nature of its existence, is "in" truth, and only because it is "in" truth does it have the possibility of being "in" untruth. Being is given only if truth, hence if Dasein, exists. (*BPP* 18–19/25, translation modified)

Being is first and foremost, at the most fundamental level, what provokes us in experience and calls forth our thinking. Heidegger here, as in *Being and Time*, insists that there is a more fundamental, a prior, notion of "truth," as that dynamic by way of which the world's beings are always already appearing to us and presenting themselves, or being *erschlossen*, "disclosed, unconcealed." For this initial disclosure in fact subtends and opens up the site within which truth can exist as traditionally conceived, namely as *adequatio intellectus et rei*, or as the correspondence between the re-presentation in a given subject's thought or statement and an objectively real or present state of affairs. Truth in the sense of disclosure is what has always already occurred in Dasein, in being-there where beings show themselves to us and call forth our thinking as "things that *are*." Whenever philosophizing has begun wondering about what is appearing, beings, the world has already disclosed itself to Dasein. We live in this disclosive "truth" and the world has appeared to us and established a connection between itself and us, even if there is still required here clarification, explanation, or refinement in understanding.

Heidegger then remarks: "it is precisely the analysis of the truth-character of Being, which shows that Being also is, as it were, based in a being, namely, in Dasein. Being is given only if the understanding of Being, hence Dasein, exists" (*BPP* 19/26). That is, if the Being that calls forth our questioning and thinking is understood, not as what is objectively and independently real or existing, but rather as what has arisen into view by way of this more primordial dynamic of truth as disclosure, then the Being we are asking about in philosophizing is always already connected to and indeed inseparable from the particular Dasein or human "being there" who receives that appearing. Heidegger writes:

> This implies at the same time that ontology cannot be established in a purely ontological manner. Its possibility is referred back to a being, that is, to something ontic—Dasein. Ontology has an ontic foundation . . . (*BPP* 19/26)

Even if one wishes to engage in philosophy as ontology, and undertake to think the nature of Being as beyond or in excess of the beings that are always already presenting themselves in one's experience, it is impossible to simply study "Being as such." One must always study Being by way of the beings that have appeared to us, and thus as they have presented themselves to this or that concrete Dasein that we are, in the site of disclosure that is this Dasein. Ontology, as the study of Being, always initially proceeds as the study of a particular being. Given this, ontology has as its proper method *phenomenology*, as the study of the appearing of "what is" to us, as concrete and historically situated Dasein. However, according to Heidegger, this studying of Being by way of the appearances of beings to us then necessitates a certain destructive approach to our own inherited tradition.

Heidegger begins his explanation of the method of phenomenology, thus understood, by insisting that the ontological turn amounts to, in the first instance, nothing other than a radicalization or a certain extension of a prominent technique in Husserlian phenomenological method, namely, *reduction*. He writes:

> Apprehension of Being, ontological investigation, always turns, at first and necessarily, to some being; but then, *in a precise way, it is led away* from that being *and led back to its Being*. We call this basic component of phenomenological method—the leading back or re-duction of investigative vision from a naively apprehended being to Being—*phenomenological reduction*. (*BPP* 21/28, translation modified)[21]

As Heidegger explains it here and as we discussed in the "Introduction," Husserl, especially the Husserl of 1913's *Ideas Toward a Pure Phenomenology and Phenomenological Philosophy*, understood reduction as a way of leading vision away from the external world of things and events, to which one presumes to have access when seeing according to the ordinary, prephilosophical "natural attitude." This entails a certain withdrawing from the world and back into consciousness itself, to transcendental subjectivity and the ideal forms according to which what we experience is constituted as a correlate of consciousness, as intended by consciousness. Heideggerian reduction, by contrast, leads vision back from the particular being to some questioning and thoughtful encounter with the Being of that being, which must precede and in a sense support our experience of the being as a being. Though always confronted after an encounter with this or that being, in a temporal sense, Being is nonetheless to be understood as ontologically and logically *proteron* or "prior," and even as *a priori*, with respect to the being that it allows to appear and present itself as a being (*BPP* 20/26).

Indeed, one might say that the Husserlian and the Heideggerian phenomenological reductions move in emphatically opposite directions. Both begin with appearances, just as the etymology of the term "phenomenology" dictates. However, the former moves away from the world or "what is" that is initially presumed to be indicated in appearances and withdraws back into the subject and its experience-constituting structures or ideas. The latter, contrarily, moves from Dasein and the appearance of beings in the "there," which Dasein holds open and indeed is, out and down into the very source of that appearing being, the dynamic movement or emergence into appearing of beings, which as such withholds itself and remains in a sense behind or beneath those beings that have come to present themselves to us.

This Heideggerian *phenomenological reduction*, as ontological, must proceed by what Heidegger describes as a kind of double movement. Indeed, in order to accomplish the thinking of not just a being but of Being, at which it aims, its reduction requires both a *phenomenological construction* and *phenomenological destruction*.

In order to make clear the necessity of phenomenological construction, Heidegger articulates a certain feature of phenomenological reduction, a feature he had already identified, in the above-discussed 1926 course, as belonging to the "critical science" that was ancient Greek philosophy, which occasioned a *krisis* or "separation" between Being and beings.[22] Here, in the 1927 course, it is phenomenological reduction, in its peculiar Heideggerian ontological mode, that occasions such a *krisis* between Being and beings.

Heidegger writes:

> Phenomenological reduction as the leading of our vision from beings back to Being nevertheless is not the only basic component of phenomenological method; in fact, it is not even the central component. For this guidance of vision back from beings to Being requires at the same time that we should bring ourselves forward positively toward Being itself . . . [However,] Being does not become accessible like beings. We do not simply find it in front of us . . . It must each time be brought into view in a free projection [*jeweils in einem freien Entwurf*]. This projecting of the antecedently given being upon its Being and the structures of its Being we call *phenomenological construction* [phänomenologische Konstruktion]. (*BPP* 21/29, translation modified)

Once again Being is described as not presenting itself to us directly, but as nonetheless always already "co-understood," available obliquely, as it were, in our experience and thinking of beings. This is not the non-appearance that belongs to beings, which are in principle available to experience, understanding, and mastery, and are only occasionally accidentally distant or unavailable. Being is not like a mountain that happens to be obscured from view by another, more proximate mountain.

Rather, in the case of Being, its inaccessibility is constitutive, for, insofar as it is not a being among others but the source of these and their appearing to us, Being is as such not viewable, not thinkable by whatever traditional means are fit for the viewing and thinking of beings. It is to be thought of as "beyond" or "excessive" *per definitionem*. In order for the reduction or the "leading back" from beings to Being to occur, given the starting place of Dasein as always among beings and given the radical inaccessibility of Being as such, what is required is an *Entwurf*, a "projection" or literally a "throwing out," a "casting out." *Entwurf* also means a "draft," a preliminary "sketch," and this is also in play here, it seems, insofar as the thinking that relates properly to Being will involve a casting out from the pre-given being toward its as-yet unviewed and ungrasped ground in Being, and this thinking will be *essentially and insuperably preliminary*, not definitive or exhaustive.

CHAPTER 2

What is truly extraordinary in Heidegger's discussion of method here, and what we must take very seriously, is that this preliminary casting-out or projecting from beings and beyond beings *is itself understood as the mode of approaching and thinking that is proper to Being*, i.e., that does not reduce Being to a being. Heideggerian phenomenological reduction, as *involving* phenomenological construction, investigates and even thinks Being as an essentially and each time preliminary projecting or casting-out beyond the beings that give themselves in our experience and, thus, beyond what is known and knowable. It is not a construction in the sense of a subjective invention or a fiction, but it is a view of Being that is co-structured or co-constituted by going beyond our specific experience of beings as this Dasein and the unfolding of those beings into presence that is Being itself.

And it is precisely this contribution of our specific Dasein to the construction of our view of Being that necessitates the third and last component of the thinking of Being. Heidegger observes:

> The method of phenomenology is likewise not exhausted by phenomenological construction. We have heard that every projecting or casting out [*Entwerfen*] of Being occurs in a reductive recursion from beings. The consideration of Being takes its start from beings. And this is obviously always determined by one's factual experience of beings and the range of possibilities of experience that at any time are peculiar to a factual Dasein, and hence to the historical situation of a philosophical investigation. (*BPP* 22/30, translation modified)

At any moment, as Dasein, we are experiencing and thinking beings in their appearing to us. If we undertake a phenomenological reduction in this Heideggerian ontological mode, we attempt to move our gaze from beings to Being, as their source. Given that we still operate in the shadow of that Greek metaphysical thinking of Being which found its culminating expression in Aristotle, we must also undertake a *destruction* of our tradition.

Heidegger thus draws the conclusion:

> To the conceptual interpretation of Being and its structures, i.e., to the reductive construction of Being, there necessarily belongs a *destruction*, i.e., a critical de-constructing [*ein kritischer Abbau*] of traditional concepts, which at first must necessarily be employed, down to the sources [*auf die Quellen*] out of which they were created [*aus denen sie geschöpft sind*]. Only by means of this destruction can ontology fully assure itself in a phenom-

enological way of the genuineness of its concepts. (*BPP* 22–23/31–32, translation modified)

Destruction emerges here once again as a critical disrupting of our inherited concepts, tracing them back to the *Quellen* or "sources" out of which they were once, by the Greeks, unfolded. Two things are vital for the present discussion.

First, destruction is, like construction, not a prior step to be completed and set aside before real ontology, that is, a conceptual analysis of Being, can begin. Not at all, as Heidegger later remarks:

> These three basic components of phenomenological method—reduction, construction, destruction—belong together in their content and must be grounded [*begründet*] in their belonging together. Construction in philosophy is necessarily destruction, that is to say, a de-constructing of traditional concepts carried out in a historical recursion to the tradition. And this is not a negation of the tradition or a condemnation of it as worthless; quite the reverse, it signifies precisely a positive appropriation of tradition. Because destruction belongs to construction, philosophical cognition is essentially at the same time, in a certain sense, historical cognition. (*BPP* 23/31)

In other words, thinking Being as beyond beings, *phenomenological reduction*, is nothing other than casting out beyond one's historically situated initial experience of beings, or *phenomenological construction*, along with *phenomenological destruction*, an engagement with one's own inherited concepts by way of a critical reading of one's traditionary texts, a reading that digs down through the concepts or content of the text to the source or ground of those concepts and takes up an open engagement with that source or ground.

Second, we must note the way in which we find ourselves related to Being in the double movement of construction and destruction. We think Being properly, according to Heidegger in *Basic Problems of Phenomenology*, insofar as we cast out beyond the beings we are experiencing and project something in excess of these and, in service of that construction, insofar as we disrupt our traditional concepts, and their equation of "what is" with the collection of present beings, by tracing those concepts back to their historical origin. In projecting out beyond our ordinary experience of beings, we are directed in our construction of Being not by something there in our world, but by what destruction excavates back beneath the concepts that the Greeks generated and passed down to us.[23]

Heidegger had tried in 1926's *Basic Concepts of Ancient Philosophy* to describe a posture of thinking itself that would acknowledge and sustain that very *krisis* or "separation" which we expressly experience in questioning and wondering. And in 1924's "Being-There and Being-True According to Aristotle" he had spoken of destruction's listening afresh to what Aristotle says in order to hear "what is not there" and "what is unspoken" in the text. Here in 1927, Heidegger characterizes this same task as a combination of phenomenological construction and phenomenological destruction that uncovers the source of the metaphysical tradition—Being as what first drew forth Greek philosophical questioning and thinking—in order to cast our own thinking today out beyond the present beings that this tradition insists are all that "is."

*

In conclusion, one insight we derive from our interpretation of these passages from Heidegger's courses and lectures of the 1920s is this: Heidegger insists throughout that the destruction of the tradition *alone* can accomplish the thinking of Being otherwise than metaphysics. We do not encounter Being as something more than present beings in our everyday experience of the world, for that experience is always already *exhaustively* organized by concepts and principles derived from within the horizon of Western metaphysical thought. We *only* encounter Being as an excess of presence in the destructive reading of the traditionary text, and perhaps most acutely, in reading the texts of Aristotle.

And even there, as we have seen, we do not find ourselves able to grasp and give an exhaustively illuminating account of this extrametaphysical sense of Being. Indeed, we do not bring it to language in any traditional philosophical manner. Rather, we claim in destruction only to *mark its withdrawal* in the Aristotelian text, insofar as we find traces or oblique indications in the initiating moment of critical questioning and searching. As Heidegger will say in the 1955 lecture "What Is Philosophy?" in a profoundly revealing passage that acts as a sort of retrospective summary of his experiments with the project of destruction over the decade of the 1920s:

> We find the answer to the question, what philosophy might be, not through historical information about the definitions of philosophy but through the conversation with that which has delivered itself to us as the Being of beings. This way to the answer for our question is not a break with history, not a repudiation of history, but an appropriation and a transformation of what the tradition has delivered [*eine Aneignung und*

> *Verwandlung des Überlieferten*]. Such an appropriation is what is meant by the title "destruction." The meaning of this word has been clearly circumscribed in *Being and Time* [§ 6]. Destruction does not mean a destroying but rather a de-constructing [*Abbauen*], demolishing [*Abtragen*], setting-aside [*Auf-die-Seite-stellen*], namely of the merely historical information about the history of philosophy. Destruction means: opening our ears, freeing ourselves for what addresses us in the tradition as the Being of beings. By listening to this spoken appeal [*auf diesen Zuspruch hören*], we reach correspondence [*Entsprechung*]. ("WP" 70–73, translation modified)

As we have seen, in returning to Aristotle, co-philosophizing along with him, and reading his text destructively, we accomplish philosophizing itself. We do so neither by simple repetition nor by rejection, but only insofar as we engage in an *Aneignung* and a *Verwandlung*, literally a "becoming proper to" or "making one's own" and a "changing into" or "thorough alteration," with respect to our received Aristotelian tradition. We do not by any means set aside the text of Aristotle, so much as we dismantle it in order to expose ourselves to the *Boden* or *Grund*, the "soil" or "ground" from which and in response to which Aristotle experienced and conceived of beings as he did. By immersing ourselves in Aristotle's questioning and thinking of Being destructively, we strive to mark not only the initial *krisis* or "distinction" of Being from beings, but that deeper *krisis* within Being itself, between, on the one hand, its unfolding there in Aristotle's thought as the presencing of present beings and, on the other hand, its role as the irremediably withdrawn and unarticulated funding and dynamic source of that presencing.

3

Three Aristotelian Concepts Destroyed

In the forgoing discussions, we have identified the basic dynamics or elements of the destructive interpretation of the Aristotelian text. First, there is the distinguishing of the experiential and conceptual registers in the text, whereby the concepts that Aristotle creates are exhibited as arising out of and in response to a complex, multiple, and often conflicting set of ordinary Greek experiences. Second, the destruction of the text digs down beneath the experiential level to its ground, namely the self-showing of beings by which they give themselves to experience in a historically and linguistically situated way. At the level of that grounding, Heidegger lays bare a double *krisis* or "separation, rift" that he locates "in" the Aristotelian text. Initially, he marks the separation between the present beings that are appearing to experience and their Being, their presence, which Aristotle succeeds in thinking and conceptualizing. Furthermore, in focusing intensely on what shows itself in the text in the interrogative moment, the moment of questioning and wondering about Being, Heidegger locates traces in the text of a deeper *krisis*, the distinction between the Being that is distributed among present beings and the infinitely questionable and self-occluding aspect of Being—that which first drew forth questioning with the dynamic emergence of beings into appearance by withholding itself beyond or behind those very beings. By the method of destructive reading, the text thereby comes to say more than it says, to hold more than it holds, as Heidegger finds gestures toward this aspect of Being, even as Aristotle neither thinks nor experiences it positively, and it is in relation to this hidden source of the traditional concepts we inherit that we might today begin to think otherwise.

All of this, I have tried to show, is already to be found at work at certain crucial moments in the lecture courses of the 1920s that present and carry out the complex hermeneutic method of destruction on the Aristotelian text. I propose here, in chapter 3, to focus on a few, as it were, "case studies" of the destruction of Aristotelian concepts—*ousia, zôon logon echon,* and *dunamis*. In Heidegger's interpretation of each of these, we will find at work each of those facets of destructive reading set out in chapters 1 and 2.

Ousia or "Substance, Beingness"

In order to fully appreciate and understand in its proper depth Heidegger's treatment of this concept, we should begin with the contrast he draws between Aristotle, as the thinker of *ousia* (usually translated as "substance"), and Plato, as the thinker of the Idea. And toward the very end of the 1926 course *Basic Concepts in Ancient Philosophy*, after offering brief treatments first of the pre-Socratics and then of Plato, that very contrast is on display as Heidegger turns to Aristotle.

Heidegger begins by addressing a prevalent "dogma" in the interpretation of Aristotle, namely that "Aristotle, by contrast with Plato, is to be characterized as a master builder. Confusing him with Thomas Aquinas." In response to the suggestion that the Aristotelian corpus presents us with a finished systematic whole, an already established set of principles arranged into a determinate structure, Heidegger protests that this is "pure fiction!" Instead, "everything is open; [there are] only basic problems [*Grundprobleme*]." Indeed, "in Aristotle, [there is] even less of a doctrinal edifice than in Plato" (*BCAncP* 121/146, 214/284–85, translation modified).[1]

Where traditional readers of the ancient Stagirite find a more or less clearly articulated and consistent set of established positions, Heidegger again and again will uncover a genuinely open, still questioning, still probing thinker at work. He reads the text of Aristotle not as a retrospective cataloging of the scientific results, but as itself the event of inquiry, a questioning still very much alive and underway on the page.

And to my mind, however unorthodox, Heidegger's assessment of the Aristotelian text here is absolutely correct. Indeed, it seems to me that only when it is viewed through the, in this respect, obscuring lens of its Scholastic reception does the *corpus aristotelicum* come to even approximate a finished system. When the actual textual remains of Aristotle's philosophy are read seriously and without that particular bias, what one finds on nearly every page is philosophical questioning in action, as it were, an inquiry starting, stopping, and restarting, over and over again. And indeed, this is precisely what one should expect, insofar as it is *dialektikê* or "dialectic" for Aristotle that explicitly plays the role of *philosophical* method, and this method is to be strenuously distinguished from the *scientific* method of *apodeixis* or "demonstration" (*Top.* 100b17–101b5).

Demonstration, discussed in detail in the *Posterior Analytics*, is for Aristotle the exclusive syllogistic form by which one produces results that qualify as *epistêmê* or "scientific knowledge"—think here of geometric proofs, syllogisms using as their premises the discipline's *archai* or first "principles," for example, its fundamental definitions, axioms, or laws

(*Post. An.* I.71b10–72b4).² By contrast, dialectic, as described in the *Topics* and then refined in the first book of the *Physics* and elsewhere,³ proceeds by the assembling of *endoxa* or "trustworthy opinions," "things that appear to be so to all, to most, or to the wise [in this area of investigation]" (*Top.* I.100a22–23), and then subjecting these to analysis, interrogation, and clarification, in part by assembling them into syllogisms and evaluating the conclusions produced against other *endoxa*. Aristotle then clarifies that, while demonstration is the method to be employed within an established science, it is dialectic that is to be used when moving "toward sciences in accord with philosophy [*pros tas kata philosophian epistêmês*]" (*Top.* 101a22–23). And dialectic is useful in philosophizing, precisely because it moves

> toward the first of the things concerning each science. For, from the principles proper to a given science it is not possible to say anything concerning those [principles], since the principles are the first of all things; rather, it is necessary concerning those [principles] to go through the trustworthy opinions [*dia tôn endoxôn*] concerning each [subject matter]. And it is this that is peculiar to and most proper to dialectic. For, being a thorough examination of something, it holds a path toward the principles of all investigations [*pros tas hapasôn tôn methodôn archas hodon echei*]. (*Top.* I.101a35–b5)

Aristotle's insistence on dialectic as the proper method for philosophical thinking exhibits what I would describe as a certain emphatically "premodern" confidence in the as-yet unverified and unsecured pre-philosophical opinions and dispositions of everyday life. In dramatic contrast with most philosophy as it has been pursued from Descartes onward in the West, which we have discussed in some detail in the "Introduction," Aristotle insists that *endoxa* provide a perfectly legitimate starting point for philosophizing. Indeed, his confidence that one can arrive at the ultimate sources, causes, and elements that constitute and give order to "what is" by nothing other than a clarification, analysis, and development of what is appearing to most or to all or to the wise in pre-philosophical experience, indicates quite clearly that, for Aristotle, the initial pre-philosophical appearing of things is necessarily *a real appearance*, even if it almost always requires philosophical, i.e., dialectical, clarification or refinement.⁴ Finally, the fact that philosophy is dialectical in this Aristotelian sense also means that it lives *in the movement from everyday appearances toward their principles or sources*, and not (as philosophy) in the drawing out of the systematic consequences of those principles once established. The latter is the project of science proper.

And the open and questioning posture of Aristotelian dialectical philosophy is nowhere more evident than in his approach to *ousia*, that most central and fundamental of Aristotelian concepts. Though we have already discussed some aspects of this term and its place in Aristotle's ontology, we might just begin here by reminding ourselves that *ousia*, in its technical sense for Aristotle, is most often translated into English as "substance," though other renderings are possible, such as "being," "essence," "reality," "thing," or even "thinghood." And as we have noted, given that the term is constructed by joining the present participle of the verb *einai*, "*on*" or "being," with the suffix that generates abstract conditions, "*-ia*," the term would have been heard immediately by the Greek ear as something like "being-ness" or perhaps "be-ity."

There is no doubt that this is the etymological sense of the term. What complicates matters here is that most scholars since Werner Jaeger's landmark 1923 study, *Aristotle: Fundamentals of the History of His Development*, find in the *corpus aristotelicum* evidence for a development, that is, for some shifts in his fundamental positions over time, and many find strong evidence for a change in what the term "*ousia*" most properly applies to for Aristotle.[5] To be sure, Jaeger's developmental thesis is complicated by the fact that Aristotle's most important philosophical texts seem to be lecture notes rather than works polished and finalized for publication, and specifically lectures that were likely revised over the course of Aristotle's life, and then cobbled together by an editor centuries after the thinker's death into the texts we have today. Nonetheless, an important shift in the concept of *ousia* seems evident as one moves from the likely early *Categories*, to the likely middle-period *Physics*, and finally to the likely very late-central stretch of the *Metaphysics* sometimes referred to as the "Ousiology," namely Books Zeta, Eta, and Theta (books VII, VIII, IX).

In the *Categories*, Aristotle explicitly identifies *ousia* as a *concrete particular thing*, this horse here or that human being there, and he takes this for something that possesses an *eidos* or a "species form." This motivates Aristotle to refer to the *eidos* in this text as explicitly ontologically secondary (*Cat.* 2a10–18). Other *onta* or "beings, things that are," in addition to concrete particular things and the forms they possess, are recognized in the *Categories*, beings such as qualities, quantities, relations, places, times, actions, affects, postures, and possessions, but these too are, as with form, ontologically secondary, dependent for their being and their intelligibility in each case on a given *ousia*. That is, they only *are*, and can only be understood, insofar as they belong to some concrete particular thing. There can be no "blue," no "four-inches-tall," no "more beautiful than," no "on the feeder," no "right now," no "singing," no "being startled," no "being perched," and no "having a nest," unless there are such things as, for example, indigo buntings in the world to which these things are predicated. And likewise, for Aristotle, the species form only exists insofar as it is possessed by a particular member of that species. In the *Physics*, when *phusis* or "nature" becomes the explicit focus of Aristotle's inquiry, along with the seemingly ubiquitous and constitutive *kinêsis* and *genesis*, or "movement" and "coming-to-be" (*Phys.* I.185a1–2, II.192b820), which seem constitutive of natural beings, *ousia* still seems to refer first and foremost to the concrete particular thing, in the technical sense arrived at through Aristotelian philosophical analysis and clarification.[6] However, this thing is now understood explicitly as a composite of two *aitia* or "causes," *eidos* and *hulê*, or "form" and "matter," which are joined to one another by the work of a third moving or efficient cause and by being directed toward a fourth end or final cause (*Phys.* II.194b18–195a3). These three additional causes of the being of the particular thing, in addition to the species form already identified in the *Categories*, represent important innovations in making beings intelligible, though the basic notion of *ousia* seems more or less unchanged.

In those apparently late-central books of the *Metaphysics*, however, we find Aristotle opening up anew the question of what should properly qualify as *ousia*, what deserves to be called "*ousia*" in its technical sense, which, let us recall, would be heard etymologically as something like "being-ness," and thus as "what *is* most of all," or "what *is*" in some central or fundamental way. It is here that many have located an important shift in Aristotle's thinking. He opens the discussion, stating, "in fact, what has been sought long ago and now and always, and what is always a source of impasses, namely the question 'What is being [*ti to on*]?,' is just the question 'What is *ousia*?'" (*Meta.* VII.1028b3–5). And he sets out over the course of the next three books to determine what properly deserves this designation.

Proceeding dialectically, Aristotle moves from the way that whatever "*ousia*" names initially appears to us, and then seeks simply to clarify what is appearing there. He initially identifies four candidates that seem to present themselves as most deserving the name "*ousia*": (1) *to ti ên einai* or "the what it was to be," usually translated as the "essence" of the thing, (2) *to katholou* or "the universal" instantiated in a given set of like particulars, (3) the *genos* or "genus" to which a given being belongs, and (4) *to hupokeimenon* or literally "the underlying thing," usually translated as the "subject." Aristotle then pauses immediately to complicate the fourth candidate by acknowledging three things that might appear to us as "underlying" all other things which are, things like qualities, quantities, and so on, namely (4a) the *hulê* or "matter" in the composite concrete particular thing, (4b) the *eidos* or "form" that the composite shows us in presenting itself as "what it is," for example, as a "horse" or as a "human being," and (4c) the composite thing itself, comprised of matter and form (*Meta.* VII.1028b33–1029a8).

Over the course of the digressive, often vexing discussion that follows, Aristotle takes up and seriously entertains these initial appearances of *ousia*, supplementing them with others along the way, discussing why each might seem to be "what *is* most of all," indicating their shortcomings, and showing the ways in which they conflict with one another. Although the specific steps in the argument and their significance for the discussion as a whole are subject to much scholarly disagreement, what is clear is that, by the end of Book Zeta, Aristotle is ready to pose his central question anew, apparently understanding the issue to have been somewhat clarified through the dialectical scrutiny given to its initial appearances thus far. The last chapter of Book Zeta thus opens with Aristotle stating, characteristically, "But what one ought to say *ousia* is, and of what sort it is, let us discuss anew, as though making another start" (*Meta.* VII.1041a6–7). What seems to have become clear to Aristotle in the foregoing discussion is that whatever *ousia* is, whatever qualifies as "what *is* most of all," it must not be the composite concrete particular thing itself, for this is evidently dependent for its "being what it is" upon its *eidos* and *hulê*, its "form" and "matter," and must be seen then as ontologically secondary to both (*Meta.* VII.1029a30–32). Thus, Aristotle concludes, since it seems clear that the *eidos* is the *aitia* and *archê*, the "cause" and "source," of a given sum of material's actually qualifying as whatever "being" it is (*Meta.* VII.1041a6–b9), it is the *eidos* that should most properly be understood as the *ousia*, *eidos* here being explicitly identified with a thing's *ti ên einai* or "essence" and its *phusis* or "nature" (*Meta.* VII.1041b31).

Aristotle has apparently shifted the emphasis in his understanding of *ousia* since the *Categories* and *Physics*, and he now holds that it is not the concrete individual thing that deserves the name "*ousia*," but rather the *immanent ordering formal cause* of that thing's being what it is. He concludes: "What is being sought after [as *ousia*] is the cause of the matter being 'what it is,' and this is the form [*to aition zêteitai tês hulês esti to eidos*]" (*Meta.* VII.1041b7–9). Aristotle's reasoning seems to be that it is the presence of, for instance, the form "house" in a given thing that qualifies this bunch of bricks and stones *as being a house* and that saves them from being merely a heap or a huddle of material.

And it is in precisely this shift in the Aristotelian thinking of *ousia* that Heidegger finds Aristotle's refinement of ordinary experience into a concept, as well as the trace of an aspect of Being that Aristotle never experiences, much less thinks, but which can be intimated here through a destructive reading. Heidegger begins by noting that Aristotle's ultimate concept of *ousia* or "substance" and his identification of "what is most of all" as the essential form that makes a given concrete particular thing what it is, will inform the entire history of "substance metaphysics" that unfolds out of Aristotle,[7] that transforms itself in myriad ways over the millennia, and that we in a certain sense continue to inherit today, as discussed above in the "Introduction."[8] It is thus precisely this Aristotelian inheritance that we are most compelled to disrupt destructively.

Of course, we must avoid seeing this destruction as revealing something like an *error* in the thinking of Aristotle, even if we hope ultimately to find a hint or an indication of something he did not experience or think. It is not the case, according to Heidegger, that Aristotle arrived at the concept of *ousia* through some simple failure of attention, some mistake in thinking, or some purely subjective invention or imposition that marks a fateful wrong turn in the course of Western thinking. As Heidegger remarks in 1924, "the Greek being-concept did not fall from the sky, but had a definite ground [*Grund*]" (*BCArP* 29/40). Aristotle's conception of *ousia* as "what is most of all" reflects and derives directly from its "ground," namely, the way beings are presenting themselves to Greek pre-philosophical experience.

Moving on then to distinguish the experiential from the conceptual register of the text, Heidegger appeals to a certain distinction in the meaning of *ousia*:

> The expression οὐσία, as the fundamental term of Aristotelian research, stems from an expression that has a *customary meaning* in natural language. The customary meaning is that which a word has *in natural speaking*... The *customariness* of meaning and expressing means, further, that it operates in the *averageness of understanding*. It is suitable for being circulated as self-evident... With οὐσία it is not the case that the terminological meaning has arisen out of the customary meaning while the customary disappeared. Rather, for Aristotle, the customary meaning exists constantly and simultaneously alongside the terminological meaning. And, according to its customary meaning, οὐσία means "property, possession, possessions and goods, estate"... [If] we examine this customary meaning, we may discover what the Greeks meant in general by "being." (*BCArP* 18/23–24)

Heidegger opposes here the *customary meaning*, the sense the term has in ordinary pre-philosophical discourse, to the *terminological* or *scientific meaning* at which Aristotle ultimately arrives and then passes along to the tradition. And that customary meaning, in its "averageness," points us toward the content of pre-conceptual experience in this case.

What is worthy of praise in the way Aristotle arrives at the concept here, for Heidegger, is his evident tolerance of ambiguity, the frankness of his text in presenting the work of refining the concept of *ousia* from a complex of competing experiential elements. It is imperative that we, as destructive readers, do not excise or overlook that original and originating complexity. Rather, we must attend to it, mark it, and thereby understand Aristotle's concept of *ousia*, as we saw in chapter 1, "in its conceptuality." Heidegger notes:

> That even a *fundamental word* like οὐσία and others like it are freighted with an *ambiguity* [Vieldeutigkeit] should not diminish its appropriateness as the title term to be investigated. On the contrary. *Everything depends on the multiplicity* [Vielfältigkeit] *of meaning being understood as such* . . . Insofar as degrees of meaning are, *each in its origin, held fast* and determined from out of matters experienced and interpreted in such and such a way, the ambiguity [*Vieldeutigkeit*] is *substantively oriented* and fixed as such; it is a *multifariousness* [Vielfachheit]. And it is precisely if it is held fast as this, and not coifed up and leveled out [*frisiert und nivelliert*] on the basis of unsubstantive systematic tendencies into an artificial uniformity of meaning, only then, as a multifariousness [*Vielfachheit*] of meaning, does it have the proper suitability to convey an *understanding of the concretion of matters* [Verständnis der Konkretion der Sachen]. (*BCArP* 232/343, translation modified)

Even as one meaning steps to the fore for Aristotle and ultimately determines the initiating metaphysical reduction of Being to presence, Heidegger sees Aristotle as, laudably, acknowledging an original multiplicity as such, recording it in his text, confronting it, and thinking in relation to it. Heidegger writes: "Aristotle had an *explicitly positive consciousness* of the multifariousness of meaning [*Vielfachheit des Bedeutens*], and particularly in the field of basic concepts [such as *ousia*]" (*BCArP* 232/344). And it remains a proper response to that initial multiplicity, when Aristotle allows one driving customary meaning to elevate itself and determine the technical meaning or the concept of *ousia* and thereby, the meaning of Being both for himself and for the rest of the tradition.

In ordinary fourth-century BCE Greek, thanks to its etymology, one might well have been able to hear the term "*ousia*" to some extent and in certain contexts as something like "being" or "thing," and also perhaps as the "essential nature" of a thing, or even the "reality" facing us. And it is surely associations such as these that determine the list of candidates for *ousia* that Aristotle generates at the outset of Book Zeta, as we saw above—essence, universal, genus, and underlying thing. But, so observes

Heidegger, the ordinary Greek speaker would have understood the term "*ousia*" most readily as something like "means" (as in the phrase "a person of means"), or as "possessions" and "goods" belonging to an individual, and finally as one's "property, household stock," or even "estate."[9] And this customary meaning drives Aristotle's conceptualization of *ousia*, Heidegger argues, for there is a certain specific way of being that these beings exhibit in everyday experience.

These are beings that *are*, first and foremost, *brauchbar* or "usable" by us, Heidegger observes. As such, they present themselves as "being right there before us" and "available" entirely. Our means, goods, possessions, and property are things we understand ourselves to possess, control, and determine without remainder. We own them. They *are* by being emphatically *ours*. These beings do not present themselves to us as essentially mysterious, question-worthy, or inaccessible in their being. They do not appear to us as intrinsically resistant to our understanding or mastery. Nor are they experienced as ontologically in process, or in the act of *accomplishing their being* or *emerging into being*. No, as pieces of property, as our goods and possessions, they present themselves first and foremost as finished, completed, and fully *there* before us, to be held, made use of, evaluated, even quantifiably so, and exchanged. It may be Aristotle who fatefully reduces Being to being present, but he does so on the basis of a latent tendency in Greek experience, one that pushes him to approach and then interpret all beings, insofar as they are beings, on the model of *ousia*, which may be etymologically "what *is* most of all," but in its customary meaning is more familiarly "property, holdings, possessions."

Toward the end of his discussion of *ousia*, Heidegger poses a question to his students about the destructive method they have been employing and what precisely it entails. He asks:

> What happened when we returned to the customary meaning in order to gain direction regarding the meaning of οὐσία, there, "being there" [*Da*, "*Dasein*"]? This return [*Rückgang*] is nothing other than an *eavesdropping on the speaking* [Abhören des Sprechens] of natural Dasein to its own world, of the way the communication of Dasein speaks with itself about beings that are there, of what being means in this natural intelligibility. (*BCArP* 29–30/41, translation modified)

When "eavesdropping" on the way that natural Greek Dasein speaks about beings, what we hear and what Aristotle himself hears when he attends to this experiential register in trying to generate the concept of *ousia*, is a *vital multiplicity*, a number of divergent meanings. Nevertheless, even given these multiple possible associations, the term "*ousia*" most of all evokes beings with the mode of present, finished, identifiable, estimable, exchangeable, masterable things.

Within that multiplicity, however, Heidegger hears one crucial divergence, a road that Aristotle's text indicates but does not take. Heidegger cites a line from the "Ousiology," in Book Eta, where, even after the above-cited result arrived at in Book Zeta, Aristotle once again restlessly reopens the discussion, returning to two primary candidates to consider whether they deserve the name "*ousia.*" Aristotle writes, in Heidegger's rendering with his parenthetical commentary on the text preserved in brackets,

> There results from the λόγοι themselves [from the investigation or λόγος as phenomenon] that something else or something different is οὐσία—ἄλλαι οὐσίαι [more than one!]—τὸ τί ἦν εἶναι and ὑποκείμενον. (*Meta.* VIII.1042a12–13)

For Heidegger, Aristotle is here entertaining the two most important and fundamentally opposed candidates that present themselves initially as *ousia*. On the one hand, as we saw, our ordinary experience of beings tells us that "what *is* most of all" is *to ti ên einai*, the "essence" and the *eidos*, the "form" of substantial beings, which makes them what they are and knowable as such. On the other hand, however, and in a powerful respect, what also seems to Aristotle initially "to be most of all" and, thus, to most deserve the name *ousia*, is the *hupokeimenon*, literally the "underlying thing," what is beneath or what subtends and holds together all the discrete properties and features of the things we experience. And as Aristotle makes clear in Book Zeta, if we were to define the concept *ousia* as the ultimate *hupokeimenon*, this would mean that "what is most of all" would be the underlying pure materiality of the thing, its material brute "there-ness," before and without any form whatsoever, before any qualities, any determination at all (*Meta.* VII.1029a8–b12).[10] Presented with this ambivalence at the level of experience, Aristotle decides in favor of identifying the concept of *ousia* with the essence and form.

It is precisely here, for Heidegger, that we see that second *krisis* in the Being which grounds both Greek experience and Aristotelian thinking—an indication of Being, not as the presence of present beings, but as what withholds itself behind such beings as the essentially question-worthy dynamic event of emergence into presence. Let us tarry here at this moment of questioning with Aristotle, at the openness to a complex multiplicity of meanings in the experiential register that seems to characterize the Aristotelian text just prior to when a definitive and fateful conception of Being as presence is generated. If we do so, Heidegger shows, we will see in *Metaphysics* Zeta and Eta the slight trace of an aspect of Being that remains unexperienced and unthought.

Heidegger will find here a kind of struggle between a Platonic impulse toward the transcendence of everyday experience and a resistance to that impulse, a contrary tendency toward immanence, toward abiding with and merely clarifying the world as we usually experience it. On the one hand, Heidegger sees in Aristotle echoes of that Platonizing force which first suggested that the material, changing, temporal, imperfect, sensible things that populate our everyday world are perhaps not ultimately real, not "what *is*" most of all. Rather, "what *is*" are the *eidê*, the "Forms" or "Ideas," the immaterial, unchanging, eternal, perfect, intelligible paradigms that sensible material things point toward and depend upon. When Aristotle feels compelled to identify *ousia* with the *eidos* or *essence* of the particular thing, even if the Aristotelian form now exists within the material thing rather than transcending it, Heidegger sees the Platonic impulse at work.

There is, on the other hand, present in the text a properly Aristotelian tendency as well, which Heidegger calls a "genuine *counterthrust* [Gegenstoß] *to Platonic philosophy*" (*BCArP* 27/37). It is this tendency that fuels the potential identification of *ousia* with the *hupokeimenon*, the "underlying thing," that subtends everything else and which ultimately underlies the *eidos* itself for Aristotle. The world that we are challenged to think and concern ourselves with, according to this notion of *ousia* as "what is" most of all, would *not* be related back to the intelligible and masterable forms that beings present us with. Rather, beings would point back to what underlies everything that is experienceable and knowable about them, a force of brute, essentially hidden and inarticulate material thereness. On the basis of this ontology, Being would not be identified with a collection of complete, intelligible, masterable present beings, but would involve a grounding in the impenetrable dynamic according to which the thing first emerged into view and provoked one's thinking and questioning. To explain what things are would require somehow thinking those things along with the quasi-miraculous fact of their being there at all.

In a section of the 1924 course specifically devoted to *Metaphysics* Zeta, Eta, and Theta, Heidegger reads these books as an account of the Platonic impulse gaining the upper hand, of *eidos* and essence ultimately winning out and seizing the mantle of *ousia*. If we could, through destructive reading, uncover that Aristotelian counter-Platonic thrust and follow its directive, we might reverse the trend by which "there-ness, presence, was effaced, vanished [*Dahaftigkeit, Präsenz, erwischt, verschwunden*]" (*BCArP* 237/351). Indeed, we might be able to return thoughtfully to that *da*, that "there," in which beings first emerge and present themselves and in relation to which Aristotle genuinely attempts to think. We would thereby be able to note the way in which with Aristotle,

> the interpretation of beings is drawn back to Being within the horizon of the immediate, explicitly, and precisely thereby the outlook toward Being in a radical sense, while *Plato*, taking only a side-glance at the being-that-is-right-there [*mit einem Seitenblick auf Daseiendes*], had been caught up fantastically in λόγος and thus, consequently and in a Greek manner, went astray [*dabei, griechisch, konsequent verfährt*] . . . The immediate, what is known, is the *average* and in this way *general*. In it everything is seen, addressed, and interpreted on its basis. (*BCArP* 238/352, translation modified)

What would it mean that, by identifying "what is" with the immaterial intelligible Forms and thereby being "caught up in a fantastical *logos*," Plato "consequently and in a Greek manner, goes astray"?[11] How so, exactly? Although we have rejected the notion that, in Heidegger's view, any of these Greek thinkers makes a mistake in putting forward the metaphysics of presence, Plato can nonetheless apparently be said to *sich verfahren* or "lose his way," for he fails to attend sufficiently to "the being-that-is-right-there," to which Aristotle displayed a great sensitivity. This going astray, which presents itself to the destructive reader as a moving toward a certain complete intelligibility of Being, is utterly Greek, which is to say, consistent with the way Being is presenting itself to Greek experience at that moment. Plato begins with the way beings present themselves immediately, in the manner in which they are already known, the average and usual way they are experienced, and out of this he conceptualizes Being as presence, as the being present of a being. The most present, the most persistently present and exhaustively accessible beings, Plato comes to believe, however, are not the concrete things of everyday life, but the Ideas of these, their ideal abstract essences, for these are not caught up in coming-to-be and passing-away, nor are they situated in concrete, transfiguring contexts of relations (*R* V.476a-b, V.479d), but seem to be eternally there and available for intellection, pure and simple.[12]

Aristotle, by contrast, seems to have been more focused on the "being-that-is-right-there," at least to the point that he resists for a moment the Platonic, and apparently quintessentially Greek, tendency toward abstraction and the reduction of Being to presence and availability. Aristotle's text shows him entertaining at least the association of Being with the *hupokeimenon*, with the ultimate underlying and supporting reality that funds the world of beings which emerge into view and present themselves to us. Of course, as it must, the Greek and originally Platonic conception of Being ultimately wins the day, insofar as Aristotle, following Plato most of the way, elevates the more customary and more available meaning of *ousia* as the completed essence or form of the present being to his concept of Being itself. In the end, he abandons the counter-Platonic impulse to which his thinking was for a moment susceptible, but that susceptibility offers to Heidegger's destructive reading a hint, an indication of Being's association with an underlying, inaccessible, unknowable source of beings.

This is not the materiality that Aristotle will eventually conceptualize in the context of his interpretation of hylomorphic beings—the material potency of the body that is actualized by the ordering power of the *eidos* or "form." Rather, what destruction can reveal here is the irremediably withdrawn and hidden ground of the present being's appearing and announcing itself as what it is—what Heidegger called (as quoted above) its *Dahaftigkeit* or brute "being-thereness," which briefly presents itself and causes Aristotle to pause before following the Platonic and Greek tendency. Indeed, in the 1924–25 course on Plato's *Sophist*, Heidegger describes what must have been the minor undercurrent of association which suggested to Aristotle, at least for a moment, that *ousia* might be most fundamentally the *hupokeimenon* or "what underlies," rather than the *eidos* or essence that a being presents us with. He writes:

> οὐσία, the basic determination of ὄν, had the character of ὑποκείμενον, of what is already there in advance, of utter and primary presence [*was im vorhinein schon vorliegt, der ganz primären Anwesenheit*]. (PS 155/224)

This primary presencing, prior to any emergence of form, is what first provokes wonder and questioning. Before the being is identified, defined, exhaustively known, and put to use, before its coming to presence *as* this or that species of being, there is its brute being there at all. Its prior emergence *as such*. To think beings in relation to that mysterious dynamic and source would amount to an initial breach of the levee that constrains metaphysical thinking and that demands the exhaustive identification of Being with the mode of being of present beings. Heidegger's destructive intervention draws attention to this deeper aspect of the ground of Aristotelian thinking, that second *krisis* in the critical science of Being in Aristotle that we heard about in chapter 2, which leaves only the faintest of traces in the still open and not yet resolved initial moments of the Aristotelian discussion.

Zôon Logon Echon or the "Animal Having Logos"

There are a number of places in the 1920s where Heidegger takes up Aristotle's essential definition of the human being as the *zôon logon echon*, usually translated as the "animal having language or reason" or "rational animal" (*Pol.* I.1253a10–18). Let us begin with one of the most extensive discussions, which occurs in Heidegger's course on the *Sophist*, that late dialogue in which Plato is at pains to distinguish two easily confused ways in which human beings take up the *logos*, namely, philosophy and sophistry. Here, a figure referred to only as the Stranger from Elea leads his young interlocutor, Theaetetus, through multiple definitions of the sophist, ultimately identifying that figure as one who fashions false appearances of anything and everything in language. This definition triggers a lengthy substantive digression in which the Stranger must show that, contra Parmenides, it is possible for the sophist to say "what is not" and thus to speak falsely at all.

Of course, this dialogue will provide Heidegger with that passage concerning the forgetting of the meaning of Being which serves as the epigraph for *Being and Time* (*Soph.* 244a–b). And given the complex of fundamental themes discussed in the dialogue—being and not-being, *logos*, truth and falsity, the nature of philosophy itself—it is no surprise that the young Heidegger would take up this work in his destructive project. What is surprising here is Heidegger's statement at the outset of the course that it is necessary to approach the Platonic text *by way of Aristotle*. This is the justification for the 160-page preliminary discussion of book VI of the *Nicomachean Ethics* (in connection with passages from a number of other Aristotelian texts). We will return later to the significance of this approach. I will simply note here at the outset that this is often read as expressing a simple, and not entirely justifiable, preference for Aristotle over Plato. To the contrary, I suggest in what follows that, while Heidegger does seem to exhibit such a preference, the hermeneutic principle as it is articulated by him here actually entails something much more profound concerning the very nature and limits of philosophical thinking itself. More on this later.

Before proceeding through Aristotle's treatment of the intellectual virtues in book VI of the *Nicomachean Ethics*, Heidegger first focuses on Aristotle's categorization of all these virtues as modes of *alêtheuein*. This is a verb built on the Greek word *alêtheia*, which is usually translated as "truth," so that the verb in the active voice would have to mean something like "to true" or "truing." Digging further into the etymology here,

Heidegger observes that although we usually translate *alêtheia* as "truth" quite straightforwardly, it would certainly have been heard by the ordinary Greek as something like "unconcealment" or "unforgetting." As the early Heidegger often notes, and continues to reference over the course of his career, the word is produced by taking the root *lêth-*, "forgetting, concealment," and affixing to it the negating "*a-*" prefix, the *alpha privativum*, and the suffix "*-ia*," which forms nouns from word roots in order to refer to a state, condition, or quality. Heidegger finds himself wondering again and again over the years what precisely would be entailed by the fact that every time one said or heard the word "truth," one could also hear "unconcealment, unforgetting."

For Heidegger, this seems to entail that the Greeks stand in an altogether different relation to their world than do those of us thinking after them, in their wake. Indeed, in a subsection of the *Sophist* course entitled "The history of the concept of truth," Heidegger traces the steps in the transformation from the original Greek notion of truth as *alêtheia* to the conventional notion of truth that Aristotle will definitively generate and pass along to the subsequent tradition.

> Ἀληθές means literally "uncovered." It is primarily things, the πράγματα, that are uncovered. Τὸ πρᾶγμα ἀληθές ["the thing is true"]. This uncoveredness does not apply to things insofar as they are, but insofar as they are encountered, insofar as they are objects of concern. Accordingly, uncoveredness is a specific accomplishment of Dasein, which has its Being in the soul: ἀληθεύει ἡ ψυχή ["the soul trues"]. Now, the most immediate kind of uncovering is speaking about things. That is, a determination of life, a determination which can be conceived as λόγος, primarily takes over the function of ἀληθεύειν. Ἀληθεύει ὁ λόγος, and precisely λόγος as λέγειν ["speaking, discoursing with others"]. Insofar now as each λόγος is a self-expression and a communication, λόγος acquires at once the meaning of the λεγόμενον ["the thing said, statement"]. Hence λόγος means on the one hand speaking, λέγειν, and then also the spoken, λεγόμενον. And insofar as it is λόγος which ἀληθεύει ["trues"], λόγος qua λεγόμενον is ἀληθής ["discourse" qua "statement" is "true"]. But strictly taken this is not the case. (*PS* 17/24–25)

Here, in tracing the historical development in the understanding of the term *alêtheia* from an original early Greek notion to what we find in the text of Aristotle, Heidegger draws open once again that distinction between the experiential and the conceptual registers in the text being read destructively. The earlier notions of *alêtheia* and *logos*, with their grounding in lived human experience, give rise to but are ultimately also partly obscured by the concepts of truth and language that emerge from them. A formerly lived notion of truth as a property of beings—namely their emerging into view, their being unconcealed in the sense of simply appearing or presenting themselves to human experience, primarily in the context of humans speaking with one another or making things appear to one another in speech—is eclipsed by a kind of truth that belongs exclusively to statements. Thus, already in Aristotle, *alêtheia* gives way to something approaching *adequatio*, the term that will ultimately appear in Thomas Aquinas's definition of truth as the *adequatio rei et intellectus*, the correspondence between present beings and their re-presentation in thought.

But it is the transformation in the nature of *logos*, and thus of the concept of the human being as *zôon logon echon*, that is our focus here. As with truth, *logos* has undergone a process of conceptualization and definition in Greek thought, culminating with Aristotle and his identification of the statement or proposition as the fundamental linguistic unit and the basic element of truth or falsity (*De int.* 17a1–3). And here too, behind or beneath this Aristotelian definition of truth as a feature of statements, Heidegger finds an original complex experience of *logos*. He writes:

> It is not the case that words first flutter about in isolation and then are taken together, whence δηλοῦν ["manifesting, making evident"] arises. On the contrary, δηλοῦν is primary. It is the fundamental phenomenon. And only with reference to it does there exist the possibility of a deficient mode, of isolated merely recited words. The δηλοῦν, which harbors the possibility of discourse, is a constitutive determination of Being-in-the-world or Being-in. (*PS* 411/593)

In experience, *logos* is not in the first instance a sum of vocal or written signs that can be brought together in meaningful combinations or sentences, which may or may not be accurate re-presentations of present beings and the relations among them. Rather, when we begin to reflect upon what *logos* is, language has always already appeared as a speaking with one another by way of which beings become clear; that is, in which the world is always already appearing. This lived activity of speaking with one another about the world around us is called by Aristotle, most fundamentally, *dêloun*, which derives from the adjective *dêlos*, meaning "clear, manifest, evident," and thus means fundamentally something like "to make clear, make manifest, make evident." It is only because we live together in language in this way, as the site or medium for our shared relating to the world, that we can then suspend that activity and turn our attention to utterances or individual words severed from their original and defining function of manifesting beings.

As we saw already at the outset of this study, in the "Introduction," insofar as the world has always appeared to human beings in their ordinary lived discoursing activities, Heidegger wants to refer to the mode of being of humans as "being-in-the-world." And as we noted, it is vital that we understand this not as a merely spatial relation between a vessel (world) and its contents (human beings). Rather, in the Greek notions of truth as *alêtheia* and language as *dêloun*, it is suggested that the Greeks originally experienced the human as having a completely different way of being than we imagine today according to our metaphysical worldview. For the Greeks originally, the human was not a present being situated in relation to other present beings, but rather a being whose being is accomplished in *logos*, which (we should recall) is not to be understood as a set of signs or symbols, but as a medium or site for the appearance of beings. The human is essentially defined by the reception of the world's appearing in language, which entails that the human is in its mode of being, in a sense, always outside itself, drawn out toward the world through its initial appearing.

So long as we think of the *zôon logon echon* definition strictly in Aristotelian terms, as a genus (living thing) with a species-defining difference (language or reason), we miss the ontological significance of *logos* that emerged through the consideration of the experiential register of the Aristotelian text, as indicated for Heidegger here in the etymologies of Aristotle's fundamental terms (*alêtheia* or "unconcealment," *dêloun* as "discoursing, making manifest," and *legein* as "speaking" but more fundamentally as a "gathering" of things together in order to bring them forth and present them). The human does not exist as a living thing, to which we then add the faculty of language or reason. Rather, its very mode of being is its receiving of the world's appearing in and through language.

And this *worldliness* of human beings, as it were, is not a radical departure from, but a sort of modification or intensification of the way of being of the *zôon* or "living thing."

> Ζωή is a concept of being: "life" refers to a *mode of being* [Seinsweise], indeed a mode of *being-in-the-world* [Sein-in-der-Welt]. A living thing is not simply at hand [*vorhanden*], but is in the world in that it has its world [*daß es seine Welt hat*]. An animal is not simply moving down the road, pushed along by some mechanism. It is in the world in the manner of "having it [the world]" [*in der Welt in der Weise des Sie-Habens*]. (*BCArP* 14/18)

Though elsewhere Heidegger may be inclined to amplify the difference between the human and the animal, even declaring the latter "poor in world" (*FCM* 195/283–84), here in 1924 he emphasizes the continuity in their way of being, and even a fundamental likeness between them. Like the human being, a living thing is also not to be understood as something "at hand," a present being taking up space, to which would be added the characteristic activity of "living." Rather, living beings *accomplish their being* and *are living* only insofar as they are essentially and constitutively related to what is in their environment. The living thing, in living, is open to its world, not only responding to what occurs and touches it immediately, as one billiard ball knocked by another, but anticipating, stretching out toward, desiring, avoiding, recoiling from other beings in its surroundings and orienting itself accordingly. Living things simply in being what they are already *have* other beings and even *have* the entire world in which they find themselves, receiving the appearances of these and containing them in a sense in their concerned activities.

Logos is to be understood, then, as simply one peculiar modification of the way in which all living things have their world. The human not only relates essentially and constitutively to beings in various modes, but relates to them *as* what they are, *as* this or that kind of being—identifying, naming, and categorizing the beings that populate its world. Though the "as"-structure peculiar to human experience will produce a vital distinction for Heidegger in other contexts, here he emphasizes the continuity between animal and human ways of being—both are modes of being-in-the-world, of having one's world. Summing up, he writes:

> The *being-in-the-world of the human being* is determined in its ground [*im Grunde bestimmt*] *through speaking.* The fundamental mode of being by which the human is in its world is in speaking with it, about it, of it. Thus is the human being determined precisely through the *logos.* (*BCArP* 14/18)

Destruction proceeds here, once again, by showing this deeper, richer experience of human life, which is simplified and thinned out by way of the Aristotelian definition, even though that essential definition responds to the basic mode of life, speaking about the world, with which the Greeks are thoroughly familiar. The concept of the human being we inherit today, the animal with a certain faculty of reason or speech, is thereby destabilized, and shown to be a reduction and a loss with respect to the experiential ground out of which it arose.

Beyond this, we again see Heidegger in this thematic context marking an essential excess of thinking, something beyond the beings that present themselves to be understood and mastered and beyond even the universal notion of Being in which they all share. We have found destruction revealing again and again the trace of that excess, but let us recall here two different contexts. On the one hand, in 1924's *Basic Concepts of Aristotelian Philosophy*, Heidegger insisted on the *insuperable incompletion* that belongs to *sophia* or "wisdom" with respect to Being, identifying *sophia* with *philosophia*, that is, with "philosophizing, desiring or loving wisdom" (*BCAncP* 8/11). And in *Basic Problems of Phenomenology*, Heidegger made clear that the phenomenological approach to the thinking of Being requires not only a reduction and destruction, but a *projection* and even a *construction*—thinking Being must go beyond what presents itself directly to be thought, and essentially project out beyond present beings in their presence toward a withdrawn source (*BPP* 21/29).

We find a resonant characterization of philosophizing here in the *Sophist* lecture course, at precisely that moment when Heidegger declares the absolute necessity of approaching the Platonic text by way of Aristotle. To be sure, Heidegger introduces this as a hermeneutic principle, insisting that interpreters should proceed "from the clear into the obscure," and not the other way around. This makes it seem as though Aristotle is simply clearer than Plato, perhaps because the former writes in straightforward philosophical prose while the latter never published in his own voice, offering instead dramas complicated by their dramatic contexts, as well as offering philosophical positions and arguments that are only ever voiced by speakers with specific perspectives and personalities.[13] But if we read on a bit and attend closely to Heidegger's characterization of the hermeneutic principle, we find something deeper and more surprising here. Heidegger writes:

> Previously it was usual to interpret Platonic philosophy by proceeding from Socrates and the Pre-Socratics to Plato. We wish to strike out in the opposite direction, from Aristotle back to Plato. This way is not unprecedented. It follows the old principle of hermeneutics, namely that interpretation should proceed from the clear into the obscure. We will presuppose that Aristotle understood Plato. Even those who have only a rough acquaintance with Aristotle will see from the level of this work that it is no bold assertion to maintain that Aristotle understood Plato. No more than it is to say in general on the question of understanding that the later ones always understand their predecessors better than the predecessors understood themselves. Precisely here lies the element of creative research [*das Elementare der schöpferischen Forschung*], that in what is most decisive this research does not understand itself. (*PS* 8/11)

Note that the thinking Heidegger finds at work here among the Greeks is specifically a *schöpferische Forschung* or "creative investigation" into Being, and this creativity is not at all presented as a philosophical deficiency. Indeed, it would seem that something about thinking Being properly even requires creativity. As we saw above, it seems to demand a certain going beyond the positive scientific study of beings and even beyond the initial critical scientific study of the universal Being of beings, both of which would approach beings as completely and thoroughly knowable in a traditional sense. What Heidegger seems to see in Plato here, and presumably in Aristotle, is a creative response to Being, a response to Being in its provocation of wonder and questioning, insofar as it holds itself in excess of the beings it allows to arise into appearance. Indeed, this thinking, precisely as creative, abdicates an exhaustive understanding of itself with respect to what is most decisive for it, namely Being.

And in case we are tempted to think that this lack of self-understanding would be a kind of deficiency, to which for instance Aristotle (as later and clearer) or Heidegger himself (as even later and even clearer, presumably) might not be susceptible, we should take note of a comment Heidegger makes much later on, as he is transitioning from Aristotle to Plato. He writes:

> The Romantic appreciation of Plato within the history of philosophy precisely does not see what is properly positive in him, i.e., what is not well-rounded, what is fragmentary, what remains underway. That is the genuinely positive element in all research [*Forschung*]. (*PS* 285/412–13)

Again, it is the remaining underway, the incompletion, of Platonic philosophizing that can point the destructive reader beyond beings and the Being of beings, to that aspect of Being according to which it holds itself back and remains irremediably question-worthy.

Dunamis or "Potency"

Toward the end of the introduction to *Being and Time*, after explaining that his method in the book will be properly, essentially phenomenological, even as it departs quite profoundly from the Husserlian method "in its actuality as a philosophical movement," Heidegger makes the following broad and radical pronouncement: "Higher than actuality stands *possibility*" (*BT* 63/38). In addition to serving as a kind of dismissal of Husserlian phenomenology, this statement is surely intended as a sort of rebuttal to Aristotle and the metaphysical thinking Heidegger sees emerging with him. It was after all Aristotle who, in inaugurating that tradition, stated, "It is clear that actuality is prior to potency [*phaneron hoti proteron energeia dunameôs estin*]" (*Meta.* IX.1049b5), and he intended this priority as both ontological and epistemological. That is, for Aristotle, *dunamis* or "potency" both is "what it is" and is knowable as such only *as organized toward* a condition of *energeia* or *entelecheia*, both of which are often translated as "act, actuality, or actualization," but which mean according to their respective etymologies "being-at-work" (*en-* or "in" + *ergon* or "work, function") and "holding-itself-in-its-end" (*en-* + *telos* or "end, aim" + *echein* or "holding").[14] An acorn, as acorn, is "what it is" and is definable as such only as "potentially an oak," while an oak in its essence is not and need not be defined as "having been an acorn."

Now, although the line cited above from *Being and Time* does seem to represent a direct rejection of Aristotle's prioritization of actuality over potency, it simultaneously marks a sort of retrieval and appropriation of Aristotle's recognition of *dunamis* as a legitimate mode of being at all. That is, for Aristotle, it must be acknowledged, something that *is* only in the mode of *dunamis* or "potentially" nevertheless still *is*. It *has being* and *as such is part of reality*. The potential oakness in the acorn is real and it does work in the world as such, for Aristotle, even though it is not yet actual and, thus, not yet present. Most commentators will wash over this radical ontological feature of Aristotle's teleological theory—the future end or aim toward which a being is unfolding has being and is working as a cause, precisely as non-present. Aristotle writes in Book Delta's philosophical lexicon, "'to be' and 'being' [*to einai . . . kai to on*] signify sometimes that what is spoken of is potentially, and sometimes that it is actually" (*Meta.* V.1017a35–b1).[15] And thus, even if Aristotle will ultimately subordinate *dunamis* to *energeia*, at least he grants it ontological legitimacy, which is more, much more, than the subsequent tradition and its metaphysics of presence will grant to merely potential being.[16]

And this is a major focus of Heidegger's treatment of *dunamis* in his 1924 course,[17] for here he makes two radical interpretive claims that involve recognizing Aristotle's affirmation of the ontological legitimacy or being of "what is potentially." Namely, Heidegger will claim that (1) according to Aristotle, all natural beings, that is, all living things and perhaps even all material things, have as their fundamental way of being *kinêsis*, which is usually rendered as "motion," but which sometimes must be understood in an expanded sense to mean something like "change." And Heidegger will insist that (2) all natural things according to Aristotle, as essentially "moving" or "changing" in the very specific and subtle sense Heidegger develops here, *are potentially* or *are what they are by way of potency*. That is, they are in their very mode of being *constituted by non-presence*. These are radical claims indeed and they require clarification.

In the first interpretive move, Heidegger insists that for natural beings, to be is to move or change. They are what they are only by way of *kinêsis*. This is a claim about all sublunary beings, all beings that are composed of elemental matter (earth, air, fire, and water) with an organizing form, or all natural beings in the sense of *Physics*' book II, which "have within themselves a source of movement and rest" (*Phys.* II.192b8–20). We would usually imagine that something has to exist, that is, it has to be what it is, and only then could it be said to move and undergo change. Heidegger finds in Aristotle a more fundamental notion of *kinêsis*, one that is not posterior to existence, but is the way in which natural beings are what they are, the way they accomplish their being. Heidegger puts this central claim succinctly:

> φύσις, world. κίνησις is not merely one state among others, but is an *essential determination*. Therefore *motion as a mode of Being is fundamental*. World, beings pure and simple, wherein each and every being is. Motion is ontologically central, even as something ontic. On the basis of motion: the ontological analysis is not a mere expansion and supplementation of what has preceded; on the contrary, it is a fundamental and more radical apprehension of these beings, the φύσει ὄντα [beings by nature] and, as such, of a pan-dynamics of *Being in general* [*Pandynamik* des Seins überhaupt]. (*BCAncP* 142–43/170–71)

The last phrase, a "pan-dynamics of Being in general," was actually so striking that it caused the German editor of the text to place a vexed little question mark after it. And his surprise is justified too, as there is entailed here a quite unexpected claim indeed. In both 1924 and 1926, Heidegger is insisting that natural beings, everything in the world of our experience, are what they are *by changing, by moving* in some sense. Are we to hear in this that Aristotle's anti-Platonism has pushed him so far as to embrace Heracliteanism? Is Aristotle to be understood as embracing the principle of *panta rhei* or "everything flows," which stands at the heart of the philosophy of the "Obscure One" himself? Not really. Even as Heidegger's Aristotle insists on the ontological function of *kinêsis*, he identifies and presents the *archai* or "principles, sources" that are at work in every event of natural change, even in coming-to-be and passing away, such that these ontologically constitutive events of change or movement can be accounted for and made intelligible (*Phys.* I.189b30–192b4). But there is nevertheless, by Heidegger's destructive reading, a moment in excess of metaphysics here, at least to the extent that the identification of *kinêsis* as the mode of being of natural beings leads Aristotle to confirm the legitimate ontological status, and indeed the participation *in Being* of non-presence.

It should be noted that, for anyone who knows Aristotle fairly well, Heidegger's understanding of *kinêsis* as the mode of being of natural beings faces some heavy resistance. In *Physics* book III, Aristotle takes up the task of giving an account of *kinêsis*, having observed that, according to all of his predecessors save Parmenides, motion or change seem to be a fundamental feature of the natural world, which it is after all the task of the *Physics* to explain and make intelligible. This presents a problem because motion or change seems to be "something indefinite, and a host of negative principles [such as otherness, non-identity, and non-being] seem also to be indefinite, since none of them is a 'this [*tode*]' or a quality, nor do they belong to any of the other ways of attributing being" (*Phys.* III.201b24–27). The natural world, then, threatens to become a sea of unintelligible alteration, approaching simple non-being, which is precisely what drove Plato to posit the Ideas above and beyond the apparent Heraclitean flux of the natural world and grant these Ideas alone true Being and intelligibility. Aristotle, by contrast, declares that although *kinêsis* is indeed in a sense "indefinite," it is nonetheless intelligible as a certain play of *dunamis* and *energeia*, a certain dynamic according to which natural beings are what they are by actualizing their potency to be.

However, this then requires Aristotle to distinguish two different ways in which potency is actualized, for in both the process by which a thing changes or comes-to-be and in that thing's just persisting, being the thing it is, Aristotle sees the actualization of a potency. Consider the stones that will be used to construct a temple, for instance. Those stones have the potential to undergo the process of construction—they can become otherwise, be moved and carved and assembled, ultimately taking on the form of a temple. This is *kinêsis*, change or motion, and Aristotle famously declares, "the actualization of a being in potency, as potency, is *kinêsis* [*hê dunamei ontow entelecheia, hê(i) toiouton, kinêsis estin*]" (*Phys.* III.201a10–11). However, once the temple is constructed, as it stands there on the hilltop, simply being a temple, this too is the actualization of its material's potency, not its potency as potency or its potency to change and become other than it is, but its potency to be a temple. Thus, *both* in changing or coming to be *and* in being, Aristotle finds the *energeia* of *dunamis*, the actualization or more literally the "putting to work" of a potency, but in explicitly different ways. In order to capture this distinction, Aristotle ultimately declares that, as opposed to *einai* or "being," "*kinêsis* seems to be some sort of *energeia*, but an incomplete one [*atelês*]" (*Phys.* III.202a32–33).

When Heidegger declares that natural beings *are what they are* by way of a kind of *kinêsis*, he must thus be expanding the notion of *kinêsis* beyond the strict sense it has in the technical definition of the term by which Aristotle distinguishes it from Being in book III of the *Physics*. Why would Heidegger want to do so? Because, notwithstanding the above emphatic and clear distinction between changing and Being, Heidegger sees, in Aristotle's thinking of the way of being of natural beings, an initial recognition of a kind of essential incompletion there as well, even if this must be distinguished from the incompletion of *kinêsis* strictly speaking.

This is the second radical interpretive move, for Heidegger sees Aristotle as observing natural beings—in the way the form orders the material into a way of being, or the soul actualizes the body's potency, into a way of life for living things—and he finds Aristotle's text here gesturing to a moment of non-presence. This is the case and it is detectible through destructive reading, even if Aristotle ultimately sets aside such non-presence and affirms the metaphysics of presence that he will pass down to the tradition through the concepts he establishes. Consider the following.

Heidegger writes:

> A being thus in the world is there and can, at the same time be something usable. Δύναμις, "not yet," can mean: is usable for . . . transformable into . . . This being that is there thus, as there completed and usable for . . . is characterized by διχῶς [doubleness, duplicity] as a being . . . Even a house is for the most part in everydayness in such a way that something is lacking in it, characterized by στέρησις [privation]. Aristotle proceeds from this point in determining movement. (*BCArP* 212/313)

That is, insofar as natural beings are what they are through the actualization of potency, they are both present, sitting there before us, *and* essentially lacking, constituted in their very being by what is *not present*, by a "not yet."[18] Moreover, Heidegger sees Aristotle's questioning insight into this duplicity of natural beings, their double way of being, as emerging explicitly from his attending to a feature of things as they themselves present in everyday experience. In this being potentially usable there is an ontological lack, and there Heidegger wants to see a certain kind of "movement" or dynamism, a kinetic way of being (even if this cannot be the technical sense of *kinêsis* that Aristotle distinguishes emphatically from the *einai* or "being" of a natural being).

Heidegger clarifies what is entailed by the account of this kinetic way of being, writing:

> Since Aristotle emphasizes this important point in the preparation of the definition of movement . . . it becomes visible that beings themselves are grasped in their ability-to-be as "from . . . toward . . .". (*BCArP* 211/312)

It is very clear here that, for Heidegger, at least at the level of everyday experience and what Aristotle is receiving from that register, natural beings present a mode of being that is something other than simple persisting self-sameness or presence. Rather, they *are* what they are insofar as they emerge "from" a potency, by actualizing their material's potential to be a being of that sort (e.g., the form's actualizing the stones' ability to be a temple), and they unfold "toward" a *telos* or "aim, end," toward performing a certain function (e.g., the temple's serving as a site to ritually honor a deity). Heidegger concludes, "Κίνησις is the 'there' of the 'from . . . to . . .' as such [*das Da des 'von . . . zu . . .' als solchen*] (*BCArP* 254/376).

Thinking back to the discussion of *ousia* earlier, this could certainly trouble that function of *eidos* or "form" as the *ousia* or "beingness" of concrete beings, which Heidegger saw as ultimately playing a role in the metaphysical understanding of Being as reducible to the sum of wholly present, available beings. Heidegger observes: "Therefore, εἶδος, appearing as presence, presence in the look, is *possible absence* [mögliche Abwesenheit]—a mode of being present and precisely as follows: of something about which I say, 'But it lacks something [*Etwas fehlt*]'" (*BCArP* 254/376). Heidegger is playing on the etymology of the term *eidos*, which stems from the verb *idein* or "to see, look at" and thus means fundamentally, the "look" something presents us with such that we recognize it as the being it is and then as the "form" the thing has. Heidegger is suggesting here that, because the *eidos* of natural beings functions as *ousia* precisely by ordering or forming the material potency that constitutes the being and because that potency then persists in the being of the natural being, there is a potential not-being, a potential absence as well that constitutes the being *in its very way of being*. And given the fact that, as Heidegger observes, "for the Greeks, movement shows itself as ἀόριστον [indeterminate, indefinite, undelimited]" (*BCArP* 216/320), this indeterminacy is in the end not something to be overcome by understanding the natural being completely. As Aristotle himself remarks in *Physics*' book III, after offering his analysis of the phenomenon of *kinêsis* by reference to the principles of *dunamis* and *energeia*, *kinêsis* is something "difficult to bring into view, but possible to be" (*Phys.* III.202a2–3).[19]

This thinking of natural beings as "not yet," specifically in the sense of "usable for . . ." or "transformable into . . . ," and indeed this double mode of being that beings have, being here before us and yet pointing beyond themselves toward what they could become, how they could serve—this could easily evoke for readers of *Being and Time* that mode of being of *Zeug* or "equipment." Indeed, Heidegger is suggesting there that perhaps the equipment we use in our everyday going about in the world might in and of itself pose some resistance to the exclusive metaphysical identification of Being with present beings. And when he makes this point, he appeals to the Greek experience of beings and a specific term in Greek that is often translated as "being," namely "*pragma.*" Heidegger writes:

> The Greeks have an appropriate term for "things": πράγματα—that is to say, that which one has to do with in one's concernful dealings (πρᾶξις [goal-directed action]). But ontologically, the specifically "pragmatic" character of the πράγματα is just what the Greeks left in obscurity; they thought of these "proximallly" as "mere things." We shall call those beings which we encounter in concern "*equipment*" . . . Equipment is essentially "something in order to" ["*etwas um-zu*"]. (*BT* 96–97/68)

Although the exact dynamic is somewhat different, in 1927 the word "equipment" refers in its way of being to the aim at which our concerned employment of it is directed; and in 1924 a natural being, as the putting to work of a *dunamis*, refers back to the material out of which it arose and forward to what it might become or how it might serve. Thus, there does seem to be a real resonance between the two discussions, at least insofar as they both observe an ontologically constitutive referential or relational, quasi-ecstatic structure in beings.

However, I would suggest that there is an even more powerful resonance with a later work of Heidegger's, with respect to the insistence in 1924 that natural beings are constituted in their way of being by *Abwesenheit* or "absence, lack, and being-away." That is, there is something more radical in the early discussion than the mere reference to another being, more than the reference to a totality of other equipment, which is indeed what we find in *Being and Time* and which would ultimately entail only a kind of mild or provisional non-presence in the way of being of these beings.[20]

Insofar as Heidegger finds in Aristotle a more radical participation of non-being, we might find a kind of foreshadowing of the thinking Heidegger calls for in his 1929 essay "What Is Metaphysics?" There he remarks:

> The nothing does not merely serve as the counter-concept of beings, but rather it originally belongs to their essential unfolding as such. In the being of beings, the nihilation of the nothing occurs. ("WM" 91/12)

I am not suggesting that in 1924's destruction of the texts of Aristotle there is already fully at work this later thinking of beings in relation to "the nothing" out of which they emerge and present themselves. But Heidegger does seem to suggest that we encounter, through that destruction, a trace of an ontologically legitimate non-being and non-presence prior to Aristotle's inauguration of metaphysics and the conceptualization of *ousia* and *dunamis*, prior to the reduction of the former to a present and utterly available being and of the latter to the mere not-yet-a-reality of possibility.

In the end, destruction points to a dynamic and kinetic way of being, rather than the customary meaning of *ousia*, by distinguishing an *experiential register* from the *conceptual register*, as we have seen now again and again. That is, Heidegger draws here the crucial distinction between, on the one hand, Aristotle's lived involvement with movement as the being of natural beings and, on the other, the generation of the concept of *dunamis* that is passed along to the tradition. Indeed, in this discussion in particular, Heidegger makes a special appeal to his students, arguing for the need to dig back into the pre-conceptual register of experience, in order to understand the precise function and sometimes surprising radicality of the concepts Aristotle is creating. He writes:

> One must be clear as to . . . the fact that previously [prior to Aristotle's research into these matters] the decisive categories were not yet familiar. For us, the concepts δύναμις, ἐνέργεια, ἐντελέχεια are so worn out that one is not at all capable of seeing what was at stake in the fundamental meaning of these concepts. We must work to insert ourselves into the time when the concepts δύναμις and ἐνέργεια were first being cultivated. (*BCArP* 198–99/293, translation modified)

Heidegger has done just this by taking Aristotle's examples seriously, chasing down implications in the etymologies of the terms, and trying to suspend as much as possible the time-worn whittled-down definitions of these concepts as they have been delivered over to us by the tradition.

And, in Aristotle's radical thinking of *dunamis* and natural beings as essentially *dynamic* in this sense, Heidegger sees an indication or a trace of the relation to Being as beyond beings, as non-being. This is so, even if once again Aristotle himself does not think or even experience that withdrawn source of beings, but ultimately reduces beings to present beings, anchoring their dynamic and essentially potential mode of being in an actualization that makes them intelligible and gives them ontological stability. Aristotle himself did not sense these implications concerning the ontologically fundamental force of *dunamis* in the everyday appearing of natural, moving, material beings. Only we uncover them, through the work of destructive reading. And having no experiential access, Aristotle ultimately tamed the dynamism of natural being by grounding it back in the ontology of *ousia*. Commenting on a passage from the *Metaphysics* in which Aristotle indicates that all categories of being (*ousia* of course, but also quantities, qualities, etc.) can be said to be either in the mode of potency or in the mode of actualization, Heidegger writes:

> Insofar as δύναμις and ἐνέργεια determine οὐσία as such, which is the primary category and to which the others are related *analogously*, then δύναμις and ἐνέργεια also extend, as modifications, to all the remaining categories. In this way, everything is led back to οὐσία as the basic phenomenon, specifically such that ἐνέργεια is the *highest kind of presence-at-hand* [höchste Art des Vorhandenseins]. (*BCAncP* 151/180)

Heidegger seems to be saying that, had the relation between *dunamis* and *energeia* won the day and ultimately presented itself as fundamental, and had Aristotle then been able to allow these to determine his ontology, he might have ended up with something other than a metaphysics of presence. But this was not to be, for according to Heidegger here, the Greek experience of the world that led to Aristotle's fateful positing of *ousiai* or "substances" as the fundamental constituents of the world also ultimately required that he subordinate *dunamis* and *energeia* to the concept of substance; that is, ultimately to the *eidos* or en-forming activity of concrete, present, completed beings in their presence-at-hand and utter availability for human knowing and mastery.

Conclusion

The Turn and a "More Faithful Adherence to the Principle" of Destruction

> The beginning acts as a divinity among human beings—she is the savior of all things, so long as she receives her due honor.
> —Plato, *Laws* VI.775e2–4

One significant aspect of the oft-discussed *Kehre* or "turn" that takes place in Heidegger's thinking from 1930 on is his apparent abandoning of the term "destruction" to refer to the method one should employ in approaching the texts of one's tradition. In this respect, "destruction" and "phenomenology" share a common fate, for Heidegger also ceases to refer to his project as "phenomenological" more or less immediately after 1927's *Being and Time*. In both cases, however, I would suggest that Heidegger's turn should be understood less as a major revision or change of course, and more as a *radicalizing* of already existing aims and tendencies.

Indeed, Heidegger himself says as much in the 1962 letter to William Richardson that serves as the preface to the latter's seminal volume, *Heidegger: Through Phenomenology to Thought*. In his response to Richardson's questions, Heidegger largely consents to the latter's distinction between a "Heidegger I" and a "Heidegger II" and agrees that he had at a certain point moved away from a more traditional phenomenological method toward a less traditional, less scientific mode that might be referred to somewhat vaguely as "thinking." Heidegger does suggest a small but important amendment to Richardson's heuristic, however, an amendment reflected in the eventual title of Richardson's monograph. That is, Heidegger tells us there that he sees himself as having moved not so much away *from* phenomenology as *through* it. He agrees that fairly early on he began to put aside Husserl's particular focus on intentional consciousness and the transcendental subject, eventually abandoning as well as its quasi-scientific aspirations and vocabulary. Nevertheless, Heidegger insists that the work of the 1930s and after is characterized by a "more faithful adherence to the principle of phenomenology" ("Pref." xiv). I would suggest that we understand this according to Heidegger's own tendency in defining "phenomenology," for throughout the 1920s he will discuss his own phenomenological project less according to the letter of Husserl's technical method and more according to the term's etymology (e.g., *BT* §7, 48–63/17–39).[1] In more faithfully adhering to the principle of phenomenology in the later period, Heidegger would still be attempting to bring forth or mark in *logos* or "language, discourse" all that is involved in the self-presentation of beings, in their *phainesthai* or "appearing," even if that selfsame project came to require of his thinking ever more dramatic and groundbreaking departures from traditional philosophizing.[2]

I would suggest that something very similar takes place with respect to the project of destruction. Although Heidegger largely (but not entirely, as we shall see) ceases to use the term itself, although the general vocabulary and the tone of his historical engagements become more evocative and open, and although he begins to proceed by a less rigorously articulated method than we have uncovered here in these pages, the approach to the past in the work of the later Heidegger amounts nevertheless to a kind of faithful adherence to the principle of the earlier destructive project. For in both the earlier and the later periods, Heidegger sees his task as (1) a destabilizing of the received tradition and its concepts and values, which exposes the tradition's original generative source, namely the first unfolding of Being into questionability among the Greeks; and (2) a pointing beyond or perhaps beneath the region opened up for thinking by the Greek metaphysical reduction of Being, a pointing toward something still covered over and preserved in that source, a subtending, insuperably question-worthy aspect of Being that remained unexperienced and unthought by the Greeks themselves. At least, as I have been arguing throughout, this can be found indicated at certain moments in those early lecture courses and papers, even if there are also contrary tendencies and divergent articulations in the early project, which Heidegger will later explicitly reject as "inappropriate" and "naive."[3] Even as Heidegger becomes increasingly aware of precisely how much of the traditional philosophical techniques and presuppositions must be called into question in order to carry out his project, with respect to at least these fundamentals, the project itself remains unchanged throughout the 1920s and into the 1930s and beyond.

CONCLUSION

The Turn toward Self-Destructing Texts

Indeed, it might even be argued that the disappearance of the term "destruction" from Heidegger's work after 1928 is more than anything a consequence of a certain threefold shift in the type of traditionary text that Heidegger becomes primarily interested in reading. First, Heidegger's interest in language as the medium or site for the appearing of beings, already evident in his early readings of Aristotle's *zôon logon echon*, begins to move away from a focus on traditional scientific or philosophical discourse as promising to properly illuminate Being and moves toward a privileging of poetry for this task. This means that he is somewhat less focused on the conceptual and concept-generating philosophical works of the philosophical canon. And second, this growing interest in the power of the poetic word in the period after *Being and Time* runs parallel to another development, according to which Heidegger seems to locate the emergence of the metaphysical interpretation of beings, and the concomitant forgetting of the question of Being, earlier and earlier in the history of Greek philosophy. A threshold once located predominantly in the texts of Aristotle seems to move back through Plato and then is ultimately situated among the pre-Socratics.[4] And finally, third, there is the growing seriousness of Heidegger's fascination with Nietzsche as the last great and culminating thinker of the metaphysical tradition, a figure whose style and mode of philosophizing is, to say the least, unorthodox.

During this later period, then, Heidegger seems to be turning frequently to poets, on the one hand, and on the other hand to thinkers who are working *at or just beyond the margins of the metaphysical worldview*; all these are figures who come close to or perhaps even succeed to some extent in speaking and thinking in excess of the tradition's exclusive view of Being as the presence of present beings. In these respects, the Heidegger of the 1930s and beyond finds himself dealing more and more with what I would call *self-destructing* texts from the tradition.

In the fragmentary remains of Anaximander, Heraclitus, and Parmenides, in the odes, hymns, and elegies of Hölderlin,[5] but also in the poetic works of Sophocles,[6] Rilke, George, Trakl, and others, and in Nietzsche's aphorisms, stylized essays, and disjointed unpublished remains, the later Heidegger finds discourses of Being that claim for themselves less conceptual clarity, and which consequently require less of a technically destructive intervention in order to be interpreted in such a way as to trouble the uniformity and ubiquity of the traditional metaphysical understanding of the world. All of these figures already stand, as it were, at the very edge of the metaphysical world, looking outward with sometimes more and sometimes less receptivity. Aristotle too stood at the edge of the metaphysical world, but only the destructive interpretive method can unearth and activate the slight indications of a receding excess there. With the self-destructing texts of these poets and unconventional thinkers, Heidegger is able to inhabit the site of their poetizing and thinking, partly with them, partly against them, pushing his own thinking beyond the traditional interpretation of beings, without having to introduce the methodologically more rigorous hermeneutic of destruction.

The First Beginning and the Other Beginning

And yet, even if it is helpful to identify a certain shift toward self-destructing texts, and even if this shift entails a host of important associated alterations in the character and approach of Heidegger's thinking, I would still like to insist on a profound continuity between the early and the later periods with respect to the aims and dynamics of destruction. Briefly and by way of conclusion, I would like to indicate a certain persistence of the destructive project, comparing some of the elements we have highlighted about the project of the early lecture courses on Aristotle with the project of thinking presented in *Contributions to Philosophy (Of the Event)*, that extremely challenging text written between 1936 and 1938 which, though unpublished in Heidegger's lifetime, is often referred to as his second magnum opus and is viewed as the central work of his later period.[7] I will argue for a deep resonance between the earlier and later incarnations of the Heideggerian project, focused specifically on the theme of the *Anfang* or the "inception." For the dynamic of beginning or inception is surprisingly central and powerful in Heidegger's thinking in both these periods, from what all it entails, to what it requires, to what it offers.

Let us recall here a few specific themes or moments from our discussion so far of the earlier Heidegger's project of destruction, as well as a few of the most striking passages on which we focused. In the "Introduction," we heard that destruction is "a critical de-constructing [*ein kritischer Abbau*] of traditional concepts . . . down to the sources [*Quellen*] out of which they were created" (*BPP* 32/23). Furthermore, any such destruction was never intended to be a purely negative "shaking off [*Abschüttelung*] of the ontological tradition," but instead, "should mark it out in its positive possibilities, which is to say, within its *limits* [Grenzen]," and these limits "are given factically with the posing of the question [*Fragestellung*] each time and with the consequently prescribed delimitation of the field of investigation" (*BT* 44/22). To be clear, destruction is said to proceed here by focusing in on *the initial moments of Aristotle's philosophical response* to the self-presentation of beings, and it traces both the emergence of concepts from out of pre-conceptual experiences and the limits on the field of what is available to investigation and thinking; destruction attempts to find both what is positively articulable within those limits (present beings) and an indication or trace of what is beyond those limits, as yet unthinkable and unavailable, but glimmering in the initial question-worthiness of and wonder at the emergence of present beings in their presence.

In chapter 1, we saw Heidegger focused on the concepts created by Aristotle and insisting that "it is the *soil* [Boden] that must be seen, that out of which these fundamental concepts grow" (*BCArP* 4/4). And in thinking down to and then out of that ground or soil of Aristotle's concepts, Heideggerian destruction entailed that we "cooperate with [*mitmachen*] the *first decisive beginning of philosophy* [das erste entscheidende Anfangen]" among the Greeks in general and Aristotle in particular, and far from rejecting or dismissing it, we must "*repeat* it [wiederholen]" (*BCAncP* 8/11). We heard as well that this repetition of the first beginning of philosophizing was to take place with an emphatically *affective dimension*: "we offer *no philosophy*, much less a history of philosophy. If *philology* means the *passion* [Leidenschaft] *for knowledge of what has been expressed*, then what we are doing is philology" (*BCArP* 4/5).

In chapter 2, we found that in order to allow the historical past to give "*a jolt* [einen Stoß] *to the present or, better yet, to the future*" (*BCArP* 5/6), it is necessary to dig down beneath even the basic experiences of beings that are reported in the Aristotelian text, and gain a kind of access ultimately "to what is meant in the concepts" (*BCAncP* 1/1). That ground or floor of Aristotle's philosophical concepts is not, then, merely the beings he experiences, but ultimately Being, as "what does not lie there for natural experience, but is rather hidden, what never lies before and is nevertheless always understood" (*BCAncP* 6/7). This *krisis* or "separation, rift" turned out to be double, however. On the one hand, it is that between the Being of beings and beings, and on the other hand, it is that between the Being of beings, the presence of present beings, and that aspect of Being that is visible only in its initial calling-forth of questioning and thinking, its being "initially unknown, closed off, inaccessible [*zunächst unbekannt, verschlossen, unzugänglich*]" (*BCAncP* 8/6). This Being in its essential inaccessibility, which is neither experienced nor thought as such in the Aristotelian text, is nevertheless detectible by the destructive reader as a trace there. In order to properly think or come to know beings in their relation to this aspect of Being, Heidegger suggests that it would be necessary to eliminate the distinction between *sophia* and *philosophia*, between the possession of "wisdom" and the "desire for wisdom," so that one who would respond thoughtfully to the second *krisis* of Being, one who is *sophos* or "wise" with respect to Being, would be

> not simply in secure possession of that to which he is devoted, what he "loves"—φιλεῖν—but rather he searches and must constantly search [*sondern sucht und muß standig suchen*]. Σοφία, the opening up [*Erschließung*] of the Being of beings, is φιλοσοφία, a searching questioning after this, [a questioning] that as such places itself under the most radical critique. (*BCAncP* 8/11)

This would entail an extraordinarily taxing searching without the intention of finding and possessing, a questioning without the hope of definitively answering, a beginning without the hope of ending. Moreover, all of this is already there in the thinking that the early Heidegger hopes to provoke in the destructive repetition of Aristotle's first articulating of metaphysical concepts. Insofar as this thinking explicitly and emphatically embraces its own limits, I have suggested, it already points to a notion of Being as withholding itself *essentially*, as always out beyond or covered over beneath beings in their apparently exhaustive availability.

Another place we found this irremediable inaccessibility of Being acknowledged in the project of the early lecture courses is Heidegger's insistence that the thinking of Being provoked by destruction must involve "a free projection" or a "projecting of the antecedently given being upon its Being and the structures of its Being," a process which Heidegger calls "*phenomenological construction*" (*BPP* 21/29, translation modified). We even heard this destructive thinking of Being described as a form of "creative research [*die schöpferische Forschung*]," such that "this research does not understand itself in respect to what is most decisive" (*PS* 8/11).

Vital here is the fact that none of these aspects of the destructive thinking called for in the early lecture courses is to be overcome. None of these are merely provisional—not such thinking's searching, questioning, free projecting or creative character, or its self-alienation. Rather, all of these belong to the extra-metaphysical thinking of Being as such, according to the passages assembled here. This is surely why Heidegger can remark in the 1924–25 *Sophist* course, when confronting "what is not well-rounded, what is fragmentary, what remains underway [*unterwegs*]" in the Platonic text, that precisely this is "the genuinely positive element in all research" (*PS* 285/412–13). The key already for the early Heidegger, then, at least at certain moments, would seem to be to somehow incorporate this incompleteness and "underway" character into thinking itself, indeed into truth itself, in such a way that these aspects are no longer thought of as initial flaws or shortcomings to be eventually overcome, but rather as necessary features of a thinking that properly and truthfully responds to a certain insuperable inaccessibility in Being itself.

Once these features have been brought to the fore in the early Heidegger's destructive project, as I hope the foregoing discussions have accomplished, I would suggest that we hear a very strong resonance on these points with the project initiated in the *Contributions to Philosophy*. In this text, Heidegger undertakes to respond in an experimental and highly unorthodox manner to what has long been his basic problem: what makes beings be is not itself a being, and is not even available among beings. If we are to think beings from out of such a source, such a grounding ontological dynamism, an event of emergence by which beings come to be, and if our traditional modes of philosophical or scientific thinking are exclusively aimed at re-presenting, objectively and with more or less clarity and precision, present beings, then do we not need an entirely new, nontraditional mode of interrogating and thinking beings? How might we begin to think beings in their relation to any such essentially withdrawn and inaccessible source of being? Or better, how might we think beings in relation to a source, the proper reception of which might be precisely the marking of its withdrawal?

In *Contributions to Philosophy*, Heidegger sometimes refers to this essentially question-worthy source of beings as *Seyn* or "Beyng," using an arcane spelling to distinguish this from the metaphysical tradition's Being of present beings. At other times he refers to it as *Ereignis*, which means most commonly something like "event," but which with its root *eigen-* or "own" also seems to evoke associations of "ownness, propriety, and appropriation."[8] The subtitle of the *Contributions* announces the attempt to think *Vom Ereignis* or "of/from out of the event," that is, to think not from beings exclusively, but out of the dynamic, always historically and linguistically situated unfolding or emerging into view of beings.

To bring into relation this project and the destructive project of the 1920s, we note the fact that the mode of thinking Heidegger presents in the *Contributions* as responsive to the essentially withdrawn or self-eclipsing character of this event-like Being is what he calls *anfängliches Denken* or "inceptual thinking." And of this, he writes:

> Inceptual thinking is the inventive thinking [*Er-denken*] of the truth of Beyng and thus is the inventive grounding of the ground [*Er-gründung des Grundes*] ... Yet how is the inventive thinking of Beyng a resting on the ground [*Aufruhen*]? By opening up what is most question-worthy, it carries out the honoring and thereby the highest transfiguration of that in which the questioning rests, i.e., *does not stop* [*Verklärung von jenem, worin das Fragen aufruht, d.h. nicht* aufhört]. (*CP* 46/56–57, translation modified)

Note here the clear points of resonance with the philosophizing wisdom, the *philo-sophia* that Heidegger explicitly equates with *sophia* in the passage cited earlier (*BCAncP* 8/11). The mode of thinking that Heidegger is calling for in both periods is precisely one that enters into a proper relation to the ground through a quasi-creative power. This is captured in the German by the distinction between *er-denken*, rendered well by the translators as "inventive thinking," as opposed to simply *denken* or "thinking." (One cannot help but think here of the distinction between *finden*, "to find," and *erfinden*, "to discover, invent.") There is an overt sense of creativity here,[9] which is not to say that this response to Beyng as the event-like emergence of beings is involved in fabricating a fiction, in generating an arbitrary and subjective response. Rather, it means simply that inceptual thinking takes on the provocation of this event as something in excess of present beings, acknowledging thereby the need for something more than their re-presentation. Such thinking would then engage in, as we heard above, a "free projection" or a "creative [*schöpferisch*]" mode of response, thereby marking the partial inaccessibility of what is to be thought.

Furthermore, as inceptual thinking, a thinking that is at home in the first incipient urgings of beings as they call forth our questioning and wondering, this thinking does not come to rest on the ground of that initial appearing by pushing through the appearances and laying the ground definitively bare, overcoming its initial question-worthiness. Rather, this inceptual thinking opens up the question-worthy *as such*, marking its essential withdrawal and inaccessibility, honoring it and bringing about a *Verklärung*, a "transfiguration" as it would be translated traditionally, but literally a kind of "transforming clarification" of that in which the questioning activity abides or finds its proper home. As a result, it does not finally think Beyng as event by arriving at a final and complete insight or articulation, but instead by never presuming to move beyond its searching, questioning activity. Again, we hear an echo of the unceasingly and emphatically questioning character of the thinking that the destruction of the 1920s aims to call forth and energize.

And just as contemporary original thinking required for the early Heidegger a return to and a repetition of the Greek invention of metaphysical concepts, here in the *Contributions* Heidegger speaks of the need for an "other beginning" today that grounds itself in the "first beginning" with the Greeks. He writes:

> "Thinking," in the ordinary determination that has been usual for a long time, is the representing of something in its ἰδέα ["look"] as the κοινόν ["common"], the representing of something in its generality . . . This thinking is related to the objectively present, to what has already come

to presence (a determinate interpretation of beings). Yet this thinking is therefore always *subsequent* . . . This thinking was once—in the first beginning, in Plato and Aristotle—still creative. Yet it was precisely this thinking that created the domain in which the representing of being as such later came to prevail and in which the abandonment by Being then unfolded in ever-greater concealment. Inceptual thinking is the original carrying out of resonating, interplay, leap, and grounding in their unity. (*CP* 51/63–64, translation modified)[10]

Heidegger insists here too on the complex mode in which the Greek past must be appropriated, repeated, cooperated with, even as it is subjected to the revelation of an excess and critiqued for what it left unthought. The creative generation of concepts in Plato and Aristotle, by which they articulated their response to the apparent question-worthiness of Being, must be allowed to resonate today, not as the concepts our tradition delivers over in weary self-evidence, but through an "interplay" with the creative moment, and the emergence there of those ontological concepts that provoke from us a leap into something new, an original extra-metaphysical way of thinking, even as we recognize the unification of the first and the other beginning in that original and originating source we find indicated in the creative response of Plato and Aristotle.

Finally, at one point in the *Contributions*, in an underappreciated passage, Heidegger even makes explicit the connection between the project of destruction in the 1920s and the way in which here the first beginning of the Greeks must be taken up. He writes in §90, which is titled "From the first to the other beginning: Negation":

How few understand "negation," and how seldom is it firmly grasped by those who do have some understanding of it! Negation is spontaneously taken to be sheer rejection, dismissal, disparagement, and even disintegration [*die Abweisung, die Wegesetzung, die Herabsetzung, und gar die Zersetzung*] . . . To be sure, such negation is not satisfied with leaping-away-from in the sense of merely leaving behind [the first beginning]. Rather, it unfolds itself by laying open the first beginning and its inceptual history [*den ersten Anfang und seine anfängliche Geschichte freilegt*] and by placing back into the possession of the beginning what has been laid open, which as deposited there, both now and in the future stands out above everything that ever arose in its wake and became an object of historiological reckoning. This erecting of what stands out of the first beginning [*Dieses Er-Bauen des Ragenden des ersten Anfang*] is the meaning of the "destruction [*Destruktion*]" occurring in the transition to the other beginning. (*CP* 140/178–79)

This is by no means to say that the entire intensity and novelty of the experiment undertaken in the *Contributions* is already present in the destructive project of the 1920s. Rather, I would suggest here in closing only that we find Heidegger in those early texts groping toward and occasionally brushing up against what he will come in the *Contributions* to more fully articulate as "inceptual thinking" and as the resonating echo and play between the first and the other beginning.

Indeed, we might invoke here a later remark of Heidegger's, from 1959's "Dialogue on Language," where he finds occasion to recall the project of a course he had given way back in 1920. Thinking back, Heidegger writes that this course remained nothing more than an "intimation [*Andeutung*]" of what it was trying to think, and that in the course he only ever "followed an unclear trace of a path [*Wegspur*]." He sums up by saying that there, in the early 1920s, the "trace [*Spur*]" he was following was nothing more than "an almost imperceptible promise announcing a release into the open [*eine Befreiung ins Freie*]" (OWL 6/137). So too, perhaps, I have tried to suggest here, in certain fascinating passages in his early destructive readings of Aristotle, we find a Heidegger following the trace of something still very much unclear, indeed just vaguely intimated, something that, though he will not "clarify" it, he will later bring more fully to thought and language as he comes to recognize the peculiar demands, and indeed the utter strangeness, of thinking beings in relation to that dynamic event of emergence that is their essentially and irremediably self-eclipsing source.

If there is, as I have suggested here in the conclusion and throughout, a substantial continuity between the early Heidegger's destructive project and the later Heidegger's "history of Beyng," what should we make of this fact? That is, if I am right that there are some moments where Heidegger early on, in his destructive interpretations of Aristotle, suggests the need to think Being as essentially and constitutively involving some withdrawal or concealment, and if the later discussions of the history of Being's unfolding and the call for a renewed thinking of Being share some fundamental dynamics and elements with his earlier destructive approach, what does that mean for us as we consider the significance of this Heideggerian mode of interpreting our inherited tradition today? Is there more to be taken from these concluding suggestions than the observation that Heidegger's philosophizing exhibits greater consistency over the course of his entire career than might initially seem to be the case?

Indeed, I believe there is. For we might make the more fundamental observation here that while it is possible to utilize Heidegger's method of destruction in taking on one's own tradition today and to do so in the more regimented mode we found at work in those early lecture courses

CONCLUSION

and papers, it is also possible to expand or contract the method, shift its features or change the materials on which it is trained, or even to dramatically alter the style and the linguistic elements with which the method is expressed and push it in new directions, all the while maintaining an adherence to the principle of the method, as I have suggested Heidegger himself did after the "turn." So long as one remains committed to a serious and deep critical reading of one's tradition, a reading that inhabits the text, trains its gaze on the text's creative impulses and philosophical drives and questioning, and then problematizes that text in such a way as to reveal the traces of unincorporated and yet still vital sources of thinking there, so long as that adamantly ambivalent relation to past figures and texts is successfully maintained, one can be said to be "destroying" one's tradition in the manner this book has attempted to elucidate and, indeed, to celebrate. And insofar as this is the case, and one meets head-on the challenge of this taxing ambivalence between co-philosophizing with one's tradition and critiquing it, between repeating and dismantling it, one will necessarily avoid the ahistoricality, superficiality, and self-satisfaction that pose real and constant dangers to the attempt to respond philosophically to the urgent personal, social, and political issues that demand our attention today.

Acknowledgments

This study was made possible by the support of DePaul's University Research Council (URC), in the form of one Paid Research Leave and two Faculty Summer Research Grants. It benefited as well from access to the collections at the following institutions, toiling away on my manuscript as I tagged along with my wife, Lisa Mahoney, on her art-historical research trips: the W. F. Albright Institute in Jerusalem, the École Biblique et Archéologique Française de Jérusalem, and the Cyprus American Archeological Research Institute in Nicosia. I would like to express my sincere gratitude to the administrators and staff at those research centers for their exemplary hospitality.

As I discussed in a bit more detail in the preface, this project stretches back to my years writing a dissertation under Professor Klaus Held at the University of Wuppertal. While I had already been exposed to Heidegger and to phenomenology more generally in the seminars of Francois Raffoul and Edward Casey at Stony Brook, for me it was with Professor Held and the rest of the faculty at Wuppertal that I began to understand the complexity and richness of Heidegger's readings of the texts of Western philosophy, and of Aristotle in particular. Along with Professor Held, it was Heinrich Hüni (†), Peter Trawny, and Georg Siegmann who modeled for me how one might think one's way into the past along with Heidegger . . . and from Professor Baum, no Heideggerian, I saw that a truly encyclopedic knowledge of the arguments of the Western canon was possible.

I consider myself very fortunate to have the colleagues I do here at DePaul, in the Department of Philosophy and in other departments across the university. I regularly benefit from too many of them to list here. Specific to this project, I must express my gratitude to Will McNeill, a true *Kenner* when it comes to Heidegger, as he read a complete early draft and commented on it with his characteristic care and thoughtfulness. I would mention specifically as well Peg Birmingham, Pascale-Anne Brault, Matthew Girson, Avery Goldman, Liam Heneghan, David Farrell Krell, Rick Lee, Danielle Meijer, Elizabeth Millán Brusslan, Michael Naas, Elizabeth Rottenberg, Fanny Söderbäck, Peter Steeves, and Kevin Thompson, all of whom have discussed various aspects of this material with me in recent years.

Beyond DePaul, I am especially grateful to the members of the North Texas Heidegger Symposium and the Heidegger Circle for the questions, comments, and conversations that took place at their annual meetings after my presentations of some of these pages. Friends and colleagues too numerous to mention at other institutions have been generous enough to share their, often much superior, expertise in Heidegger, so I acknowledge them here en masse. Malek Moazzam-Doulat read parts of this manuscript and it was improved considerably as a result. I have gone to Andrew J. Mitchell, Peter Trawny, and Marcia Cavalcante in various contexts over the years for expert opinions on thorny issues in the interpretation of this thinker. And this project would simply not have been possible had it not been for the groundbreaking scholarly work of Ted Kisiel (†), who I had the opportunity to meet and spend time with before his recent passing.

At Northwestern University Press, I would like to thank Trevor Perri, who initially accepted and supported in the project, Faith Wilson Stein, who brought it to its conclusion and improved the manuscript substantially with her judicious editorial interventions, and the excellent copy editor, Paul Mendelson, who saved me from many stylistic infelicities, grammatical blunders, and bibliographical confusions. Also, a special thanks to "anonymous reader 1," whose admirable care and precision in commenting on the first draft led to many genuine improvements in the final version.

Finally, my wife Lisa read much of this manuscript, improving the clarity of the writing and argument (as much as the quality of the source material allowed). For this, as for most good things in my life, I am very much in her debt.

The errors and oversights that persist in these pages, despite the contributions of all these fine people, are obviously down to me.

Notes

Preface

1. That thesis, which certainly reflected my deep exposure to the phenomenological tradition at Wuppertal, was defended in 2004 and eventually came out in a thoroughly revised form as Sean D. Kirkland, *The Ontology of Socratic Questioning in Plato's Early Dialogues* (Albany, NY: State University of New York Press, 2012).

2. During the years I was at Wuppertal, there were among the faculty of the Philosophical Seminar no fewer than *four* editors of volumes in Heidegger's *Gesamtausgabe*: my *Doktorvater* Klaus Held, as well as Heinrich Hüni, Claudius Strube, and Peter Trawny. Since my time there, it has become home to the Martin Heidegger Institute, under the energetic direction of Trawny.

3. "Traditionary text" is a term introduced by the translators of Hans-Georg Gadamer's *Wahrheit und Methode* into English. Joel Weinsheimer and Donald Marshall use the term to render the German "*Überlieferung*," literally "that which is being delivered over" to us, usually translated as "tradition, custom." The term is intended to capture the way in which some historical texts seem to bear one's tradition and to be responsible, through their influence, for passing along the content of that tradition down to one's present historical context. Some texts from the history of thought or literature seem actively still at work in passing down to us the concepts and values we inherit today as our own—their interpretation, appropriation, or critique arises for us, then, not as a possible preoccupation, but as a pressing task. They are, in this sense, traditionary, not merely traditional. For a discussion of the term, see the "Translators' Preface" in Hans-Georg Gadamer, *Truth and Method*, trans. J. Weisheimer and D. G. Marshall (London: Continuum, 1975/1989), xvi.

4. Perhaps we can persist a while in the "abeyance" Jacques Derrida describes in the last of a series of short essays or meditations that he contributed to a collection of photographs by Jean-François Bonhomme—Jacques Derrida, *Athens, Still Remains*, trans. Pascale-Anne Brault and Michael Naas (New York: Fordham University Press, 2010). Derrida's contributions open, on the very first page, with the line "Nous nous devons à la mort," translated into English as "We owe ourselves to death" (Derrida, *Athens*, 1). And on the final page, Derrida is still asking, "We? What 'we'? And, first of all, who is included in this we? Like a negative still in the camera, an impressed question remains in abeyance, still pending. Will it ever be developed? Who will have signed the *nous*, whether the first or the

second, of this *nous nous devons à la mort*? Me, you, she, he, all of you? And who will have inherited it in the end?" (Derrida, *Athens*, 69).

5. Paul Ricoeur, *Freud and Philosophy: An Essay on Interpretation*, trans. D. Savage (New Haven, CT: Yale University Press, 1965/1970), 32.

6. This puts me in the unenviable position of having to disagree, respectfully, with the position stated in Audre Lorde's influential essay, which is indeed right there in its title: "The Master's Tools Will Never Dismantle the Master's House," in Audre Lorde, *Sister Outsider* (Berkeley, CA: Crossing, 1984/2007). I suppose I share Søren Kierkegaard's hope that, "In the hands of philosophy, history might rejuvenate itself into a divine youthfulness." This line appears in a section entitled "Selected Entries from the Journals and Papers," in Søren Kierkegaard, *The Concept of Irony*, ed. and trans. E. and H. Hong (Princeton, NJ: Princeton University Press, 1841/1989), 443.

7. There has been in recent years a veritable explosion of interest in this question. Two works that I have found particularly thoughtful and illuminating on this subject are Peter Trawny's *Freedom to Fail: Heidegger's Anarchy*, trans. I. A. Moore and C. Turner (Cambridge: Polity, 2014/2015) and his *Heidegger and the Myth of a Jewish World Conspiracy*, trans. A. J. Mitchell (Chicago: University of Chicago Press, 2014/2016). The former is a deep meditation on the perhaps essential relationship between philosophizing and a fundamental form of errancy; and the latter is a revelation of the fact that, in Heidegger's tracing of the narrative of the ancient forgetting and possible future recovery of the question of Being, the protagonists in the story, the Greeks and the Germans, appear in the *Black Notebooks* as fundamentally and perhaps constitutively opposed to an antagonist, namely "world Judaism." Also see Jean-Luc Nancy, *The Banality of Heidegger*, trans. J. Fort (New York: Fordham University Press, 2015/2017); and Barbara Cassin and Alain Badiou, *Heidegger: The Withdrawal of Being*, trans. S. Spitzer (New York: Columbia University Press, 2010/2016).

8. For a subtle and insightful account of this historical development, and specifically of the relation between Enlightenment thinking and the turn to history as an epistemological and ontological principle, see Peter H. Reill, *The German Enlightenment and the Rise of Historicism* (Berkeley: University of California Press, 2018). And for the direct influence of this line of development on Heidegger, see Robert Scharff, *How History Matters to Philosophy: Reconsidering Philosophy's Part after Positivism* (New York: Routledge, 2015).

9. It is my hope that destruction could be added to the list of powerful philosophical tools that thinkers engaged in various critical projects are already explicitly deriving from the phenomenological tradition that includes Heidegger. To give just a sense of the impressive spectrum of such appropriations, they range from feminist theorists such as Simone de Beauvoir and Luce Irigaray to Afropessimists like Frank B. Wilderson and Calvin Warren, from de-colonial thinkers such as Frantz Fanon to queer theorists like Sara Ahmed, and to theorists of disability like S. Kay Toombs and Joel Michael Reynolds. See Simone de Beauvoir, *The Second Sex*, ed. and trans. H. M. Parshley (New York: Vintage, 1949/1989); Luce Irigaray, *The Forgetting of Air in Martin Heidegger*, trans. M. B. Mader (Austin: University of Texas Press, 1983/1989); Frank B. Wilderson III, *Afropessimism*. (New York: Norton, 2020); Calvin Warren, *Ontological Terror: Blackness, Nihilism, Eman-*

cipation (Durham, NC: Duke University Press, 2018); Frantz Fanon, *Black Skin, White Masks*, trans. R. Philcox (New York: Grove, 1952/2008); Sara Ahmed, *Queer Phenomenology: Orientations, Objects, Others* (Durham, NC: Duke University Press, 2006); S. Kay Toombs, "The Lived Experience of Disability," *Human Studies* 18, no. 1 (Jan. 1995): 9-23; and Joel Michael Reynolds, "Heidegger, Embodiment, Disability," *Epoché* 26, no. 1 (2021): 183–201.

10. I thank one of the anonymous readers at Northwestern University Press for bringing to my attention the way in which Heidegger's destructive interpretive approach "participates in the modernist *esprit* of the time." Avant-garde artistic movements such as cubism, futurism, and Dada all saw the need for something like a destructive treatment of the traditions they were inheriting and reacting against. It would be interesting to undertake a broad study of the period on precisely this point, in order to see whether anything like the fascinatingly rich and complex play of rejection and recuperation, which I find in Heideggerian destruction, is present in any of these movements as well.

11. Indeed, we confront immediately the true strangeness and radicality of Heidegger's project when we understand that in response to the question, "What is it that the Greeks failed to think?" one answer Heidegger gives is, "Nothing." That is, in the forgetting of Being that occurred with the Greek inauguration of metaphysical thinking, what was missed was not a thing at all, not a being or region of beings that was simply left out, unattended to in Greek thought. Rather, if what was left unthought there, in a culminating way with Aristotle, is no thing, then the thinking that can incorporate *this* into its approach to beings is a peculiar one indeed. Heidegger famously thematizes just this link between Being and "the Nothing," of course, in his 1929 essay "What Is Metaphysics?" to which we will return briefly in chapters 2 and 3.

12. Joan Stambaugh, translator's preface to Martin Heidegger, *Being and Time: A Revised Edition of the Stambaugh Translation*, trans. J. Stambaugh and D. Schmidt (Albany, NY: State University of New York Press, 1996/2010), xxiv.

Introduction

1. Indeed, after a period in which he understood himself primarily as a student of Christian theology, busying himself with medieval mysticism, Augustine, Luther, Kierkegaard, and Schleiermacher, among others, Heidegger turned to philosophy as such and over the course of the 1920s engaged deeply with Plato, Leibniz, Kant, Hegel, Dilthey, and others. Nevertheless, I would argue that, of the historical figures with whom Heidegger was engaged during this period, Aristotle plays the most pivotal role in the radicalization of the phenomenology he inherited from Husserl, by which Heidegger arrives at his own original philosophical contribution. On the significance specifically of Aristotle for the early development of Heidegger's philosophical approach, see Thomas Sheehan, "Heidegger's Early Years," in *Heidegger: The Man and the Thinker*, ed. T. Sheehan (Chicago: Precedent, 1981), 3–19; Theodore Kisiel, "What Did Heidegger Find in Aristotle?" chapter 5 of *The Genesis of "Being and Time"* (Berkeley: University of

California Press, 1993), 227–75; and Franco Volpi, "*Being and Time*: A 'Translation' of the *Nicomachean Ethics*?" in *Reading Heidegger from the Start: Essays in His Earliest Thought*, ed. T. Kisiel and J. Van Buren (Albany, NY: State University of New York Press, 1994), 195–213. Finally, Francisco Gonzalez makes a forceful argument for the importance of Heidegger's early engagement with Aristotle in "Whose Metaphysics of Presence? Heidegger's Interpretation of *Energeia* and *Dunamis* in Aristotle," *Southern Journal of Philosophy* 44 (2006): 533–68. Gonzalez counts twelve seminars dealing exclusively or largely with Aristotle during the 1920s, and then meticulously reconstructs the first of these from the less-than-ideal accounts contained in student notes taken during the seminar. On this basis, he shows that, among a host of other foreshadowing moments, one sees a precursor to the phenomenological study of everyday experience in *Being and Time* in Heidegger's explicit refusal to abide by scholarly convention, and his insistence instead on moving seamlessly between passages articulating the psychology of *De anima* and those articulating Aristotle's ontology from the *Physics* and *Metaphysics*. Gonzalez observes: "We of course see here already the project of *Being and Time*: to arrive at an understanding of being as such through an analysis of a particular but in some way privileged way of being, that is, Dasein" (Gonzalez, "The Birth of *Being and Time*: Heidegger's Pivotal 1921 Reading of Aristotle's *On the Soul*," *Southern Journal of Philosophy* 56, no. 2 [2018]: 219). Contrarily, John Van Buren does make a compelling case for there being three *equally* vital touchstones for Heidegger in initiating his philosophical trajectory: Christian thinkers and the lived experience of Christianity, phenomenology, and Aristotle. John Van Buren, "Heidegger's Early Freiburg Courses, 1915–1923," *Research in Phenomenology* 23, no. 1 (1993): 145–46.

2. In the short autobiographical essay entitled "My Way into Phenomenology," a seventy-four-year-old Heidegger offers another, later retrospective view of the same period. The first two philosophical works that he mentions there as seminal influences are Edmund Husserl's *Logical Investigations*, an inaugurating work for twentieth-century phenomenology, and Franz Brentano's dissertation on Aristotle's *Metaphysics* ("MWP" 74). Heidegger writes of Brentano's dissertation, *On the Several Senses of Being in Aristotle*, which is in fact a straightforward presentation of Aristotelian metaphysics, that it "had been the chief help and guide of my first awkward attempts to penetrate into philosophy" ("MWP" 74). See Edmund Husserl, *Logical Investigations I & II*, trans. J. N. Findlay (London: Routledge, 1900–1901/1970); and Franz Brentano, *On the Several Senses of Being in Aristotle*, trans. R. George (Berkeley: University of California Press, 1862/1977).

3. Walter Brogan, *Heidegger and Aristotle: The Twofoldness of Being* (Albany, NY: State University of New York Press, 2005), 1. Also, "Aristotle has influenced [Heidegger] more than any other thinker" (William Richardson, *Heidegger: Through Phenomenology to Thought* [The Hague: Nijhoff, 1963], 309); "Aristotle appears directly or indirectly on virtually every page of *Being and Time*" (Thomas Sheehan, "Heidegger, Aristotle, and Phenomenology," *Philosophy Today* 19 [Summer 1974]: 87); and "Mit der Wendung zu Aristoteles gewinnt Heidegger die eigentümliche Stellung seines Philosophierens" (Günter Figal, "Heidegger als Aristoteliker," in *Heidegger und Aristoteles: Heidegger Jahrbuch 3*, ed. A. Denker et al. [Freiburg: Karl Alber, 2007], 54).

4. When I use the term "radical" (or "radically") here and throughout, I intend it to describe not merely something "extreme" or "far-reaching," but rather something that produces an innovation specifically by returning to the *radix* or "root" of a previous movement, position, or theory.

5. The phrase used here, to "take on" Aristotle, is actually borrowed from my colleague and friend Michael Naas, who used it in its ambivalence to great effect in his study *Taking on the Tradition: Jacques Derrida and the Legacies of Deconstruction* (Stanford, CA: Stanford University Press, 2002). Naas elaborates on the two senses of the phrase: both to take something on by taking it up, taking possession of it, or incorporating it, and to take something on by contesting or battling against it. This is precisely the ambivalence that we shall find in the Heideggerian posture toward Aristotle, and indeed toward the tradition as a whole.

6. Indeed, one eminent Heidegger specialist even asks, "After all, wasn't the gesture with which Privatdozent Heidegger came onto the scene generally destructive?" Otto Pöggeler, "Destruction and Moment," in Kisiel and Van Buren, *Reading Heidegger*, 137.

7. Sometimes Heidegger also employs the terms *Abbau* or "de-construction," *Abtragen* or "carrying away," and *Auf-die-Seite-stellen* or literally a "setting-to-the-side." Indeed, Heidegger's terminology for this undertaking shifts from one context to another, and occasionally a number of terms are assembled even in a single passage to clarify or emphasize certain aspects of the method. Some of the earliest substantive uses of the term *"Destruktion,"* as referring to an approach to interpretation that disrupts original and obscuring metaphysical structures, are to be found in *Phenomenology of Intuition and Expression* and in *Phenomenology of Religious Life*. The former was a lecture course held in Freiburg in 1920, and the latter is a volume comprised of two lecture courses Heidegger held in Freiburg between 1920 and 1921, as well a course he intended for 1918–19, but never delivered. In the first volume, *"Destruktion"* is clarified as not a *Zertrümmern* or "demolition" (*PIE* 143/183), but rather an *Abbau* or "un-building, de-construction," and in the second volume it is linked to its near synonym in ordinary German, *"Zerstörung"* (*PRL* 236/311). In a later retrospective reference to the project of destructive reading, in 1955's lecture "What Is Philosophy?" which looks back specifically at §6 of *Being and Time*, we find the above-mentioned terms (*Abbau, Abtragen, Auf-die-Seite-stellen,* and *Destruktion*) all brought together in a single discussion ("WP" 70–73). We will return to this passage at the close of chapter 2.

8. No doubt we can see the 1927 lecture course, *Basic Problems of Phenomenology*, as tracing something very much like the basic trajectory of the destructive project planned for part 2 of *Being and Time*. It describes an essential component of its phenomenological method explicitly as "destruction," and it moves from Kant back to Aristotle by way of a consideration of the Cartesian *res cogitans*. We can also think of *Kant and the Problem of Metaphysics*, published just two years after *Being and Time*, as accomplishing something like the planned first step in part 2's systematic destruction of the Western tradition. Albert Hofstadter remarks, in the "Translator's Introduction" to *Basic Problems of Phenomenology*: "If we put together *Being and Time* as published, *Kant and the Problem of Metaphysics*, and our present volume . . . we have in three volumes the entire treatise which Heidegger had originally wished to call 'Being and Time'—even if not quite in the form

then imagined" (*BPP* xvii.). A somewhat more thorough destruction of Descartes had already been carried out in the middle section of the 1923 lecture course, *Introduction to Phenomenological Research*, the alternative title of which was *The Beginning of Modern Philosophy*.

9. Indeed, rather than approach the existing text of *Being and Time* as, centrally, a call for destruction, both its champions and its detractors tend to move through the text as a more or less freestanding phenomenological analysis of lived human life.

10. Robert Bernasconi makes a similar observation, noting that although the first half of the projected whole of *Being and Time* was "understood as only provisional, awaiting the destructuring [Bernasconi's translation for '*Destruktion*'] that was set to take place in the book's second part," nonetheless the book "has usually been read without reference to this rubric," and "the way in which the work was supposed to contribute to a destructuring of the history of ontology has been left virtually unclarified or, worse still, the notion of destructuring has been given a wholly negative sense, contrary to Heidegger's own explicit warnings to the contrary" (Bernasconi, "Repetition and Tradition: Heidegger's Destructuring of the Distinction between Essence and Existence in *Basic Problems of Phenomenology*," in *Reading Heidegger from the Start*, ed. T. Kisiel and J. Van Buren, 123).

11. The Stambaugh and Schmidt translation of *Being and Time* refers to it as an "[Exergue]" (with square brackets) when listing it among the preliminary contents (along with the translator's preface and the author's preface for the seventh edition), but there is no mention of it at all among the contents listed in the German original or in the Macquarrie and Robinson translation. (Note: I recognize the many advances and virtues of the Stambaugh and Schmidt translation, and I have myself benefited from it, even if I tend to return when quoting to the older translation out of habit and a comfort with its terminology.)

12. To be clear, the metaphysical tradition does acknowledge the "ontological difference" after a fashion, but it sees Being as nothing but a feature or a predicate attached to beings. That is, Being is, for metaphysics, entirely distributed over the class "beings," with no remainder. Heidegger is ultimately trying to provoke a questioning that wonders if Being is perhaps in excess of the totality of beings, and is then suggesting that only a radically transformed mode of thinking would be able to properly take up that excess as such.

13. In the course of his analysis of everyday experience in *Being and Time*, Heidegger shows that whereas the tradition tends to think of beings existing fundamentally in the mode of *Vorhandenheit* or "presence-at-hand," there is a more original and primary way in which things present themselves, *Zuhandenheit* or "readiness-to-hand," a kind of useability or serviceability with respect to our aims or projects, and the former is actually secondary to and derivative of the latter (*BT* 95–107/66–76). With this, Heidegger wishes to destabilize the privileged status and presumed fundamentality of the former, which he sees as having been established already with the Greeks. However, even if it is explanatorily prior to presence-at-hand, the readiness-to-hand of instruments or tools uncovered in the analytic of everyday life in *Being and Time* is not yet the experience of an extra-metaphysical way of being, as some readers seem to presume, and indeed

the revelation of the explanatory priority of readiness-to-hand is not the organizing aim of Heidegger's project in *Being and Time*. After all, the tools that *are* in the mode of readiness-to-hand refer to an entire equipmental totality in which they exist, and this does not entail anything like a moment of the fundamental and necessary withdrawal of Being, which is what must be recognized in order think or experience beings extra-metaphysically for Heidegger. Furthermore, see Sacha Golob, chapter 4, "'Being,' Realism, and Truth," in *Heidegger on Concepts, Freedom and Normativity* (Cambridge: Cambridge University Press, 2014), 156–79, where Golob argues against those who see a sort of idealism in Heidegger's prioritizing of readiness-to-hand over presence-at-hand, in that the former would seem to be explicitly the way the world shows itself to a subject relative to that subject's pursuing certain aims. For a representative reading of Heidegger as an idealist, see William Blattner, *Heidegger's Temporal Idealism* (Cambridge: Cambridge University Press, 1999). And John Searle, for another, attacks Heidegger on precisely this point in "The Phenomenological Illusion," in *Experience and Analysis*, ed. M. Reicher and J. Marek (Kirchberg am Wechsel: Austrian Ludwig Wittgenstein Society, 2004), 17–36. Searle's criticism is that it is simply very obvious that "the observer independent is ontologically prior" and "the observer dependent is derivative," and so we can claim without further ado that, in prioritizing readiness-to-hand over presence-at-hand in *Being and Time*, "*Heidegger has the ontology exactly backwards*" (Searle, "Phenomenological Illusion," 25, Searle's emphasis). Golob admits that Heidegger's attempt to offer a "non-naturalistic, non-reductive account of the nature of Dasein's intentionality" (Golob, *Heidegger on Concepts*, 161), that is, an account exclusively interested in the world of beings showing itself in experience (or to "intentionality" in Golob's terms), means that Heidegger has "little to say about Dasein's determination by the natural world (162). But Golob, to my mind, rightly rejects the implication that because he resists appealing to causal explanations based in some presumed observer-independent natural world, Heidegger must be some kind of idealist, even if there are some passages where Heidegger seems to suggest as much—"Of course, only as long as Dasein is . . . 'is there' Being" (*BT* 255/212). Heidegger's own retrospective assessment of the project of *Being and Time* in 1946's "Letter on Humanism" gives us, to my mind, the best response to these concerns about idealism and realism. Indeed, citing this very passage, Heidegger tells us: "This means that only so long as the clearing of Being eventuates itself [*sich ereignet*] does Being convey itself to human beings" ("LH" 256/167, translation modified). This is not the place to enter into an extended discussion of *Lichtung* or "clearing" and *Ereignis* or "event, event of appropriation," terms that will later be associated with what is approached in 1927 simply as Being. But we might simply say that, in Heidegger's retrospective assessment, the Being that *Being and Time* is calling us to wonder at and to begin to think is not the "observer-independent" natural world, nor is it "observer-dependent," in the sense that its features are determined by the structures or limitations of our subjectivity, our consciousness. Rather, Being is that encompassing opening within which we find ourselves, where beings emerge into appearance and present themselves to us, such that Being is the condition for their being beings at all *and* for their being recognized and understood by us as beings. Though this is not the focus of our discussion here, the presentation of Heidegger's departure from Husserl below will have a bit more to say about Heidegger's status as neither an idealist nor a realist in any traditional sense.

14. The German ear would ordinarily have heard the term "*Dasein*" as something like "reality" or "existence."

15. Although it requires a departure from the central task of this introduction, we should probably take a moment, in what will effectively be a sort of appendix, to discuss the sources on the basis of which the young Heidegger theorizes the *Geschichtlichkeit* or "historicality" of Dasein. Let us turn to his 1924 lecture to the Cologne Kant Society, where Heidegger remarks that "it is entirely up to us whether we get a clearer sense of the historical foundations [*Gründen*] of how we see, think, and interpret, or whether we instead treat history as a mere collection of antiquities. We must understand that history does not lie behind us like some object, but rather that *we ourselves are history*, and consequently that we bear the responsibility for how we deal with it" ("BTBT" 219, translation modified). It is necessary to address the claim here that we *are* history with the utmost seriousness. The past, in this light, is not a formerly present state of affairs that has now passed away and been replaced by the present state of affairs. Rather, given the fundamentally ecstatic "temporality" and "historicality" of human being discussed above, the past is first and foremost a feature of our present way of being. *Historie* or "historiology," the science of history, imagines that its scientific methods allow it privileged access to an objective reality that once was, to the way things actually were at this or that moment in past time. However, for Heidegger, what is thereby accessed is secondary to the primary *Geschichte* or "history" that unfolds in our way of being in the world as stretching out beyond our present into our past and future, having emerged out of the former and finding ourselves drawn out into the latter. Heidegger will write in *Being and Time*: "Insofar as Dasein's Being is historical—that is to say, insofar as by reason of its ecstatico-horizonal temporality, it is open in its character of 'having-been'—the way is in general prepared for such thematizing of the 'past' as can be accomplished in existence. And because Dasein, *and only Dasein*, is primordially historical, that which historiological thematizing presents as a possible object for research, must have the kind of Being of *Dasein which has-been-there*" (*BT* 445/383). Only because we *are* in such a way as to stretch ourselves back into the past from which we emerge can we then first thematize the dynamic of inheriting our tradition "in existence," that is, in living our lives. And only because that is possible for us can we then, secondarily, objectify the past as a no-longer-present reality and study it quasi-scientifically, meticulously cataloging its features and elements. Heidegger makes it quite clear in *Being and Time* that his understanding of the historicality of human being had been influenced by Count Yorck von Wartenburg's correspondence with Wilhelm Dilthey, which was first published in 1923. To be sure, some of *Being and Time*'s most illuminating passages on human life's essential and constitutive relation to its past come in §77, which amounts to a running citation from Count Yorck with commentary. One of the letters from Yorck provides Heidegger with the impetus for the striking formulation above, "We are history [*Wir sind Geschichte*]." Yorck writes to Dilthey: "The entire given psycho-physical reality is not something that

is, but something that lives: that is the germ cell of historicity. And self-reflection, which is directed not at an abstract I, but the entirety of my own self, will find that I am historically determined, just as physics grasps me as determined by the cosmos. Just as I am nature, I am history. And in this decisive sense we have to understand Goethe's dictum of [our] having lived [*Gelebthaben*] for at least three thousand years. Conversely, it follows that history as a scientific discipline exists only as psychology of history." See Erich Rothacker, ed., *Briefwechsel zwischen Wilhelm Dilthey und dem Grafen Yorck v. Wartenburg* (Halle: Max Niemeyer, 1923), 71. Living is here placed in opposition to mere being, which seems to be for Yorck a kind of ahistorical ontological condition. Human life, by contrast, would involve for Yorck an essential emerging out of a past and into the future, which would provide the "germ cell" of historicity, of reflecting on oneself, one's life, and thereby one's past and one's having been determined. That influencing, ordering past is thus part of "my whole self" and in this sense, "I am history." The study of my tradition, then, stretching all the way back to the Greeks, can be understood as a "psychology of history," insofar as it reveals features and dynamics of my present mind, and determines historical elements and forces that are even now to be found working their way through me, in my experience of and thinking about my world. The thinking of history will bring to light not the objective character of events and figures belonging to a long-dead past present, but rather the past that is currently at work in my own *psychê*, emerging out of the possibilities for experience and thinking that unfold toward me out of the future. Though the influence of Yorck and Dilthey on *Being and Time* is clearly indicated, we should note that already four years before the publication of their correspondence, in the 1919 text "Critical Comments on Karl Jaspers' *Psychology of Worldviews*," Heidegger is thinking along these very lines. He remarks there that "the proper experience of having-myself *extends historically into the past of the 'I.'* This past is not like an appendage that the 'I' drags along with itself. Rather, it is experienced as the past of an 'I' that experiences it historically within a horizon of *expectations placed ahead of itself* by itself, in which the 'I' has itself once in a 'selfly' as well as historical way . . . For the historical is not merely something of which we have knowledge and about which we write books; rather, *we ourselves are the historical that we ourselves bear and carry as a responsibility*" ("Comm." 139–40/23).

16. In fact, the cause of our falling away from Being is twofold. On the one hand, as an ontological structure of Dasein itself, we lose ourselves in the world of beings and confuse our own mode of being with what often seems to be their simple persistence and presence before us. On the other hand, we inherit a traditional understanding of Being that we then, without reflection or interrogation, allow to organize our experience of beings, of one another, and of ourselves. On this, see Will McNeill, "From *Destruktion* to the History of Being," *Gatherings* 2 (2012): 28.

17. Robert Scharff sees Heidegger (and Dilthey and Nietzsche somewhat less successfully) as offering a much-needed correction of a certain self-deception that characterizes analytic philosophy in the wake of positivism, insofar as it ignores or even vigorously denies what Scharff sees as the irremediably historically situated character of all philosophizing. Scharff offers a compelling reading of

the second of Nietzsche's *Untimely Meditations*, which finds Nietzsche laying out a fairly robust notion of that temporality that grounds the three modes of history to which we will turn later on in the "Introduction." More relevant at this point is Scharff's focus in two chapters on the Heidegger of the 1920s and his insistence on the condition of historicity within which the phenomenological project must be self-consciously carried out. See Scharff, *How History Matters*. See also Pascal Massie's review of Scharff's book, in which Massie eventually raises the problem of a fascinating division between two "ontological regions," namely "a cosmic (natural) one and a human one (psychological/historical/cultural) one," which he sees as threatening Scharff's (and Heidegger's) project. Massie then suggests a way in which the notion of the "life-world" might be expanded to re-situate the human world within the natural material one, stretching back into deep history. See Massie, "Review of *How History Matters to Philosophy*," *Philosophy Today* 62, no. 2 (Spring 2018): 653–60. This is a brief but highly suggestive discussion.

18. "Authentic historicality," for Heidegger, would entail resolutely taking up that historical inheritance, engaging in a *Wiederholung*, which is sometimes translated as a "repetition." This is misleading, however, insofar as it suggests the production of a likeness or sameness, a taking up of the views and the values one has inherited and simply reproducing them in one's future actions, only now intentionally. But Heidegger has no such simple repetition in mind. Indeed, I would suggest an alternative translation for *Wiederholung*: "retrieval." This could then even entail a destruction of our tradition and the content it passes along to us in the service of a retrieval of something from our past. What that is, we have not yet made clear, but it seems to me that this must be what authentic historizing entails.

19. For Heidegger, it is of no significance that Aristotle himself never used the term "metaphysics" (μεταφυσική), the term only being introduced later as the title for Aristotle's work on the "science of being as being," perhaps by the first-century BCE editor and commentator Andronicus of Rhodes as he arranged Aristotle's corpus into a definitive edition after they had been brought to Rome.

20. Helmuth Vetter observes that "als eines der Grundstücke der Phänomenologie gehört die Destruktion in die Hermeneutik der Faktizität" (Helmuth Vetter, "Heideggers Destruktion der Tradition am Beispiel des Aristoteles," in *Heidegger und Aristoteles*, ed. Denker et al., 79).

21. I would argue that Books Zeta, Eta, and Theta of the *Metaphysics*, sometimes referred to as the "Ousiology," present a quasi-phenomenological study of *ousia*. That discussion begins with Aristotle observing that "while being is said in many ways, it is apparent [*phaneron*] that the way that is first among these is 'the what-it-is' [*to ti estin*], which indicates *ousia* [*sêmainei tên ousian*]" (*Meta.* VII.1028a13–15). Aristotle employs here his technical philosophical method, *dialektikê* or "dialectic," and this proceeds by assembling how the subject matter *appears* pre-philosophically and then attempting to clarify what presents itself in those appearances. In this case, Aristotle is hoping to provide a foundation for the study of being as being (*Meta.* IV.1003a21–22).

22. To be clear, this is not to say that the individual thinker Aristotle is responsible, much less *culpable*, for imposing substance ontology on the sub-

sequent tradition. Rather, the world of beings was presenting itself to him in fourth-century BCE Greece in such a way that his conceptualizing of it in terms of *ousiai* was powerfully satisfying. We might say, rather, that he was singularly brilliant in his perception, description, and conceptualization of the received phenomenal content presenting itself to him and his contemporaries at that historical moment.

23. Indeed, this is why, to cite just a couple of important examples, when Simone de Beauvoir wants to revolutionize the way we conceive of the sexes in *The Second Sex*, she has to take on the Aristotelian concept of essence and the Aristotelian form-matter composite, and when Judith Butler wants to revolutionize the way we think of gender in *Gender Trouble*, she has to take on the Aristotelian concept of substance. See de Beauvoir, *The Second Sex*; and Judith Butler, *Gender Trouble: Feminism and the Subversion of Identity* (New York: Routledge, 1990).

24. Note that this paper was contemporaneous with the 1924–25 lecture course *Plato's "Sophist,"* and it bears a close connection to the treatment of Aristotle's *Ethics* there. See chapter 2 below for a discussion of that course.

25. It may well be the case that, in the fields of post-Newtonian physics and quantum theory, scientists have begun to entertain modes of being that are conceived of as legitimately *non-present*, either temporally or epistemologically. The "block universe" theory, sometimes called "eternalism," surely suggests that all of time has equal ontological status and time should not be thought of as unfolding from the future through the present into the past, but rather as the fourth dimension of an unchanging space-time whole (hence, a "block"). In this model, past and future events *are* in the same sense that the present *is*. And, for instance, Heisenberg's uncertainty principle in quantum mechanics would seem to set an insuperable limit at the ontological level to the presence (or accessibility and knowability) of material reality, insofar as it maintains that certain values regarding a given subatomic particle are fundamentally and irremediably undeterminable. Heidegger does mention Heisenberg by name in 1935, seemingly exempting him from a general critique of science and its exclusive focus on present entities (*WTKLG* 67). And one might well recall here that something like a friendship blossomed between Heidegger and Heisenberg, after the latter visited the *Hütte* in Todtnauberg in 1935. And Heisenberg eventually made a contribution to Heidegger's 1959 *Festschrift* (Werner Heisenberg Grundlegende Voraussetzungen in der Physik der Elementarteilchen," in *Martin Heidegger zum Siebzigsten Geburstag*, ed. Günther Neske [Pfüllingen: Neske, 1959], 291–97). For more on their relationship, however, see Otto Pöggeler, "The Hermeneutics of the Technological World: The Heidegger-Heisenberg Dispute," trans. M. Kane and K. Pfefferkorn-Forbath, *International Journal of Philosophical Studies* 1, no. 1 (1993): 21–48.

26. Heidegger remarks, in a letter to Elizabeth Blochmann, "I don't believe we will find ourselves again so long as we keep chasing after the "current situation," instead of turning our backs to it in the knowledge that the beginning of the history of our essential being, in antiquity, must speak in what we ourselves can be as existing beings." The letter is dated 20. December, 1931, from Freiburg, and it appears in Martin Heidegger and Elizabeth Blochmann, *Briefwechsel, 1918–1969*, ed. J. W. Storch (Marbach am Neckar: Deutsche Schillergesellschaft, 1989).

27. Heidegger's critical remarks sometimes seem to misrepresent the content, commitments, and implications of Husserlian phenomenology. Indeed, at certain points in Husserl's work, some of Heidegger's presumed innovations may well be anticipated. For instance, in the third of the *Cartesian Meditations*, we hear Husserl suggesting that the focus on the contents and structures of consciousness accomplished through the *epochê* is ultimately to be set aside, and that ontology, and an insistence on thinking the reality that is appearing to consciousness, are put back on the table (Husserl, *Cartesian Meditations*, §§23–24). Moreover, in Husserl's late *Crisis of the European Sciences and Transcendental Phenomenology*, the role of history and tradition in the constitution of the "life-world" are undeniable. I do not believe we find moments where Husserl anticipates anything like the essential and insuperable concealment that Heidegger sees as belonging to Being itself, but perhaps it could be argued that something moving in this direction is at least implicit when Husserl attributes an interminability or infinite striving to philosophical understanding itself. In any case, we should proceed with caution when Heidegger rejects the phenomenological project of his former mentor as definitively and utterly non-ontological, ahistorical, and epistemologically naive.

28. Another way of describing the position at which Heidegger arrives would be to say that he is opposed to any disjunctive approach to experience and that he endorses something akin to externalism. "Disjunctivism" describes any theory of perception which denies that the same account belongs to all three types of perceptual experience: veridical perception, illusion, and hallucination. "Externalism," in the context of philosophy of mind at least, entails that what occurs in a given individual's mind is not exhaustively determined by or explicable in terms of what occurs in the associated material brain. This can mean either that the mental content or what presents itself to consciousness is taken to be in part external (content externalism), or that some aspect of the subject or bearer of the mental content is taken to be in part external (extended mind).

29. Samuel IJsseling, "Heidegger and the Destruction of Ontology," *Man and World* 15 (1982): 4.

30. The terms "objective" and "object," in their technical senses for Descartes and Kant respectively, depart from the commonsense notion of objective on which I am relying above. In the course of his first proof for God's existence in the "Third Meditation," Descartes observes a distinction among his ideas, specifically between those ideas that have more and those that have less *réalité objective*, in the French, or *realitas objectiva*, in the Latin, that is, "objective reality." The idea of a substance is then declared to have more objective reality than the idea of a mode or an accident, and the idea of a supreme, omnipotent, creator God is declared to "clearly" have more objective reality than the ideas of finite substances. Given this, it would seem, according to Descartes's reasoning, that objective reality has something to do with independence or self-sufficiency. The idea of an accident, say, a color, depends on the idea of a substance to which that accident belongs. The idea of a finite substance, as an *ens creatum*, depends on the idea of a God, as an *ens increatum* and the cause or ground of its being. The relative objective reality of ideas is then contrasted with their "actual or formal reality," in French *réalité actuelle ou formelle* or in Latin *realitas actualis sive formalis*,

which seems to indicate something's existing externally or being in the world (something confusingly quite close to our commonsense notion of "objective reality"). In Kantian epistemology, the object is a complex notion indeed: see S. R. Palmquist, "Six Perspectives on the Object in Kant's Theory of Knowledge," *Dialectica* 40, no. 2 (1986): 121–51. At least we can say that objects, in some basic sense for Kant, are those things that we perceive and are then able to cognize or know, which do not then exist independently of consciousness, but are constituted through the imposition of the forms of intuition, space and time, and the categories of the understanding applied to raw sense data. As Heidegger himself notes in *Being and Time*, for Kant "'appearances' are, in the first place, the 'objects of empirical intuition': they are what shows itself in such intuition" (*BT* 54/30) and are thus not things-in-themselves existing independently of consciousness. For a revealing discussion of the late-medieval coining and subsequent philosophical development of the term *objectum*, see L. Dewan, "Obiectum: Notes on the Invention of a Word," *Archives d'Histoire Doctrinale et Littéraire de Moyen Âge* 56 (1981): 37–96.

31. One standard starting point in interpretations of Kantian idealism would be that the objects we perceive and intend have the properties they do, for example, their spatiotemporal character, due to certain features or requirements of our minds, which would then seem to entail that there are either (A) two regions of objects or, minimally, (B) two fundamentally distinct ways of approaching one region of beings, as "appearances" to us or as "things in themselves." Above I am describing Kant in terms of A and suggesting how Heidegger would assess that standard account of transcendental idealism. It should be noted, however, that in his own interpretation of the *Critique of Pure Reason*, Heidegger clearly reads Kant in terms of B, even to the point of rejecting the "idealism" usually attributed to Kant and bringing him, in a sense generously, a bit closer to his own, that is, Heidegger's, ontology. After citing Kant's suggestion that philosophy might make better progress if, rather than assuming that knowledge must conform to objects, it assumes that "objects must conform to our knowledge" (*Critique of Pure Reason* B, xvi), Heidegger writes: "With this Kant wants to say: not 'all knowledge' is ontic, and where there is such knowledge, it is only possible through ontological knowledge. Through the Copernican Revolution, the 'old' concept of truth in the sense of the 'correspondence' (*adequation*) of knowledge to the being is so little shaken that it [the Copernican Revolution] actually presupposes it [the old concept of truth], indeed even grounds it for the first time. Ontic knowledge can only correspond to beings ('objects') if this being as being is already first apparent [*offenbar*], i.e., it is already first known in the constitution of its Being. Appearances of beings (ontic truth) revolve around the unveiledness of the constitution of the Being of beings (ontological truth)" (*KPM* 8/12). See Immanuel Kant, *Critique of Pure Reason*, trans. N. K. Smith [New York: St. Martin's, 1781/1965]. For Heidegger's Kant, ontic knowledge knows its spatiotemporal and categorically ordered objects against a backdrop of the Being of beings, their emerging into appearance before us. Indeed, in *Being and Time*, Heidegger even goes so far as to rehabilitate, as it were, the term "idealism," writing that "if what the term 'idealism' says, amounts to the understanding that Being can never be

explained by entities but is that which is 'transcendental' for every entity, then idealism affords the only correct possibility for a philosophical problematic. If so, Aristotle was no less an idealist than Kant. But if 'idealism' signifies tracing back every entity to a subject or consciousness whose sole distinguishing features are that it remains *indefinite* in its Being and is best characterized negatively as 'un-Thing-like,' then this idealism is not less naïve in its method than the most grossly militant realism" (*BT* 251–52/208).

32. As one commentator remarks, for Heidegger, "nature is neither appearance nor thing-in-itself," and indeed, "the very concept of the thing-in-itself is bankrupt" (William Blattner, "Heidegger's Kantian Idealism Revisited," *Inquiry: An Interdisciplinary Journal of Philosophy* 47, no. 4 [2004]: 322).

33. Brentano sums up the "intentionality" that he suggests belongs to every mental state, saying that "in presentation, something is presented, in judgement something is affirmed or denied, in love loved, in hate hated, in desire desired, and so on" (Franz Brentano, *Psychology from an Empirical Standpoint* [London: Routledge, 1874/1973], 88).

34. Given Heidegger's insistence on investigating "what is" as what has already appeared in pre-philosophical experience, perhaps the most consequential and most foundational distinction for Heideggerian thinking ends up being, rather than any of those listed above, the purportedly self-evident distinction between pre-philosophical or everyday experience and the moment of reflection or thinking, which, though it certainly renounces any presumed transcendence of everyday circumstance, nonetheless presumes to introduce a crucial wrinkle or refraction into the relation between Dasein and beings.

35. That is, even if, in the period stretching from the Greeks down to the present, that relation to Being is established entirely through Being's *withdrawal* from Dasein, its being *eclipsed* by the beings that it allows to emerge into self-presentation or appearance and itself *not appearing*.

36. One of the most illuminating and helpful discussions of *Grundstimmungen* in Heidegger, and their complex function, is Klaus Held's "Fundamental Moods and Heidegger's Critique of Contemporary Culture," trans. A. J. Steinbock, in *Reading Heidegger: Commemorations*, ed. John Sallis (Bloomington: Indiana University Press, 1993), 286–303.

37. Friedrich Nietzsche, "On the Utility and Liability of History for Life," in *Unfashionable Observations: The Complete Works of Friedrich Nietzsche*, vol. 2, trans. R. T. Gray (Stanford, CA: Stanford University Press, 1874/1997), 86, translation modified. At this point in the text, Nietzsche is describing the individual who can benefit specifically from "critical history," but I would suggest that, though all three modes of history (the monumental, antiquarian, and critical) are to be employed over time, perhaps in a complex alternating series, with each correcting the apparently inevitable excess of the last, it would seem to be specifically the critical mode that Nietzsche sees his own historical moment to be most urgently in need of.

38. In his illuminating essay on Nietzsche's method of reading historical texts, "Nietzsche, Genealogy, History," Michel Foucault draws a distinction within Nietzsche's work itself, between tracing one's inherited concepts and values

back to an *Ursprung* or "origin" and tracing them back to an *Entstehungsherd*, or "threshold of emergence." Whereas the former would claim to identify a more or less completely intelligible historical cause and source for the subsequent development, the latter would trace a contemporary value or concept back to a multiple, complex, contested, and ultimately inaccessible dynamic event of creation. It is the latter that I am emphasizing here, and which I find at work in Nietzsche's thinking from the *Birth of Tragedy* (1872) and *Philosophy in the Tragic Age of the Greeks* (1873) on. And it is precisely this tendency in Nietzsche's approach to history that I see resonating deeply with the Heideggerian destructive project. See Michel Foucault, "Nietzsche, Genealogy, History," in *Language, Counter-Memory, Practice: Selected Essays and Interviews*, ed. and trans. D. Bouchard (Ithaca, NY: Cornell University Press, 1971/1977), 139–64.

39. Nietzsche, "On the Utility and Liability of History for Life," 94.

40. In his monograph on the project of Nietzschean philosophy, Gilles Deleuze remarks: "The difference *in* the origin does not appear *at* the origin—except perhaps to a particularly practiced eye, the eye which sees from afar, the eye of the far-sighted, the eye of the genealogist" (Gilles Deleuze, *Nietzsche and Philosophy*, trans. H. Tomlinson [New York: Columbia University Press, 1962/1983], 5). This eye, according to the present interpretation, belongs to the Heideggerian destructive reader as well. It is an eye that ultimately uncovers and brings to fulfillment a differentiation, a schism, an excess in the Aristotelian text, a differentiation which Aristotle himself did not think or even experience directly, but to which his text can be read as nonetheless gesturing.

41. Jacques Derrida, "Letter to a Japanese Friend," trans. A. Benjamin and D. Wood, in *Derrida and Difference*, ed. R. Bernasconi and D. Wood (Evanston, IL: Northwestern University Press, 1988), 4. Derrida goes on to list other terms that might be "substituted" for *déconstruction—écriture, trace, différence, supplement, hymen, pharmakon, marge, entame, parergon*, and so on.

42. Jacques Derrida, *Positions*, trans. A. Bass (Chicago: University of Chicago Press, 1972/1981), 41–42.

43. Derrida, *Positions*, 41.

44. Derrida, *Positions*, 43. The term *pharmakon*, which in Greek indicates both a healing potion and a poison, is used by Socrates in Plato's *Phaedrus* to characterize the technology of writing as opposed to spoken discourse (*Phdr.* 275a), and Derrida leverages precisely that tension in his reading of the dialogue in "Plato's Pharmacy." Jacques Derrida, *Dissemination*, trans. B. Johnson (Chicago: University of Chicago Press, 1972/1981), 61–171.

45. Derrida, "Letter to a Japanese Friend," 1.

46. For studies that approach destruction primarily in light of Heidegger's own broader project of raising the question of the meaning of Being, see, for example, Walter Schulz, "Über den philosophiegeschichtlichen Ort Martin Heideggers," in *Heidegger*, ed. O. Pöggeler (Cologne: Verlag Kiepenheuer & Witsch, 1969), 95–139; Robert Bernasconi, *The Question of Language in Heidegger's History of Being* (Atlantic Highlands, NJ: Humanities, 1985); Theodore Kisiel, *Heidegger's Way of Thought*, ed. A. Denker and M. Heinz (New York: Continuum, 2002), esp. chapter 7; Jeffrey Andrew Barash, *Martin Heidegger and the Problem of Historical*

Meaning (New York: Fordham University Press, 2003); and McNeill, "From *Destruktion* to the History of Being." While scholars have, as I suggest above, largely not addressed and evaluated destruction on its own terms as a hermeneutic method, one can find some initial steps in this direction in Bernasconi, "Repetition and Tradition," 123–36; and IJsseling, "Heidegger and the Destruction of Ontology." And there are two book-length treatments of the early Heidegger, in which one does find extensive and extremely helpful discussions of the project of destruction, though these emphasize a decidedly different aspect of that project than I do here. Benjamin Crowe in *Heidegger's Religious Origins: Destruction and Authenticity* (Bloomington: Indiana University Press, 2006) and Scott Campbell in *The Early Heidegger's Philosophy of Life: Facticity, Being, and Language* (New York: Fordham University Press, 2012) both present destruction fundamentally as a means of arriving at a form of "authenticity," which is to say a means of arriving at an unfiltered or direct philosophical engagement with life and factical existence. I agree with Crowe that "few . . . have attempted to come to a thorough understanding of it [destruction], and fewer still have succeeded in the task. By and large, the term 'destruction' (or some other translation of Heidegger's term '*Destruktion*') either receives little comment or is used by commentators as if its meaning were obvious" (Crowe, *Heidegger's Religious Origins*, 2). And although Crowe does break this mold and take up destruction as a central term in need of study and interpretation, he moves the term in a very different direction than I will here. That is, as one would expect from the title of his book, Crowe foregrounds the fact that Heidegger inherits the term *Destruktion* as a Germanization of Luther's Latin word *destruktio*, and thus Crowe sees destruction in light of Heidegger's early concern with religious thought and life, and defines it as first and foremost "a philosophical practice that aims at cultivating authenticity as a concrete possibility for individual women and men" (Crowe, *Heidegger's Religious Origins*, 3). Campbell takes up Crowe's emphasis, though he insists nicely on complicating the relationship between authentic and inauthentic life, finding in *Being and Time* good reason to see authenticity as "not merely a matter of destroying or overcoming human fallenness, but, together with fallenness, it is a moment of revelation (καιρός) through insight (φρόνησις) into who we are, that is, into who the human being is as a whole" (Campbell, *The Early Heidegger's Philosophy of Life*, 212). I do not disagree with this fundamental avenue of interpretation, but it seems to me in need of a supplement indicating that the authentic freeing of oneself from one's inherited, everyday, unreflective mode of experiencing one's world, oneself, and others proceeds *not* by a simple demolition of that worldview, but rather *only* by destabilizing the historical and particularly ancient texts that record the creation of the concepts that determine and structure that worldview.

47. In a later, handwritten marginal note in one of Heidegger's own copies of the published text of *Being and Time*, on the page containing the outline for the never-completed destructive reading of the tradition, we find the following lines apparently summarizing that project: "The return into the origin [*Die Umkehr in die Herkunft*]. / Presencing from out of this origin [*Das Anwesen aus dieser Herkunft*]" (*BT* 40n.). Here, destruction would not seem to gain access to something other than the Being that was thought as presence by Aristotle.

Rather, destruction allows one to experience present beings no longer in their simple presence, but in their emergence from out of a non-presence, a ground that is unavailable and abidingly hidden, just as it was for Aristotle, only now it is experienced as such, as hidden. The copious marginal notes from Heidegger's *Hüttenexemplar* of *Sein und Zeit*, the copy he kept in his cabin in the Schwarzwald, are not included in the Macquarrie and Robinson translation, though they are preserved and translated in the Stambaugh and Schmidt version. For the note quoted here, see Heidegger, *Being and Time: A Revised Edition of the Stambaugh Translation* (35/40).

48. In his excellent essay "Heideggers Destruktion der Tradition am Beispiel des Aristoteles," Helmuth Vetter draws a helpful and illuminating connection between this aspect of Heidegger's destructive method—the leveraging of a separation in the text between the registers of experience and conceptuality—and the notion on which the early Heidegger focuses elsewhere, referred to as "formal indication." Vetter observes: "Vorhabe und Vorsicht der aristotelischen Ontologie sind vom Gehaltssinn bestimmt. Ihr Vorgriff hat seine Herkunft 'in der Selbstverständlichkeit des natürlichen Daseins' [*BCArP* 28] aus der auch die Bedeutung von οὐσία erwachsen ist. Nun ist die Destruktion als ἑρμενεύειν selbst eine Weise, wie Seiendes zumVerständnis gebracht wird. Um die Vorhabe in ihrer eingeschränkten Sichtweite destruieren zu können, muß sich der hermeneutische λόγος der Destruktion von jenen Begriffen absetzen, die aus der aristotelischen Vorhabe erwachsen sind. Die gegenruinante radikale Kritik setzt voraus, das begriffliche Artikulieren selbst zu destruieren—es 'muß radikal durchreflektiert werden, um so die Vorhabeproblematik radikal zu verstehen' [*PISPA* 52]. Diese Reflexion ergibt dieformale Anzeige als das begriffliche Instrument der Destruktion. Daß der gegenständlich bestimmte Begriff der οὐσία in seiner Ruinanz sichtbar wird, setzt voraus, daß man 'den Anzeigecharakter des Formalen, d.h. der Gegenständlichkeit als solcher, prinzipiell ansetzt'" [*PISPA* 299]" (Vetter, "Heideggers Destruktion," 91–92). Here, I would refer to Daniel Dahlstrom's clarifying discussion of the way in which the philosophical concept of philosophy's central subject matter, namely what it means "to be," must be understood as a "formal indication," in the sense of a sign or a signal pointing us toward an original, uninterrogated "having of" or "comportment toward" beings, which the philosopher must use to "enact (or more exactly, reenact) that original, unthematic 'having,' so as to appropriate it explicitly" (Daniel Dahlstrom, "Heidegger's Method: Philosophical Concepts as Formal Indications," *Review of Metaphysics* 47, no. 4 [1994]: 782).

Chapter 1

1. Some, especially those who would emphasize other influences on Heidegger's thinking prior to *Being and Time*, might claim this exaggerates the proximity of the outline of the never-published manuscript, sometimes referred to as the "Natorp Report," to Heidegger's magnum opus. Against this, I would point

to Michael Bauer's remarks in his translator's preface to the first publication in English of "Phenomenological Interpretations with Respect to Aristotle: Indication of the Hermeneutical Situation" in 1992 (after this introductory text was sent to Paul Natorp in Marburg and Georg Misch in Göttingen, it was for many years misplaced and was only located again in 1989 in the Göttingen archive): "When it comes to understanding the genesis and development of Heidegger's thought, it would be rather difficult to overestimate the importance of the 'Aristotle-Introduction' of 1922, Heidegger's 'Phenomenological Interpretations with Respect to Aristotle.' This text is both a manifesto which describes the young Heidegger's philosophical commitments, as well as a promissory note which outlines his projected future work. This 'Aristotle-Introduction' not only enunciates Heidegger's broad project of a philosophy which is both systematic and historical; it also indicates, in particular, why a principal (or fundamental) ontology can be actualized only through a destruction of the history of ontology. This text anticipates several central themes of *Being and Time* (e.g., facticity, death, falling), and also foreshadows some of the issues which were to occupy the later Heidegger (e.g., 'truth' as a heterogeneous process of unconcealment)" (Michael Bauer, translator's preface to 'Phenomenological Interpretations with Respect to Aristotle: Indication of the Hermeneutical Situation,'" *Man and World* 25 [1992]: 355). A version of Bauer's translation, revised and expanded with notes by Kisiel, appears in Theodore Kisiel and Thomas Sheehan, eds., *Becoming Heidegger: On the Trail of His Occasional Writings, 1919–1927* (Evanston, IL: Northwestern University Press, 2007), 149–79. And Kisiel and Sheehan say of that text in their introductory discussion: "The upshot is a closer fusion of two still-disparate strands in Heidegger's phenomenological approach: the 'systematic' approach to the structures of the field of factic life experience, and the 'historical' approach to the conceptual resources available in the philosophical tradition for such a phenomenological hermeneutics of facticity . . . [This text presents] for the very first time the double-pronged program familiar to us from *Being and Time* as (1) a fundamental ontology and (2) a destruction of the history of ontology" (Kisiel and Sheehan, *Becoming Heidegger*, 151). For other compelling discussions of the closeness of the projected Aristotle book to *Being and Time*, see Volpi, "*Being and Time*: A 'Translation'"; and Walter Brogan, "The Place of Aristotle in the Development of Heidegger's Phenomenology," in *Reading Heidegger from the Start*, ed. T. Kisiel and J. Van Buren, 195–212.

2. These remarks appear in a letter dated February 1, 1922, from Husserl to Paul Natorp, in which Husserl advocates for the young docent despite his lack of publication record and supports him for the position at Marburg that Heidegger would eventually assume in the fall of 1923. Kisiel and Sheehan, *Becoming Heidegger*, 151.

3. I am translating the German phrase "*ohne weiteres*" here in the most literal manner, as "without something further." Admittedly, more common translations would be "readily, easily, offhand, just like that, without hesitation," but I would insist that, in time, further investigation of Heidegger's project here, and specifically the unpacking of his insistence on understanding these concepts "in their conceptuality," will make good on this literal rendering.

4. On this aspect of Heidegger's project, see Rudolf Bernet's helpful essay entitled "The Limits of Conceptual Thinking," in *Phenomenology of Thinking: Philosophical Investigations into the Character of Cognitive Experiences*, ed. T. Breyer and C. Gutland (New York: Routledge, 2016), 147–64. Bernet draws very direct, and illuminating, connections between the critiques of conceptual thinking presented by Heidegger and Deleuze.

5. For a deep investigation of the relationship between experience, specifically perceptual content, and conceptual thinking, there is much of value in the MacDowell-Dreyfus debate. John MacDowell argues that even in the absence of linguistic articulability, all perceptual content can be retained in memory and considered conceptually, while Dreyfus, influenced by Heidegger, argues that unreflective action entails a fundamentally unconceptualizable experience of the world. On the debate, see J. K. Schear, ed., *Mind, Reason, and Being-in-the-World: The MacDowell-Dreyfus Debate* (New York: Routledge, 2013).

6. One cannot help but hear in this an anticipation of Deleuze and Guattari's basic definition of philosophy. They write in *What Is Philosophy?*: "The philosopher is the concept's friend; he is the potentiality of the concept. That is, philosophy is not a simple art of forming, inventing, or fabricating concepts. More rigorously, philosophy is the discipline that involves *creating concepts*" (Gilles Deleuze and Félix Guattari, *What Is Philosophy?* [New York: Columbia University Press, 1991/1994], 5). Furthermore, and explicitly referencing Nietzsche's conception of "the task of philosophy," they declare that "you will know nothing through concepts unless you have first created them—that is, constructed them in an intuition specific to them: a field, a plane, and a ground that must not be confused with them but that shelters their seeds" (Deleuze and Guattari, *What Is Philosophy?* 7). This seems very much in keeping with both the project of philosophizing that Heidegger refers to as *Begriffsbildung* or "concept formation" (*BCAncP* 8/11), which he claims to find at work in the texts of the tradition, and his insistence that we immerse ourselves in those texts and "co-philosophize" with the authors, that is, "cooperate" in the creation of concepts, experiencing the movement by which they are drawn out of their ground. And although Deleuze and Guattari insist on a kind of "constructivism" with regard to philosophical truth, they would nevertheless reject that this creation is a matter of caprice or merely subjective will or desire. The creation is not arbitrary, but rather is provoked and even necessitated by the plane or field from which the concept will emerge and in which it must find its place. Heidegger too writes of the philosopher as one "*who has accepted responsibility for the concept* [die Verantwortlichkeit für den Begriff übernommen]" (*BCArP* 5/6), but clarifies that acceptance of this responsibility is not tantamount to claiming any sort of absolute control or power over the concept's emergence. Rather, creating concepts would always mean responding properly to "*the fundamental exigencies of scientific research* [die Grunderfordnisse jeglicher wissenschaftlichen Forschung]" (*BCArP* 4/4). That is, concepts emerge, they are formed or created, and ancient philosophers like Aristotle participate vitally in this emergence, but the emergence occurs in accord with necessitations arising from the *Grund* or "ground, foundation" to which one relates in originary experience. One forms or creates concepts only according to the manner drawn

forth by the mode of appearing of beings, and Being, at one's specific historical moment.

7. As close as Aristotle's *to kath' hekaston* and *to katholou* may seem to Kant's *representatio singularis* and *representatio per notas communes*, it is imperative to remember that the movement these thinkers see taking place between these two poles is emphatically in opposite directions.

8. See *PIA/PR* 14–15/17, where in 1921-22 Heidegger calls into question the genus/differentia model of definition, declaring that according to the "original sense of definition," from which the genus/differentia model is "but a particular derivative," "the full definition is not merely its content, the proposition."

9. Aristotle in fact has a variety of ways of thinking about definition, and even a variety of terms that might in certain contexts be translated as "definition"—*horismos*, as we saw above, is the technical term for a definition, but there are also *horos* and *logos*, which are probably better understood as types of "accounts." Of the technical sense of "definition," Aristotle tells us in the *Posterior Analytics*: "A definition . . . is said to be an account of the 'what is' [*Horismos d'* . . . *legetai einai logos tou ti esti*]" (*Post. An.* II.93b29–30), which, he then clarifies, is not in the most original sense merely the meaning of a word, nor is it simply stating the facts about a given thing, but instead requires stating *to ti ên einai* or literally "the what-it-was-to-be," or as it is often rendered, the "essence." Ultimately, it seems that in the Aristotelian universe, only the *eidos* or the "species form" can be defined in the most technical sense, for its essential character can be rendered as the *genos* or "genus" plus the *diaphora* or "differentia." For a thorough discussion collecting all the references to this technical mode of definition, see E. H. Granger, "Aristotle on Genus and Differentia," in *Essays in Ancient Greek Philosophy V: Aristotle's Ontology*, ed. T. Preus (Albany, NY: State University of New York Press, 1992), 69–93.

10. In his 1924 "review article" for the journal *Deutsche Vierteljahrschrift für Literarurwissenschaft und Geistesgeschichte*, an essay entitled "The Concept of Time," sometimes referred to as the "Dilthey Draft" of *Being and Time*, Heidegger describes the task of destruction in very similar terms, namely as having to test ancient Greek concepts, which are our inherited concepts, for their authenticity with respect to the experiences from which they arose. He closes the essay with the following: "The dominance [*Herrschaft*] of Greek ontology—within both our interpretational tradition [cf. Hegel's *Logic*] and the history of our own Dasein—blocks ontological access to Dasein. To gain access means to dismantle [*abtragen*] this Greek ontology whose self-evident status obscures its dominance, or to dismantle those research strategies influenced by this ontology in such a way that we bring out its true foundations. We must see to it that the ontology of Dasein, as destruction [*Destruktion*], seizes the opportunity to determine the provenance and adequacy of traditional categories. In doing so, one ensures that the positive explanation of phenomena proceeds on a firm and steady footing. The phenomenological destruction of ontology and logic amounts to a critique of present time, but not a critique of Greek ontology. We begin to see the positive aspects of this ontology and can now correctly appropriate it as the ontology of the world in which every Dasein exists. As a thing of the past, we can unlock the historical po-

tential of this ontology for a contemporary age that aims to understand itself. The ontology of Dasein is historiological knowledge [*historisches Erkennen*] because the basic constitution of Dasein is historicity [*Geschichtlichkeit*], which determines the scope of Dasein's interpretations at any given time" (CT2 88/102–3). In determining the "provenance" and the "adequacy" of our inherited Greek concepts, destruction is also described here as itself the "ontology of Dasein," insofar as Dasein is essentially historical, constituted in its very being by its inheriting of a past and by projecting itself out toward a future, and destruction is a mode of doing precisely that.

11. Already in 1919, Heidegger writes: "By exposing the bias built into the tradition and recognizing its consequences, we may be led to the insight that the concrete possibility of bringing the phenomena of existence into view and explicating them in a genuine [hermeneutic] conceptuality [*Begrifflichkeit*] can be opened up *only when* the concrete tradition that is seen to be still at work in one form or another has been *destroyed* [*destruiert*]. We can turn our attention to the ways and means of explicating the proper experience of the self in its world *only when*, through destruction, the motivating and effective basic experiences [*Grunderfahrungen*] are brought forth and assessed with regard to their originality [*Ursprünglichkeit*]. Such destruction is in its very sense dominated by a thoroughly historical concern that is anxious about a self that is concretely one's own" ("Comm." 142, translation modified).

12. Hans-Georg Gadamer remarks that "certainly, on the basis of any given expression of Heidegger's, one may and should try to think for oneself. But one ought never to use Heidegger's words as if they were the kind of words we had thought of already" (Hans-Georg Gadamer, "Martin Heidegger's One Path," trans. P. C. Smith, in *Reading Heidegger from the Start*, ed. T. Kisiel and J. Van Buren, 31).

13. For a thorough study of the indebtedness to Dilthey in Heidegger's radicalization of phenomenology, see Robert Scharff's book, *Heidegger Becoming Phenomenological: Interpreting Husserl through Dilthey, 1916–1925* (New York: Rowman and Littlefield, 2019). It presents a compelling argument for the previously underappreciated centrality of Heidegger's early encounter with Dilthey, who offers a model for a kind of immanent and non-theoretically distanced thinking of historically situated life.

14. This insertion of destruction into the project of Husserlian phenomenology is more centrally discussed in the methodological introduction to the 1927 course, *Basic Problems of Phenomenology*, to which we have made reference already in the "Introduction" and to which we will have occasion to return in chapter 2.

15. Note that Heidegger pointedly remarks that what we hope to become equal to is not the conclusions or the philosophical positions of the Greeks, but specifically their *questioning*.

16. We might note that, in the above-cited *What Is Called Thinking?* (1951–52), Heidegger spends a fair amount of time quite emphatically opposing his own philosophizing to the discipline of philology (*WT* 3/5).

Chapter 2

1. Nietzsche, "On the Utility and Liability of History for Life," 87.
2. Friedrich Nietzsche, *The Gay Science*, ed. B. Williams, trans. J. Nauckhoff and A. del Caro (Cambridge: Cambridge University Press, 1882, 1887/2001), §125.
3. Nietzsche, "On the Utility and Liability of History for Life," §§2–3.
4. One finds this approach in Franco Volpi's excellent essay, provocatively titled "*Being and Time*: A 'Translation' of the *Nicomachean Ethics*?" He opens the essay by forcefully, and convincingly, contesting Jonathan Barnes's claim that, in Volpi's words, "if Aristotle were alive today, he would live in Oxford, taking a few side trips to Louvain perhaps." Against this, Volpi insists that Aristotle certainly "would have preferred philosophizing in the Black Forest with Heidegger." Volpi is focused here on the fact that Heidegger "seeks to appropriate . . . the founding questions first thought by the Greeks and especially by Aristotle, in order to obtain a fundamental doctrine" (Volpi, "*Being and Time*: A 'Translation,'" 195). Attending primarily to the "crucial ten-year silence preceding the publication of *Being and Time*," Volpi hopes in reading these lecture courses "to show how the genesis of the terminology in *Being and Time*" constitutes a "zealous appropriation of Aristotle's practical philosophy" (196).
5. Another very compelling version of this approach is presented in Ian Thompson's essay, "Ontotheology? Understanding Heidegger's *Destruktion* of Metaphysics." Thompson writes that destruction "decomposes or decompiles metaphysics' sedimented historical layers, reconstructing their hidden ontotheological structure and seeking to uncover the 'decisive experiences' responsible for this shared structure (experiences which Heidegger hopes will help us to envision a path beyond) (Ian Thompson, "Ontotheology? Understanding Heidegger's *Destruktion* of Metaphysics," *International Journal of Philosophical Studies* 8, no. 3 [2000]: 323). On my reading, it is not the content of Aristotle's pre-metaphysical experience that Heidegger's destructive reading puts us in relation to, but the source of those experiences, which is in excess of those experiences.
6. We can hear something like this negative conception of destructive reading even in the title of Otto Pöggeler's essay, "Destruction and Moment," once we understand its significance. To my mind, Pöggeler compellingly presents Heidegger as taking up Husserl's phenomenological approach and the motto "To the things themselves!" but he insists that Heidegger came to hold that "these things (the phenomena of phenomenological philosophy) manifest themselves only in a process whose motivating core must constantly be reopened through destruction" (Pöggeler, "Destruction and Moment," in *Reading Heidegger from the Start*, ed. T. Kisiel and J. Van Buren, 137). This might suggest that destruction is a matter of merely casting off traditional influences in order to experience beings purely, directly in their emergence into appearance. I would like to suggest here that something more complex occurs in destructive reading than a simple escape from the tradition that would facilitate one's reception of the content of the *Augenblick* or "moment."
7. Hans-Georg Gadamer, "Die Marburger Theologie," in *Gesammelte Werke III: Neuere Philosophie I* (Tübingen: J. C. B. Mohr, 1987), 199. And there are a

NOTES TO PAGE 55

number of scholars who have recognized the fundamental ambivalence of destruction, as well as often remarking on the failure of previous scholarship to take that ambivalence seriously. See, for instance, Samuel IJsseling, who remarks: "Although Heidegger has on several occasions expressed himself with clarity concerning the meaning of destruction, the entire project nevertheless remains somewhat ambiguous. This ambiguity shows itself, as well, in the very term 'destruction,' which literally does mean something on the order of destroying. But, in fact, its intention is to be a structural analysis of the tradition" (IJsseling, "Heidegger and the Destruction of Ontology," 5). Or consider Robert Bernasconi: "What is often treated by commentators and critics straightforwardly as Heidegger's own philosophy is rather to be read under the rubric of repetition (*Wiederholung*). Repetition is never a simple reiteration of the past; it includes reconstructing the tradition to which each of us is said to belong. To the extent that reconstruction has been carried out successfully, it does not call for acceptance or rejection . . . What Heidegger calls 'destructuring' [Bernasconi's translation of *Destruktion*], and what is often talked about by commentators as if it was a disowning, is in fact an owning or appropriation (*Aneignung*) that is not separated from the constitution of the tradition" (Bernasconi, "Repetition and Tradition," 124). And Marlène Zarader observes: "The status of the Greeks, in the course of these years at Marburg, is ambiguous . . . [They are] both solicited and criticized at one and the same time" (Marlène Zarader, "The Mirror with the Triple Reflection," in *Critical Heidegger*, ed. C. Macann [London: Routledge, 1996], 10). Finally, as we will do below, Walter Brogan traces this ambivalence back to a division in Being itself, a feature of his interpretation that is evident right in the very title of his book: *Heidegger and Aristotle: The Twofoldness of Being*. Brogan writes, with characteristic lucidity: "Heidegger understands this deconstructive reading not only as an overcoming of the bias and prejudices that arise from an unclarified relationship to the past, but as a movement between destruction and retrieval. Hermeneutics not only dismantles the tradition, it also retrieves an authentic philosophical dimension of that tradition that tends to get covered over in the uncritical way in which the tradition is handed down. This double movement of destruction and retrieval is not to be understood as two separate stages of philosophical investigation, where one moves from the first task to the second, but as a belonging together and a reciprocity between these two tasks such that this double movement is itself Heidegger's way of returning to Aristotle" (Brogan, *Heidegger and Aristotle*, 6). In chapter 2 here, our task is simply to understand with more precision how this destructive "double movement" works, what its dynamic really is, and especially how Heidegger sees this ambivalence as grounded in a certain *krisis* within the Aristotelian text, and ultimately within Being itself as asked after by Aristotle.

8. Hannah Arendt, "Martin Heidegger at Eighty," trans. A. Hofstadter, *New York Review of Books* 17, no. 6 (October 21, 1971): 51. This piece was originally published in German. See Hannah Arendt, "Martin Heidegger ist achtzig Jahre alt," *Merkur* 10 (1969): 893–902. See John Van Buren, *Heidegger: Rumor of a Hidden King* (Bloomington: Indiana University Press, 1994).

9. Here one should be reminded that, after having fled the Germany of the

1930s and after having spent a couple of decades teaching at the New School for Social Research in New York, Marx returned to Germany and ultimately assumed Heidegger's own *Lehrstuhl* at the University of Freiburg in 1964. This would surely have given some added weight to Marx's interpretation of Heidegger's project. It is also of some interest to acknowledge that, whereas Gadamer and Arendt's nuanced understanding of a certain ambivalence in Heidegger's destructive interpretation of Aristotle arose from their direct experience of Heidegger's lecture courses, the relevant courses would not yet have been published at the time Marx came out with his assessment of a more univocally negative Heideggerian treatment of Aristotle. Werner Marx, *Heidegger und die Tradition* (Stuttgart: Kohlhammer, 1961) and *Heidegger and the Tradition*, trans. T. Kisiel and M. Greene (Evanston, IL: Northwestern University Press, 1961/1971).

10. Marx, *Heidegger and the Tradition*, 19/11.

11. Marx, *Heidegger and the Tradition*, 13/6. Under this interpretation, it must be admitted that Heidegger's project appears as, in a sense, hyper-modern, and thus, by his own lights, completely metaphysical. From Descartes to Nietzsche (at least in Heidegger's reading), quintessentially modern philosophers have aimed at escaping from or overcoming their tradition and establishing a new and completely distinct foundation for thinking. Does it really seem likely that Heidegger would undertake simply another iteration of that project of overcoming and moving definitively beyond the past, which he had so deeply criticized in modern philosophy?

12. Marx, *Heidegger and the Tradition*, 18/10.

13. Marx, *Heidegger and the Tradition*, 18/10.

14. For a discussion of the importance for Heidegger of inhabiting and thinking within this intermediary space between subject and object, and indeed in a way that produces a necessary redefinition of both poles in the relation, see my "Thinking in the Between with Heidegger and Plato," *Research in Phenomenology* 37, no. 1 (2007): 95–111.

15. For an excellent treatment of the philosophical import of Heidegger's distinction, see Graeme Nicholson, "The Ontological Difference," *American Philosophical Quarterly* 33, no. 4 (1996): 357–74.

16. Mark Wrathall offers a clarifying, if potentially misleadingly spatializing, account of the difference being discussed here. In a chapter entitled "Philosophers, Thinkers, and Heidegger's Place in the History of Being," Wrathall writes: "Metaphysics . . . is the attempt to think and name the being of what is. But because metaphysicians do not understand that there is a background, which is itself not a being, that constitutes the foreground as what it is, they interpret the unity of the foreground in terms of some uniform thing or feature in terms of which everything is what it is" (Mark A. Wrathall, *Heidegger and Unconcealment: Truth, Language, and History* [Cambridge: Cambridge University Press, 2011], 181). While I do find Wrathall's language of background and foreground initially helpful in beginning to think the distinction between Being as the withdrawn, inaccessible source of beings, and the Being of beings, that universal which is distributed over all beings, I worry that the insinuation of two distinct locations or sites is ultimately misleading. The Being that the later Heidegger will attempt to

capture as *Seyn* and *Ereignis*, or "Beyng" and "event, appropriative event," is not located in some other space outside of the dynamic emergence of present beings into their being what they are. It is in a sense right there in present beings, but withdrawn as the dynamic of their emergence.

17. In 1962, in the letter to William Richardson, Heidegger makes precisely this distinction between the Being of Beings and Being as such. As he discusses and ultimately approves of Richardson's title, *Through Phenomenology to Thought*, he writes that this will be an apt description of his development so long as "thought" there is "shorn of that ambiguity which allows it to cover on the one hand metaphysical thought (the thinking of the Being of beings) and on the other hand the Being-question, sc. the thinking of Being as such (the revealedness of Being) [*Denken des Seins als solchen* (*die Offenbarkeit des Seins*)]" (Richardson, *Heidegger: Through Phenomenology to Thought*, xiv–xv). I am suggesting here that, in the work of the early Heidegger's destructive reading, a very similar distinction is already in play, between the universal Being distributed over all beings and that initial and initiating, abidingly question-worthy Being that first calls for thinking with its momentous *Selbst-Offenbarung* or "self-revelation," "showing itself as that which is to-be-thought and as that which has want of a thought corresponding to it" (Richardson, *Heidegger: Through Phenomenology to Thought*, xvi–xvii).

18. That is, in the last line of the notes on the course taken down and later transcribed by Hermann Mörchen, and included as a kind of appendix in *Basic Concepts of Ancient Philosophy* (GA 22).

19. Kisiel and Sheehan, *Becoming Heidegger*, 153.

20. Although he is focused primarily on the later Heidegger, Michel Haar remarks, in his *Song of the Earth: Heidegger and the Grounds of the History of Being*: "The very development of the History of Being from the Greek *logos* to modern Technology does not exclude, but implies, a reserve, an opacity, a reverse side which can never be exhibited. It is this withdrawing, non-manifest dimension that makes History *destiny* and not the logical unfolding that, according to Hegel, is governed by an eternal necessity" (Michel Haar, *The Song of the Earth: Heidegger and the Grounds of the History of Being*, trans. R. Lilly [Bloomington: Indiana University Press, 1987/1993], 2). Here, in the early Heidegger, we are finding at least an initial inkling of such an inexhaustible and irremediably withdrawn source of the metaphysical tradition, to which Heidegger claims we can gain access through destruction and in relation to which we might begin to think as such, which is to say, not by exhibiting it or revealing it exhaustively, but by acknowledging the source in its resistance to any such modality of thinking.

21. Heidegger goes on here to explain in more detail what distinguishes his method from the Husserlian method he is explicitly appropriating: "We are thus adopting a central term of Husserl's phenomenology in its literal wording, though not in its substantive intent. *For Husserl*, phenomenological reduction, which he worked out for the first time expressly in the *Ideas Toward a Pure Phenomenology and Phenomenological Philosophy* (1913), is the method of leading phenomenological vision from the natural attitude of the human being whose life is involved in the world of things and persons back to the transcendental life of consciousness and its noetic-noematic experiences, in which objects are constituted

as correlates of consciousness. *For us* phenomenological reduction means leading phenomenological vision back from the apprehension of a being, whatever may be the character of that apprehension, to the understanding of the Being of that being" (*BPP* 21/29, translation modified).

22. Heidegger asserts here that phenomenological reduction, in this ontological and almost contra-Husserlian mode, was in a sense a method already practiced by the ancient Greeks, He writes: "while phenomenology certainly arouses lively interest today, what it seeks and aims at was already vigorously pursued in Western philosophy from the very beginning" (*BPP* 21/28).

23. Robert Bernasconi beautifully captures the radicality of this project in *Basic Concepts of Phenomenology*, writing that destruction "is more than genealogy. The tradition initially presents itself as an obstacle to questioning, because of its tendency to impart to certain concepts an aura of self-evidence. It becomes, in the course of Heidegger's analysis, the means by which that self-evidence gives access to what, concealed, underlies it. In other words, the tradition is found to give access to what at first it seemed to obscure. What it obscures is not a beginning, a historical origin, but the unthought as the space from which previous philosophers have thought" (Bernasconi, "Repetition and Tradition," 136).

Chapter 3

1. This particular moment of the seminar is recorded in two different locations. On the one hand, there is the primary text reproduced as the main text in volume 22 of the *Gesamtausgabe*, which is based on a photocopy of Heidegger's handwritten manuscript for the lecture course held at Marbach; and on the other hand, there are the transcribed notes on the course take by Hermann Mörchen, which are included in the *Gesamtausgabe* volume as an appendix. The remarks cited above, on the abidingly asystematic, open, or aporematic character of Aristotle's corpus, combine the two accounts. In the Mörchen transcription, Heidegger is reported saying: "To speak of Plato's philosophy as a system is out of the question. But that is not a drawback. Everything is open, under way, approach, obscure; which is precisely what makes it productive, leading further on. No system; instead actual work on the matters at issue. That is why such a philosophy is ageless. The meaning of scientific research is not to disseminate finished truth, but to pose genuine problems. That is also the character of Aristotle's philosophy, which is traditionally taken to be even more of a doctrinal edifice. Aristotle attempts to appropriate positively the impulses driving Plato's philosophy" (*BCAncP* 214/284–85).

2. Aristotle also allows for demonstrative scientific syllogisms to employ premises that are ultimately or manifestly grounded in the first principles of the science as well (*Top.* 100a26–30).

3. The relevant passages are *Top.* I.101a35–b5, *Phys.* I.184a1–23, *NE* VII.1145b2–20, and *Meta.* II.993a30–995a22.

4. On these sections of the *Topics* and the *Physics*, and on the usually misunderstood character of Aristotle's philosophical method, *dialektikê* (which must be distinguished from *apodeixis* or "demonstration," the method of *epistêmê* or "science," the production of scientific knowledge), see my "Dialectic and Proto-Phenomenology in Aristotle's *Topics* and *Physics*," *Proceedings of the Boston Area Colloquium in Ancient Philosophy* 29 (2014): 185–213.

5. Jaeger's landmark work was published just one year before Heidegger's deep engagement with Aristotle in *Basic Problems of Aristotelian Philosophy* in the summer semester of 1924, and it is clear that Heidegger had read seriously and internalized the book's developmental and ultimately anti-Scholastic interpretation. Heidegger already refers to this book on the second page of the lecture, as well as referring to Jaeger's 1912 work *Studien zur Enstehungsgeschichte der Metaphysik des Aristoteles*. Indeed, he tells his students: "As for Aristotle, his philosophy, and its development, you will find everything you need in the book of the classical philologist *Jaeger*" (*BCArP* 4/5). This remark is all the more striking insofar as Heidegger will go on in the very next paragraph to declare his own aim in the course as, strictly speaking, "philological," and thus as akin to Jaeger's. See Werner Jaeger, *Aristoteles: Grundlegung einer Geschichte seiner Entwicklung* (Berlin: Weidmann, 1923); and *Studien zur Enstehungsgeschichte der Metaphysik des Aristoteles* (Berlin: Weidmann, 1912).

6. One underappreciated complication in the discussion of the meaning of any given term for Aristotle, even leaving aside developmental changes, is the fact that Aristotelian philosophizing, which is alive and in action on the page of his texts, proceeds by *dialektikê* or "dialectic," which as we heard earlier he defines quite clearly as the bringing together in *logos* of *endoxa* or "trustworthy appearances" of a given subject matter, the clarification, analysis, and comparison of which produces the *archai* or "first principles" employed by an *epistêmê* or "science" like geometry (*Top.* 100a30–101b2). This means that, with respect to a given employment of a given term, Aristotle could be using it in the ordinary pre-philosophical sense, what everyone or most people think when they hear the term *ousia*, or in his technical philosophical sense, or anywhere on the spectrum of analysis and clarification that stretches between these two poles.

7. Indeed, Heidegger writes in the above-cited letter to William Richardson that it was primarily a thinking of *alêtheia* as "un-concealment" and *ousia* as the "presence" of present beings that launched him on the first phase of his career and to the raising of the question of Being (Richardson, *Heidegger: Through Phenomenology to Thought*, viii–xxiv).

8. This fundamental ontology was apparently passed down first into the medieval period, visible perhaps in the identification of "what is" as *ens creatum*, "created being," dependent on an ultimate *ens creator* or *increatum*, a "creator being" or an "uncreated being." It reverberates further through the Cartesian distinction between *res existensa* and *res cogitans*, the "extended thing" and the "thinking thing." It surely remains at work in Spinoza's all-unifying divine substance and in Leibniz's monadic ontology as well. It continues on through the empiricist conception of a unified mind or self, all the way down to the tran-

scendental subject as foundation of experience, which Kant and Husserl share. And it still, as I suggested in the "Introduction," sets the parameters within which we experience the world and ourselves today pre-philosophically and pre-scientifically.

9. In Heidegger's German, these translation options are as follows: *Vermögen* for "means," *Hab* and *Gut* for "possessions" and "goods," *Haushalt* for "property," and *Anwesen* for "estate."

10. Aristotle decides in favor of form and essence, declaring simply that *ousia*'s being identified with the materiality and brute there-ness of beings is ultimately "impossible [*adunaton*]" because, more than being the ontological foundation of all dependent qualities, quantities, relations, actions, and so on, "what *is* most of all," *ousia*, must be recognized as above all else a "this something [*tode ti*]." That is, what really seems *to be* in some authoritative and compelling, even if not yet fully clarified, sense is something localizable and unified, a *ti* or a "something" that can be gestured at or referred to by the demonstrative pronoun *tode* or "this." And furthermore, Aristotle continues, "what *is*" presses upon us as having the character of being "separate [*chôriston*]," as something sufficiently discrete and independent, distinguished from other beings and in possession of itself (*Meta.* VII.1029a26–30). It is then, on the basis of these compelling initial, pre-philosophical associations with "what *is* most of all," that Aristotle seems to define the concept of *ousia* as the essence, the form that endows a thing with this kind of unity, this-ness, and self-sufficiency, and he rejects the claim that *ousia* is what underlies all beings, all qualities, all determinations.

11. It should be noted here that my translation of this passage is open to some criticism. On the one hand, Heidegger's text is at this point in the lecture course even more than usually elliptical and difficult to parse. On the other hand, there is a fundamental question concerning how to render the verb "*verfahren*" here, which can mean simply "to proceed, handle something" or it can mean, as I have rendered it, "to go astray, miss the way," but then only when it occurs with the reflexive pronoun. The grammatical question here is whether the reflexive pronoun, which in fact occurs here in the first half of the sentence, before the verb "*verfängt*," can be taken as distributed over the verb in the second half of the sentence, "*verfährt*," as well. If so, the sentence would read, in as literal a translation as possible, Plato "catches himself up fantastically in *logos* and thereby, Greek-ly, consequently loses his way." If the reflexive pronoun is not distributed over the second verb, then the latter part of the sentence would read, Plato "catches himself up fantastically in *logos* and thereby, Greek-ly, proceeds consequentially." I would suggest that here, given the context in which Plato is in general being treated quite critically and compared unfavorably with Aristotle on precisely this point (namely, Plato's interpreting the Ideas as "what *is*" in a paradigmatic way and thereby turning away from the notion of Being that is destructively detectible in the immediate, pre-philosophical Greek experience of the material world), we have sufficient reason to conclude that Heidegger is suggesting that Plato loses his way here. However, this is not in fact required for the interpretation I am putting forward. Heidegger's general critical assessment of Plato's tendency toward abstraction here is sufficient to make the point, which is

that Aristotle exhibits an admirable counter-Platonic tendency toward acknowledging the ontological claim of beings in their brute concrete thereness.

12. Will McNeill, in his essay "From *Destruktion* to the History of Being," focuses on Heidegger's later abandonment of the project of "destruction" in favor of what he comes to refer to as a setting out of the "history of beyng." In the context of this later project, Heidegger himself sometimes attributes a certain "naiveté" to his earlier destructive approach to the history of metaphysics. McNeill argues that destruction, up to and including its presentation in *Being and Time*, was always intended to reveal not the historical facts of a given moment in the history of metaphysics, but always the temporalizing of Dasein according to which Being presents Dasein in any given historical moment with possibilities, the opening-up of certain ways of being. What destruction reveals, then, would be that futural openness with which Being presents Dasein and draws it into its future, and not at all Dasein's own subjectively rooted projection of a given identity or character in action. This would accordingly not seem so naive, for it would indeed already point to the non-subjectively grounded destining of Being on which the later Heidegger's "history of beyng" will insist. McNeill sees Heidegger's later self-critical remarks as directed at the presumption of destruction to reveal exhaustively the original sources or experiences from which the metaphysical identification of Being with presence emerged. That is, McNeill finds Heidegger diagnosing in his earlier method a certain misplaced epistemological presumptiveness. The later Heidegger insists that the study of the history of the metaphysical thinking of Being does not completely overcome or put aside the concealment of Being that occurred there, but confronts an insuperable because constitutive concealment that belongs to the revealing and destining dynamic of Being itself. I am completely convinced by McNeill's interpretation of Heidegger's own self-criticism. However, what I have been arguing here is that, nevertheless, there are moments in the destructive project set forth in the early lecture courses where Heidegger seems to suggest that philosophical thinking would properly acknowledge and incorporate, rather than vanquish, a certain aspect of question-worthiness in Being itself.

13. Only later in his career did Heidegger seem to become comfortable with the dialogue form, but even then more with producing them than reading and interpreting them in all their dramatic complexity. He at least seemed at certain points, for example, in *Country Path Conversations* (1944–45) or in the conversation with a Japanese interlocutor in *On the Way to Language* (1959), to come to appreciate the particular power of conversational discourse. Indeed, in a letter to his wife, Elfride, at the time of composition of the former of these, Heidegger mentions having promised years earlier to write a book on Plato and dedicate it to her. He then remarks: "Only from my own experience have I now understood Plato's mode of presentation [*Art der Darstellung*], and in some form or other the Plato book intended for you must one day become reality after all" (*MLS* 235).

14. These are two terms that Aristotle often seems to use interchangeably, and even declares to be either synonymous or tending toward synonymy at *Meta.* IX.1048b18–35.

15. As we noted at the very outset of this study, it is Franz Brentano's doc-

toral dissertation, *On the Several Senses of Being in Aristotle*, that Heidegger says he worked his way through several times as a student and which he credits with first raising in him the question of Being that would guide and motivate him throughout his career (Richardson, *Heidegger: Through Phenomenology to Thought*, x). And Brentano focuses on a passage very much like the one quoted here from Book Delta, where Aristotle rehearses the various ways in which something can be said to "be," including "being potentially" (*Meta.* VI.1026a32–b2).

16. To be sure, there is a part of the tradition working in Aristotle's wake throughout the Middle Ages, for instance certain Neoplatonists and Scholastics, who accept the ontologically legitimate status of *dunamis*.

17. See also Heidegger's extensive discussion of *dunamis* in his 1931 lecture course, *Aristotle's Metaphysics Θ.1–3: On the Essence and Actuality of Force*. The editor of that *Gesamtausgabe* volume, Heinrich Hüni, writes in his short accompanying essay: "The phenomenon of force or capability, which is discussed thoroughly in its variations, becomes the nucleus for splitting up the general Greek being-concept of presence" (*AM* 196/226).

18. See Brogan, who in *Heidegger and Aristotle* places a "twofoldness of Being" right at the center of Heidegger's reading of Aristotle.

19. After arguing for the notion of ontological *kinêsis* discussed above, Heidegger's text later on returns to *kinêsis* in its more technical Aristotelian sense, the sense of *kinêsis* that Aristotle opposes to the way *dunamis* and *energeia* relate to one another in a natural being's *einai* or simply "being" what it is (see in particular *BCArP* 213–17/315–21). Francisco Gonzalez criticizes this inconsistency in his essay on the 1924 course. Indeed, he problematizes a number of details of Heidegger's reading and ultimately calls for a rejection of Heidegger's basic claim that Aristotle shows himself to be a thinker of the metaphysics of presence. I agree with Gonzalez's fundamental point that Aristotle often seems to be experiencing and thinking beings in a way that that exceeds the constraints of the metaphysical reduction of being to presence. However, I think that the inconsistency Gonzalez finds in Heidegger's course on this point can be explained by clarifying whether what is being discussed is *kinêsis* in its technical Aristotelian sense, which is differentiated from *einai*, or the more expanded ontological notion of *kinêsis* that Heidegger is introducing here, to capture the indeterminacy, incompletion, absence, and non-being that constitute the way of being of natural beings. See Gonzalez, "Whose Metaphysics of Presence?"

20. Perhaps the mode of being of the individual piece of equipment in the analysis of *Being and Time* is possessed of a greater degree of absence, or a deeper aspect of non-presence, than I am crediting it with here (and in the note on "readiness-to-hand" in the "Introduction"). Nonetheless, the talk of the world to which the piece of equipment points as a *Verweisungsganzheit* or "referential totality" (*BT* §16) seems to indicate that although a given piece of equipment is what it is by reference to the whole, and thus to what it itself is not, there is a certain ultimate or projected completion and overcoming of that absence when the entire context is taken into account.

Conclusion

1. See here, for instance, the definition of "phenomenology" in 1924, in the *Sophist* lecture course, where Heidegger defines it in terms of a *legein* of *phainomena*, and then suggests that where we might learn "the phenomenological way of consideration" is "from the simple and original considerations of the Greeks," even if in "the present era, the phenomenological mode of thought was adopted explicitly for the first time in Husserl's *Logical Investigations*" (*PS* 6/8–9).

2. Surely the farthest territory reached in this flight from traditional philosophizing is Heidegger's attempt to think things as situated within, or in the light of, what he calls the *Geviert* or "fourfold" of the earth, the sky, divinities, and mortals. To my mind, the authoritative and most helpful treatment of this attempt is Andrew J. Mitchell, *The Fourfold: Reading the Later Heidegger* (Evanston, IL: Northwestern University Press, 2015).

3. Heidegger addresses the early method of destruction and finds it wanting in the 1973 "Zähringen Seminar" (*FS* 78/133). On the precise nature of that inappropriateness and naiveté, see William McNeill's interpretation in his "From *Destruktion* to the History of Being." And see, as well, McNeill's careful tracing of Heidegger's initial embrace, radicalization, and ultimate abandonment of the term "phenomenology" in *The Fate of Phenomenology: Heidegger's Legacy* (Lanham, MD: Rowman and Littlefield, 2020). Indeed, McNeill ends the book showing that, as the task of thinking becomes identified with what Heidegger will call in the "Zähringen Seminar" of 1973 "the phenomenology of the inapparent," Heidegger suggests (in some only recently published notes) the alternative term "*phenomenophasis*," something like a "saying of appearance" that is a tautological naming and letting appear of the inapparent ground of appearing, *as inapparent*, which Heidegger associates in these notes with Parmenides. This is, for McNeill, not so much a rejection of his mentor's method as it is a return to the Greek origin of Western philosophizing in this mode. McNeill writes: "Far from being a dismissal of Husserl, then, the instituting of phenomenophasis is in fact the retrieval and preservation of his central insight into Being as the self-showing of phenomena and its recognition as the fundamental trait of Greek, Western philosophical thinking—that trait from which science first emerges" (McNeill, *Fate of Phenomenology*, 128). What was inapparent in ancient Greek philosophizing is for the first time, McNeill suggests, being said and thought as such: "It seems likely that this remarkable Greek saying of Being, of the source or wellspring (πηγή) of unconcealment, was penned by Heidegger the Greek—the Greek who was more Greek than the Greeks themselves, venturing to think and to say the unthought of Greek philosophy" (McNeill, *Fate of Phenomenology*, 133). If this project involves a recovery (and radicalization) of what the early Heidegger calls "phenomenology," I would suggest it also involves a recovery of what he calls "destruction" as well.

4. I am thinking here for instance of the essay "Plato's Doctrine of Truth," first published in 1931 and then revised in 1940 and eventually published in 1967 in *Wegmarken* (GA 9), as well as of the four essays collected in David Farrell Krell's volume, *Early Greek Thinking: The Dawn of Western Philosophy*, which focus on Anaxi-

mander, Parmenides, and Heraclitus, and which were composed between 1943 and 1954. One sees the eventual stopping point of this trajectory in Heidegger's "The End of Philosophy and the Task of Thinking," a paper presented at a conference in Paris in 1964. Early on Heidegger seemed to see the texts of Plato as the moment in the history of Greek thought when the "forgetting of Being" occurs, when *alêtheia* or "unconcealment" became reduced to *orthotês* or "correctness," while the pre-Socratics like Heraclitus and Parmenides were thinking or at least experiencing things prior to metaphysics. But in this essay he declares that even for Parmenides truth was already correctness ("EPTT" 386–92).

5. Indeed, in entertaining the kind of thinking along with the beginning of our tradition that Heidegger believes the method of destruction enables, these lines might spring to mind from Hölderlin's "The Rhine" (which Heidegger of course treats in detail much later in his 1934-35 lecture course: "What springs forth purely is a riddle. Even/Song may barely unveil it. For/ As you began, so will you remain,/ However much necessity achieves,/ And cultivation, the most is accomplished by/ birth . . . (*Ein Rätsel ist Reinentsprungenes. Auch/ Der Gesang kaum darf es enthüllen. Denn/ Wie du anfingst, wirst du bleiben,/ So viel auch wirket die Not,/ Und die Zucht, das meist nämlich/ Vermag die Geburt . . .*" (47–51) (Friedrich Hölderlin, "Der Rhein," in *Sämtliche Werke, Bd. Vier: Gedichte 1800-1806*, ed. by N. v. Hellingrath [Berlin: Propyläen, 1923], 173.).

6. See my forthcoming essay, "Heidegger and Sophocles: Antigone's *Êthos* of Intimating and Waiting," for a treatment of the privileging of poetic discourse in Heidegger's treatment of Sophocles, in A. Benjamin, ed., *Heidegger and Literature* (Oxford: Oxford University Press, forthcoming).

7. Although I present the texts of this period as a more or less unified whole here, Daniela Vallega-Neu, in what is arguably the authoritative scholarly treatment of those texts, sees a shift in course or an intensification in the project, a "new beginning" (Daniela Vallega-Neu, *Heidegger's Poietic Writings: From "Contributions to Philosophy" to "The Event"* [Bloomington: Indiana University Press, 2018], 12), taking place between the *Contributions* (GA 65) and *On the Beginning* (GA 66).

8. In the "Genealogical Glossary of Heidegger's Basic Terms" offered as one of the appendixes of his seminal work, *The Genesis of Heidegger's "Being and Time,"* Theodore Kisiel writes the following of the term *Ereignis*, which he translates as "properizing event, appropriating event": It was "clearly destined from the start to be the central 'terminus technicus' of Heidegger's entire *Denkweg* to identify the course and 'primal leap' (*Ur-sprung*) of experience," even if the term "goes into a dormancy for almost a decade after its initial thematization [in 1919]." See Kisiel, *The Genesis of Heidegger's "Being and Time,"* 494–95.

9. Vallega-Neu refers to all the works of the period surrounding the *Contributions* as "poietic writings," indicating the, in a specific sense, creativity or inventiveness that is necessitated by the task of thinking beings from Being as *Ereignis* or "event." See Vallega-Neu, *Heidegger's Poietic Writings*.

10. A bit later, in 1949's "Question concerning Technology," we hear a similar point being made about this resonance between ancient and contemporary occurences of "incipient thinking": "To the human being, the incipiently early (*das anfängliche Frühe*) only shows itself in the end. Thus, in the realm of

thinking, any effort to think through the incipient thought ever more incipiently (*das anfängliche Gedachte noch anfänglicher zu durchdenken*) is not some absurd wish to revive the past, but instead a sober preparedness to wonder at the coming of the dawn" (QCT 303/26). Lovitt's translation has been modified to emphasize the presence and repetition here of the adjective '*anfänglich*,' 'initial, incipient.' Heidegger sometimes draws a technical distinction between the German terms *Ursprung*, *Beginn*, and *Anfang*, which might be rendered as, respectively, 'origin, originary leap,' 'beginning, start,' and 'beginning, inception.' For an excellent discussion of the differences between these terms in Heidegger's thinking, see the eighth chapter, entitled "Anfang and Ursprung: The Temporal Difference," of Reiner Schürmann's study of Heidegger, which is (Reiner Schürman, *Heidegger on Being and Acting: From Principles to Anarchy* [Bloomington: Indiana University Press, 1982/1987], 120–51).

Bibliography

Works by Heidegger in German

Heidegger, Martin. *Sein und Zeit.* Tübingen: Niemeyer, 1927/1993.
———. *Kant und das Problem der Metaphysik.* GA 3. Frankfurt am Main: Klostermann, 1929/1991.
———. *Holzwege.* GA 5. Edited by F.-W. von Herrmann. Frankfurt am Main: Klostermann, 1950/1994.
———. *Was heißt Denken?* Tübingen: Niemeyer, 1954.
———. "Die Frage nach der Technik." In *Vorträge und Aufsätze.* Tübingen: Niemeyer, 1954.
———. *Unterwegs zur Sprache.* Stuttgart: Neske, 1959.
———. *Wegmarken.* GA 9. Edited by F.-W. von Herrmann. Frankfurt am Main: Klostermann, 1967/1976.
———. *Zur Sache des Denkens.* GA 14. Edited by F.-W. von Herrmann. Frankfurt am Main: Klostermann, 1969/2007.
———. "Mein Weg in die Phänomenologie." In *Zur Sache des Denkens,* 81–90. 1969/2007.
———. *Zur Sache des Denkens.* Tübingen: Niemeyer, 1969.
———. *Die Grundprobleme der Phänomenologie.* GA 24. Edited by F.-W. von Herrmann. Frankfurt am Main: Klostermann, 1975/1997.
———. *Aristoteles, Metaphysik Θ1–3: Vom Wesen und Wirklichkeit der Kraft.* GA 33. Edited by H. Hüni. Frankfurt am Main: Klostermann, 1981.
———. *Die Grundbegriffe der Metaphysik.* GA 29/30. Edited by F.-W. von Herrmann. Frankfurt am Main: Klostermann, 1983.
———. *Die Frage nach dem Ding: Zu Kants Lehre von den transzendentalen Grundsätzen.* GA 41. Edited by P. Jaeger. Frankfurt am Main: Klostermann, 1984.
———. *Phänomenologische Interpretationen zu Aristoteles: Einführung in die phänomenologische Forschung.* GA 61. Edited by W. Bröcker and K. Bröcker-Oltmans. Frankfurt am Main: Klostermann, 1985.
———. *Seminare.* GA 15. Edited by C. Ochwadt. Frankfurt am Main: Klostermann, 1986.
———. *Beiträge zur Philosophie (Vom Ereignis).* GA 65. Edited by F.-W. von Herrmann. Frankfurt am Main: Klostermann, 1989.
———, and Elizabeth Blochmann. *Briefwechsel, 1918–1969.* Edited by J. W. Storch. Marbach am Neckar: Deutsche Schillergesellschaft, 1989.

---. *Platon: Sophistes*. GA 19. Edited by E. Schüßler. Frankfurt am Main: Klostermann, 1992.

---. *Grundbegriffe der antiken Philosophie*. GA 22. Edited by F.-K. Blust. Frankfurt am Main: Klostermann, 1993.

---. *Einführung in die phänomenologische Forschung*. GA 17. Edited by F.-W. von Herrmann. Frankfurt am Main: Klostermann, 1994.

---. *Phänomenologie des religiösen Lebens*. GA 60. Edited by M. Jung, T. Regehly, and C. Strube. Frankfurt am Main: Klostermann, 1995.

---. "Anhang: Mein bisheriger Weg." In *Besinnung* (1938/39). GA 66. Edited by F.-W. von Herrmann. Frankfurt am Main: Klostermann, 1997.

---. *Grundbegriffe der aristotelischen Philosophie*. GA 18. Edited by M. Michalski. Frankfurt am Main: Klostermann, 2002.

---. *Der Begriff der Zeit*. GA 64. Edited by F.-W. von Herrmann. Frankfurt am Main: Klostermann, 2004.

---. *Phänomenologische Interpretationen ausgewählter Abhandlungen des Aristototeles zur Ontologie und Logik*. GA 62. Edited by G. Neumann. Frankfurt am Main: Klostermann, 2005.

---. *Mein liebes Seelchen! Briefe Martin Heideggers an seine Frau Elfride, 1915–1970*. Edited by G. Heidegger. Munich: Deutsche Verlags-Anstalt, 2005.

---. *Identität und Differenz*. GA 11. Edited by F.-W. von Herrmann. Frankfurt am Main: Klostermann, 2006.

---. *Phänomenologie der Anschauung und des Ausdrucks*. GA 59. Edited by C. Strube. Frankfurt am Main: Klostermann, 2007.

---. *Vorträge. Teil 1: 1915–1932*. GA 80. Edited by G. Neumann. Frankfurt am Main: Klostermann, 2016.

Works by Heidegger in English

Heidegger, Martin. *Being and Time*. Translated by J. Macquarrie and E. S. Robinson. Oxford: Blackwell, 1962.

---. *What Is Philosophy?* Translated by W. Kluback and J. T. Wilde. New Haven, CT: College and University Press, 1968. (bilingual edition)

---. *What Is Called Thinking?* Translated by J. Glenn Gray. New York: Harper and Row, 1968.

---. *On the Way to Language*. Translated by P. Hertz and J. Stambaugh. New York: Harper and Row, 1971.

---. "My Way into Phenomenology." In *On Time and Being*, translated by J. Stambaugh. New York: Harper and Row, 1972.

---. *Early Greek Thinking*. Edited by D. F. Krell, translated by D. F. Krell and F. Carpuzzi. New York: Harper and Row, 1975.

---. "The Question concerning Technology." In *Basic Writings: From "Being and Time" (1927) to "The Task of Thinking" (1964)*, edited by D. F. Krell, translated by W. Lovitt. New York: Harper and Row, 1977.

———. *Basic Problems of Phenomenology*. Translated by A. Hofstadter. Bloomington: Indiana University Press, 1982.
———. *The Concept of Time*. Translated by William McNeill. Oxford: Blackwell, 1991.
———. *Aristotle's Metaphysics Θ1–3: On the Essence and Actuality of Force*. Translated by W. Brogan and P. Warnek. Bloomington: Indiana University Press, 1995.
———. *Fundamental Concepts of Metaphysics: World, Finitude, Solitude*. Translated by W. McNeill and N. Walker. Bloomington: Indiana University Press, 1995.
———. *Being and Time: A Revised Edition of the Stambaugh Translation*. Translated by J. Stambaugh and D. Schmidt. Albany: State University of New York Press, 1996/2010.
———. *Kant and the Problem of Metaphysics*. Translated by R. Taft. Bloomington: Indiana University Press, 1997.
———. *Plato's "Sophist."* Translated by R. Rojcewicz and A. Schuwer. Bloomington: Indiana University Press, 1997.
———. *Pathmarks*. Edited by W. McNeill. Cambridge: Cambridge University Press, 1998.
———. *Phenomenological Interpretations of Aristotle: Initiation into Phenomenological Research*. Translated by R. Rojcewicz. Bloomington: Indiana University Press, 2001.
———. *Off the Beaten Track*. Edited and translated by J. Young and K. Haynes. Cambridge: Cambridge University Press, 2002.
———. *Phenomenology of Religious Life*. Translated by M. Fritsche and T. Colony. Bloomington: Indiana University Press, 2004.
———. *Introduction to Phenomenological Research*. Translated by D. Dahlstrom. Bloomington: Indiana University Press, 2005.
———. "Phenomenological Interpretations with Respect to Aristotle: Indication of the Hermeneutical Situation." Translated by M. Bauer and T. Kisiel. In *Becoming Heidegger*, edited by T. Kisiel and T. Sheehan, 149–79. Evanston, IL: Northwestern University Press, 2007.
———. *Basic Concepts of Ancient Philosophy*. Translated by R. Rojcewicz. Bloomington: Indiana University Press, 2008.
———. *Basic Concepts of Aristotelian Philosophy*. Translated by R. Metcalf and M. Tanzer. Bloomington: Indiana University Press, 2009.
———. *Phenomenology of Intuition and Expression: Theory of Philosophical Concept Formation*. Translated by T. Colony. London: Continuum, 2010.
———. *The Concept of Time*. Translated by I. Farin. London: Continuum, 2011.
———. *Contributions to Philosophy: Of the Event*. Translated by R. Rojcewicz and D. Vallega-Neu. Bloomington: Indiana University Press, 2012.
———. "Zähringen Seminar." In *Four Seminars*, translated by A. J. Mitchell and F. Raffoul. Bloomington: Indiana University Press, 2012.

Works by Other Authors

Ahmed, Sara. *Queer Phenomenology: Orientations, Objects, Others*. Durham, NC: Duke University Press, 2006.

Arendt, Hannah. "Martin Heidegger at Eighty." Translated by A. Hofstadter. *New York Review of Books* 17, no. 6 (October 21, 1971).

———. "Martin Heidegger ist achtzig Jahre alt." *Merkur* 10 (1969): 893–902.

Bambach, Charles. *Heidegger, Dilthey, and the Crisis of Historicism*. Ithaca, NY: Cornell University Press, 1995.

Barash, Jeffrey Andrew. *Martin Heidegger and the Problem of Historical Meaning*. New York: Fordham University Press, 2003.

Bauer, Michael. "Translator's Preface to 'Phenomenological Interpretations with Respect to Aristotle: Indication of the Hermeneutical Situation.'" *Man and World* 25 (1992): 355–57.

Beauvoir, Simone de. *The Prime of Life: The Autobiography of Simone de Beauvoir, 1929–1944*. Translated by P. Green. New York: Harper Collins, 1960/1962.

———. *The Second Sex*. Edited and translated by H. M. Parshley. New York: Vintage, 1949/1989.

Benjamin, A., ed. *Heidegger and Literature*. Oxford: Oxford University Press (forthcoming).

Bernasconi, Robert. "Heidegger's Destruction of Phronesis." *Southern Journal of Philosophy* 28 (1989): 127–47.

———. *The Question of Language in Heidegger's History of Being*. Atlantic Highlands, NJ: Humanities, 1985.

———. "Repetition and Tradition: Heidegger's Destructuring of the Distinction between Essence and Existence in *Basic Problems of Phenomenology*." In *Reading Heidegger from the Start*, edited by T. Kisiel and J. Van Buren, 123–36. Albany: State University of New York Press, 1994.

Bernasconi, Robert, and David Wood. *Derrida and Difference*. Evanston, IL: Northwestern University Press, 1988.

Bernet, Rudolph. "The Limits of Conceptual Thinking." In *Phenomenology of Thinking*, edited by T. Breyer and C. Gutland, 147–64. New York: Routledge, 2016.

Blattner, William. "Heidegger's Kantian Idealism Revisited." *Inquiry: An Interdisciplinary Journal of Philosophy* 47, no. 4 (2004): 321–37.

———. *Heidegger's Temporal Idealism*. Cambridge: Cambridge University Press, 1999.

Brentano, Franz. *On the Several Senses of Being in Aristotle*. Translated by R. George. Berkeley: University of California Press, 1862/1977.

———. *Psychology from an Empirical Standpoint*. London: Routledge, 1874/1973.

Breyer, Thiemo, and Christopher Gutland, eds. *Phenomenology of Thinking: Philosophical Investigations into the Character of Cognitive Experiences*. New York: Routledge, 2016.

Brogan, Walter. *Heidegger and Aristotle: The Twofoldness of Being*. Albany: State University of New York Press, 2005.

BIBLIOGRAPHY

———. "The Place of Aristotle in the Development of Heidegger's Phenomenology." In *Reading Heidegger from the Start*, edited by T. Kisiel and J. Van Buren, 195–212. Albany: State University of New York Press, 1994.
Butler, Judith. *Gender Trouble: Feminism and the Subversion of Identity*. New York: Routledge, 1990.
Campbell, Scott. *The Early Heidegger's Philosophy of Life: Facticity, Being, and Language*. New York: Fordham University Press, 2012.
———. "Early Lecture Courses." In *The Bloomsbury Companion to Heidegger*, edited by E. Nelson and F. Raffoul, 179–84. London: Bloomsbury, 2013.
Cassin, Barbara, and Alain Badiou. *Heidegger: The Withdrawal of Being*. Translated by S. Spitzer. New York: Columbia University Press, 2010/2016.
Ciccareli, Pierpaolo. "Heideggers Destruktion der ontologischen Differenz." In *Denkspuren. Festschrift für Heinrich Hüni*, edited by O. Kosmus and F. Kurbacher, 169–83. Würzburg: Königshausen & Neumann, 2008.
Crowe, Benjamin D. *Heidegger's Religious Origins: Destruction and Authenticity*. Bloomington: Indiana University Press, 2006.
Dahlstrom, Daniel. "Heidegger's Method: Philosophical Concepts as Formal Indications." *Review of Metaphysics* 47, no. 4 (1994): 775–95.
Deleuze, Gilles. *Nietzsche and Philosophy*. Translated by H. Tomlinson. New York: Columbia University Press, 1962/1983.
Deleuze, Gilles, and Félix Guattari. *What Is Philosophy?* New York: Columbia University Press, 1991/1994.
Denker, A., et al., eds. *Heidegger und Aristoteles: Heidegger Jahrbuch 3*. Freiburg: Karl Alber, 2007.
Derrida, Jacques. *Athens, Still Remains*. Translated by P.-A. Brault and M. Naas. New York: Fordham University Press, 2010.
———. *Dissemination*. Translated by B. Johnson. Chicago: University of Chicago Press, 1972/1981.
———. "Letter to a Japanese Friend." Translated by A. Benjamin and D. Wood. In *Derrida and Difference*, edited by R. Bernasconi and D. Wood, 71–82. Evanston, IL: Northwestern University Press, 1988.
———. *Positions*. Translated by A. Bass. Chicago: University of Chicago Press, 1972/1981.
Dewan, L. "Obiectum: Notes on the Invention of a Word," *Archives d'Histoire Doctrinale et Littéraire de Moyen Age* 56 (1981): 37–96.
Dreyfus, Hubert. *Being-in-the-World: A Commentary on "Being and Time," Division 1*. Cambridge, MA: MIT Press, 1991.
Fanon, Frantz. *Black Skin, White Masks*. Translated by R. Philcox. New York: Grove, 1952/2008.
Figal, Günter. "Heidegger als Aristoteliker." In *Heidegger und Aristoteles*, edited by A. Denker et al., 53–76. Freiburg: Karl Alber, 2007.
Foran, Lisa, and Rozemund Uljée. *Heidegger, Levinas, Derrida: The Question of Difference*. New York: Springer, 2016.
Foucault, Michel. "Nietzsche, Genealogy, History." In *Language, Counter-Memory, Practice: Selected Essays and Interviews*, edited and translated by D. Bouchard, 139–64. Ithaca, NY: Cornell University Press, 1971/1977.

Gadamer, Hans-Georg. "Die Marburger Theologie." In *Gesammelte Werke III: Neuere Philosophie I*. Tübingen: J. C. B. Mohr, 1987.

———. "Martin Heidegger's One Path." Translated by P. C. Smith. In *Reading Heidegger from the Start*, edited by T. Kisiel and J. Van Buren, 19–34. Albany: State University of New York Press, 1994.

———. *Truth and Method*. Translated by J. Weisheimer and D. G. Marshall. London: Continuum, 1975/1989.

Golob, Sacha. *Heidegger on Concepts, Freedom and Normativity*. Cambridge: Cambridge University Press, 2014.

Gonzalez, Francisco. "The Birth of *Being and Time*: Heidegger's Pivotal 1921 Reading of Aristotle's *On the Soul*." *Southern Journal of Philosophy* 56, no. 2 (2018): 216–39.

———. "Whose Metaphysics of Presence: Heidegger's Interpretation of *Energeia* and *Dunamis* in Aristotle." *Southern Journal of Philosophy* 44, no. 4 (2006): 533–68.

Granger, E. H. "Aristotle on Genus and Differentia." In *Essays in Ancient Greek Philosophy V: Aristotle's Ontology*, edited by A. Preus, 69–93. Albany: State University of New York Press, 1992.

Günther, H. C., and A. Rengakos, eds. *Heidegger und die Antike*. Munich: Beck, 2006.

Haar, Michel. *The Song of the Earth: Heidegger and the Grounds of the History of Being*. Translated by R. Lilly. Bloomington: Indiana University Press, 1987/1993.

Hatab, Lawrence. "The Point of Language in Heidegger's Thinking: A Call for the Revival of Formal Indication." *Gatherings* 6 (2016): 1–22.

Heisenberg, W. "Grundlegende Voraussetzungen in der Physik der Elementarteilchen." In *Martin Heidegger zum Siebzigsten Geburstag*, edited by G. Neske, 291–97. Pfüllingen: Neske, 1959.

Held, Klaus. "Fundamental Moods and Heidegger's Critique of Contemporary Culture." Translated by A. J. Steinbock. In *Reading Heidegger*, edited by J. Sallis, 286–303. Bloomington: Indiana University Press, 1993.

Henning, E. M. "Destruction and Repetition: Heidegger's Philosophy of History." *Journal of European Studies* 12, no. 48 (1982): 260–82.

Hölderlin, Friedrich. "Der Rhein." In Sämtliche Werke. Bd. Vier: Gedichte 1800–1806, 47–51. Edited by N. v. Hellingrath. Berlin: Propyläen, 1923

Husserl, Edmund. *The Cartesian Meditations: An Introduction to Phenomenology*. Translated by D. Cairns. The Hague: Martinus Nijhoff, 1931/1960.

———. *The Crisis of the European Sciences and Transcendental Phenomenology*. Translated by D. Carr. Evanston, IL: Northwestern University Press, 1936/1970.

Hyland, Drew, and J. P. Manoussakis, eds. *Heidegger and the Greeks*. Bloomington: Indiana University Press, 2006.

IJsseling, Samuel. "Heidegger and the Destruction of Ontology." *Man and World* 15 (1982): 3–16.

Irigaray, Luce. *The Forgetting of Air in Martin Heidegger*. Translated by M. B. Mader. Austin: University of Texas Press, 1983/1989.

Jaeger, Werner. *Aristoteles: Grundlegung einer Geschichte seiner Entwicklung*. Berlin: Weidmann, 1923.

———. *Studien zur Enstehungsgeschichte der Metaphysik des Aristoteles.* Berlin: Weidmann, 1912.
Kant, Immanuel. *Critique of Pure Reason.* Translated by N. K. Smith. New York: St. Martin's, 1781/1965.
Kierkegaard, Søren. *The Concept of Irony.* Edited and translated by E. Hong and H. Hong. Princeton, NJ: Princeton University Press, 1841/1989.
Kirkland, Sean D. "Dialectic and Proto-Phenomenology in Aristotle's *Topics* and *Physics.*" *Proceedings of the Boston Area Colloquium in Ancient Philosophy*, vol. 29 (2014): 185–213.
———. "Heidegger and Sophocles: Antigone's *Êthos* of Intimating and Waiting." In *Heidegger and Literature*, ed. A Benjamin (forthcoming).
———. *The Ontology of Socratic Questioning in Plato's Early Dialogues.* Albany: State University of New York Press, 2012.
———. "Thinking in the Between with Heidegger and Plato." *Research in Phenomenology* 37, no. 1 (2007): 95–111.
Kisiel, Theodore. *The Genesis of Heidegger's "Being and Time."* Berkeley: University of California Press, 1995.
———. *Heidegger's Way of Thought.* Edited by A. Denker and M. Heinz. New York: Continuum, 2002.
Kisiel, Theodore, and Thomas Sheehan, eds. *Becoming Heidegger: On the Trail of His Occasional Writings, 1919–1927.* Evanston, IL: Northwestern University Press, 2007.
Kisiel, Theodore, and John Van Buren, eds. *Reading Heidegger from the Start: Essays in his Earliest Thought.* Albany: State University of New York Press, 1994.
Lorde, Audre. *Sister Outsider.* Berkeley, CA: Crossing, 1984/2007.
Macann, Christopher, ed. *Critical Heidegger.* London: Routledge, 1996.
Maly, Kenneth. "To Re-Awaken the Matter of Being: A Review of *Sein und Zeit. Gesamtausgabe Bd. 2* by Martin Heidegger." *Research in Phenomenology* 7, "Heidegger Memorial Issue" (1977): 282–98.
Marx, Werner. *Heidegger und die Tradition.* Stuttgart: Kohlhammer, 1961.
———. *Heidegger and the Tradition* Translated by T. Kisiel and M. Greene. Evanston, IL: Northwestern University Press, 1961/1971.
Massie, Pascal. "Review of *How History Matters to Philosophy.*" *Philosophy Today* 62, no. 2 (Spring 2018): 653–60.
McNeill, William. *The Fate of Phenomenology: Heidegger's Legacy.* Lanham, MD: Rowman and Littlefield, 2020.
———. "From *Destruktion* to the History of Being." *Gatherings* 2 (2012): 24–40.
———. *The Glance of the Eye: Heidegger, Aristotle, and the Ends of History.* Albany: State University of New York Press, 1999.
———. *The Time of Life: Heidegger and Êthos.* Albany: State University of New York Press, 2006.
Michelfelder, Diane P., and Richard E. Palmer, eds. *Dialogue and Deconstruction: The Gadamer-Derrida Encounter.* Albany: State University of New York Press, 1989.
Mitchell, Andrew J. *The Fourfold: Reading the Later Heidegger.* Evanston, IL: Northwestern University Press, 2015.

Moran, Dermot. "The Early Heidegger." In *The Bloomsbury Companion to Heidegger*, edited by E. Nelson and F. Raffoul, 23–30. London: Bloomsbury, 2013.
Naas, Michael. *Taking on the Tradition: Jacques Derrida and the Legacies of Deconstruction*. Stanford, CA: Stanford University Press, 2002.
Nancy, Jean-Luc. *The Banality of Heidegger*. Translated by J. Fort. New York: Fordham University Press, 2017.
Nelson, Eric, and Francois Raffoul, eds. *The Bloomsbury Companion to Heidegger*. London: Bloomsbury, 2013.
Neske, G., ed. *Martin Heidegger zum Siebzigsten Geburstag*. Pfüllingen: Neske, 1959.
Nicholson, Graeme. "The Ontological Difference." *American Philosophical Quarterly* 33, no. 4 (1996): 357–74.
Nietzsche, Friedrich. *The Gay Science*. Edited by B. Williams, translated by J. Nauckhoff and A. del Caro. Cambridge: Cambridge University Press, 1882, 1887/2001.
———. "On the Utility and Liability of History for Life." In *Unfashionable Observations: The Complete Works of Friedrich Nietzsche*, vol. 2, translated by R. T. Gray. Stanford, CA: Stanford University Press, 1874/1997.
———. *Sämtliche Werke: Kritische Studienausgabe* (*KSA*). Vols. 1–15. Edited by G. Colli and M. Montinari. Berlin: De Gruyter, 1967–77/1988.
Palmquist, S. R. "Six Perspectives on the Object in Kant's Theory of Knowledge." *Dialectica* 40, no. 2 (1986): 121–51.
Pöggeler, Otto. "Destruction and Moment." In *Reading Heidegger from the Start*, edited by T. Kisiel and J. Van Buren, 137–56. Albany: State University of New York Press, 1994.
———, ed. *Heidegger: Perspektiven zur Deutung seines Werks*. Cologne: Verlag Kiepenheuer & Witsch, 1970.
———. "The Hermeneutics of the Technological World: The Heidegger-Heisenberg Dispute." Translated by M. Kane and K. Pfefferkorn-Forbath. *International Journal of Philosophical Studies* 1, no. 1 (1993): 21–48.
Preus, A., ed. *Essays in Ancient Greek Philosophy V: Aristotle's Ontology*. Albany: State University of New York Press, 1992.
Reicher, M., and J. Marek, eds. *Experience and Analysis*. Kirchberg am Wechsel: Austrian Ludwig Wittgenstein Society, 2004.
Reill, Peter H. *The German Enlightenment and the Rise of Historicism*. Berkeley: University of California Press, 2018.
Reynolds, Joel Michael. "Heidegger, Embodiment, Disability." *Epoché* 26, no. 1 (2021): 183–201.
Richardson, William. *Heidegger: Through Phenomenology to Thought*. The Hague: Martinus Nijhoff, 1963.
Ricoeur, Paul. *Freud and Philosophy: An Essay on Interpretation*. Translated by D. Savage. New Haven, CT: Yale University Press, 1965/1970.
Rothacker, Erich, ed. *Briefwechsel zwischen Wilhelm Dilthey und dem Grafen Yorck v. Wartenburg*. Halle: Max Niemeyer, 1923.
Sallis, John, ed. *Reading Heidegger: Commemorations*. Bloomington: Indiana University Press, 1993.
Sampath, Rajesh. "The 1924 Lecture 'The Concept of Time' as the Step beyond

Being and Time (1927) and after Deconstruction." In *Heidegger, Levinas, Derrida*, edited by L. Foran and R. Uljée, 149–62. New York: Springer, 2016.
Scharff, Robert. *Heidegger Becoming Phenomenological: Interpreting Husserl through Dilthey, 1916–1925*. New York: Rowman and Littlefield, 2019.
———. *How History Matters to Philosophy: Reconsidering Philosophy's Part after Positivism*. New York: Routledge, 2015.
Schear, Joseph K. *Mind, Reason, and Being-in-the-World: The MacDowell-Dreyfus Debate*. New York: Routledge, 2013.
Schulz, Walter. "Über den philosophiegeschichtlichen Ort Martin Heideggers." In *Heidegger*, edited by O. Pöggeler, 95–139. Cologne: Verlag Kiepenheuer & Witsch, 1970.
Schürmann, Reiner. *Heidegger on Being and Acting: From Principles to Anarchy*. Bloomington: Indiana University Press, 1982/1987.
Searle, John. "The Phenomenological Illusion." In *Experience and Analysis*, edited by M. Reicher and J. Marek, 17–36. Kirchberg am Wechsel: Austrian Ludwig Wittgenstein Society, 2004.
Sheehan, Thomas, ed. *Heidegger: The Man and the Thinker*. Chicago: Precedent, 1981.
———. "Heidegger, Aristotle, and Phenomenology." *Philosophy Today* 19 (Summer 1974): 87–94.
———. "Heidegger's Early Years: Fragments for a Philosophical Biography." In *Heidegger: The Man and the Thinker*, edited by T. Sheehan, 3–19. Chicago: Precedent, 1981.
Spanos, William V. *Heidegger and Criticism: Retrieving the Cultural Politics of Destruction*. Minneapolis: University of Minnesota Press, 1993.
Stambaugh, Joan. "Translator's Preface." In Heidegger, *Being and Time*, translated by J. Stambaugh and D. Schmidt, xxiii–xxvi. Albany: State University of New York Press, 1996/2010.
Thanassas, Panagiotis. "*Phronesis* vs. *Sophia*: On Heidegger's Ambivalent Aristotelianism." *Review of Metaphysics* 66 (September 2012): 31–59.
Thompson, Ian. "Ontotheology? Understanding Heidegger's *Destruktion* of Metaphysics." *International Journal of Philosophical Studies* 8, no. 3 (2000): 297–327.
Toombs, S. Kay. "The Lived Experience of Disability." *Human Studies* 18, no. 1 (Jan. 1995): 9–23.
Trawny, Peter. *Freedom to Fail: Heidegger's Anarchy*. Translated by I. A. Moore and C. Turner. Cambridge: Polity, 2014/2015.
———. *Heidegger and the Myth of a Jewish World Conspiracy*. Translated by A. J. Mitchell. Chicago: University of Chicago Press, 2014/2016.
Vallega-Neu, Daniela. *Heidegger's Poietic Writings: From "Contributions to Philosophy" to "The Event."* Bloomington: Indiana University Press, 2018.
Van Buren, John. *Heidegger: Rumor of a Hidden King*. Bloomington: Indiana University Press, 1994.
———. "Heidegger's Early Freiburg Courses, 1915–1923." *Research in Phenomenology* 23, no. 1 (1993): 132–52.

Vetter, Helmuth. "Heideggers Destruktion der Tradition am Beispiel des Aristoteles." In *Heidegger und Aristoteles*, edited by A. Denker et al., 77–95. Freiburg: Karl Alber, 2007.
Volpi, Franco. *"Being and Time*: A 'Translation' of the *Nicomachean Ethics*?" In *Reading Heidegger from the Start*, edited by T. Kisiel and J. Van Buren, 195–213. Albany: State University of New York Press, 1994.
Warren, Calvin. *Ontological Terror: Blackness, Nihilism, Emancipation*. Durham, NC: Duke University Press, 2018.
Weisheimer, Joel, and Donald Marshall. "Translators' Preface." In *Truth and Method*, by H.-G. Gadamer, xi–xix. London: Continuum, 1975/1989.
Wilderson, Frank B., III. *Afropessimism*. New York: Norton, 2020.
Winnubst, Shannon. "Temporality in Queer Theory and Continental Philosophy." *Philosophy Compass* 5, no. 2 (2010): 136–46.
Wittgenstein, Ludwig. *Tractatus Logic-Philosophicus*. Translated by C. K. Ogden. New York: Routledge, 1922.
Wrathall, Mark A. *Heidegger and Unconcealment: Truth, Language, and History*. Cambridge: Cambridge University Press, 2011.
Zarader, Marlène. 1996. "The Mirror with the Triple Reflection." In *Critical Heidegger*, edited by C. Macann, 7–27. London: Routledge, 1996.

Index

absence (*Abwesenheit*), 24; and the *dunamis* of natural beings, 104–6, 150n19; and equipment in *Being and Time*, 150n20
adequatio intellectus et rei. *See* truth
aitia, 84, 85
alêtheia, 93–95; as verb *alêtheuein*, 93; in relation to *logos* and *dêloun*, 95–96
ambivalence, in destructive method, 4, 54–55, 118, 142n7, 143n9; in the Aristotelian text, 69–71, 89; in Being itself, 142n7; in language, 40; at threshold of conceptuality, 43–44
animal. *See zôê*
antisemitism, x–xi
apodeixis, 81–82
archê, 85, 101
Aristotelian corpus, 15, 81; *Cat.*, 16, 83–84; *De int.*, 95; *Meta.*, 16, 21, 36, 83–85, 89–90, 100, 130n21, 146n3, 148n10, 149n14; *EN*, 93, 146n3; *Phys.*, 16, 82, 84, 101–2, 104, 146n3; *Pol.*, 93; *Post. An.*, 36, 39, 81–82, 140n8; *Top.*, 81–82, 146n3, 147n6
attunement (*Stimmung*), 20–22, 134n36; the mood evoked at the opening of *Being and Time*, 6–7, 50. *See also* distress (*Not*)
beginning (*Anfang*), first beginning, other beginning, 115–17, 152n.10; inceptual thinking (*anfängliches Denken*), 114–16
Being (*Sein*), xii–xiii, 7–8, 126n13; metaphysical vs. extra-metaphysical xii–xiii; and Dasein, 8–12; of beings, 8–9; forgetting the question of, 6–8, 11–12, 21–22, 110, 123n11, 151n4; as unthought, 66–67; as forgotten already among the Pre-Socratics, 151n4. *See also* event

Brentano, Franz, 124n2, 134n33, 149n15
canonical texts, ix, 24
colonialism, ix–x
concepts (*Begriffe*), as beyond definition, 32–33; in their conceptuality (*Begrifflichkeit*), 32–35 philosophy as creating concepts, 116, 139n6; experiential ground of, 40–42
co-philosophizing (*Mitphilosophieren*), 48, 79, 118, 139n6; with Aristotle, 65
co-understanding (*Mitverstehen*), 62, 63, 75
critical science, 45–47, 75, 92; philosophy as, 58–67
creative investigation (*schöpferische Forschung*), 69; into Being, 98–99; in later Heidegger, 152n9

Dasein, 11, 128n14; as site for the disclosure of Being, 19–20, 72–74, 134n34; and everydayness12, 18, 129n16; essential historicality of, 13, 14, 30–31, 46, 128n15; and intentionality, 126n13; Greek ontology and contemporary Dasein, 140n9
definition, Kant on definition, 35, 37–38; Aristotle on definition, 38–40, 140n8
Deleuze, Gilles, philosophy as creating concepts, 139n6; on Nietzschean genealogy, 135n40
dêloun, 95–96
Derrida, Jacques, 23–25, 121n4, 135n41
Descartes, René, 18–19, 82, 132n30, 144n11; and the subject-object split, 18–20
dialektikê, in Aristotle, 81–82
Dilthey, Wilhelm, 45–46, 141n12; the Dilthey-Yorcke correspondence, 128n15

165

INDEX

distress (*Not*), 2–7, 21
dunamis, 99–107, 150n17, 150n19

ecstasis, ecstatic being, 10–11, 105, 128n15
Einstein, Albert, 17
empiricism, 20
endoxa, 81–82, 147n6
energeia, 100, 102
entelecheia, 100
epochê, 18–19
equipment, 105, 150n20
Eurocentrism, ix
event (*Ereignis*), xii–xiii, 126n13; the event-like emergence of beings into appearance, 89; conceptuality and event-like emergence, 34; as ontological dynamism, 114; creativity in thinking Being as event-like emergence, 115; as self-eclipsing, 114, 117, 134n35; the event of Being as "nothing" in the disclosure of beings, xii–xii, 60, 105–6, 123n11, 144n16
excess, Being as excess in beings, xii, 12, 68–69, 74–75, 98–99, 111, 115; concept as in excess of definition, 32; thinking in excess of metaphysics, 44, 101–2, 110; excess belonging to the Aristotelian text, 54, 71, 135n40
existence (*Eksistenz*), 10–11
experience, 18–19, 36; and attunement, 21–22; and definition, 38; versus concept in Aristotle's text, 39–40, 41–42, 43–44
fallenness (*Verfallenheit*), 12–13, 20, 135n46
forgetting of Being. *See* Being

Gadamer, Hans-Georg, 54–5, 131n3, 141n11, 142n7, 143n9
ground (*Grund, Boden*), 24, 38, 71; fundamental concepts (*Grundbegriffe*), 32
Guattari, Félix, on philosophy as creating concepts, 139n6

Hegel, G. W. F., 17
historicality, 5, 6, 11–12, 128n15, 130n18
historicism, xi, 51–52, 122n8
history of philosophy, 48

hulê, 90–92
Hüni, Heinrich, 150n17
hupokeimenon, 90–92
Husserl, Edmund, Heidegger's critiques of, 3, 18–20, 45–46, 73–74, 99, 108–9, 124n2, 132n27, 142n6, 145n21, 151n1151n3; on Heidegger's early development, 30, 138n2;

imperialism, ix–x
inceptual thinking (*anfängliches Denken*). *See* beginning
incompletion, 98, 99, 102–3, 113–14
indeterminacy, 9, 104, 150n19
intelligibility, 20, 34, 35, 41–42, 43, 65, 83, 88, 90–91, 102, 106,
intentionality, 19, 127n13, 134n33

Jaeger, Werner, 83, 147n5
Jaspers, Karl, 15, 128n15

Kant, Immanuel, 18–19, 35–38, 132n30, 133n31, 140n7, 147n8
Kierkegaard, Soren, 122n6
kinêsis, 100–104, 150n19
krisis, 57; in critical science, 45–46; in questioning, 57, 78; double *krisis* in Being, 63–65, 68–69; in the Aristotelian text, 63–66

language, 95–97
laying beyond (*hinausliegend*), 64–65; Being beyond appearances, 18, 28; beyond beings, 42, 65, 73, 75–78, 80, 98, 99, 109, 112, 113; beyond the concept, 58–59; beyond definition, 31–34, 38; beyond experience, 59, 65; beyond science, 99; beyond the Aristotelian text, 54, 70–71
Leibniz, Gottfried Wilhelm, 17, 147
Locke, John, 17
logic, 46–47; Aristotelian versus modern mathematical, 16
logos, 93–99
love. *See philosophia*

Marx, Karl, ix
Marx, Werner, 55–58
materiality, 90–92

metaphysics of presence, xii–xiii, 12–15, 33; temporal presence, 13–14; epistemological presence, 14; Aristotle as inaugurating figure, 40, 100, 103, 123n1, 150n19
mood. *See* attunement

Natorp, Paul, 30
nature. *See phusis*
Nietzsche, Friedrich, ix, xi, 12, 22–23, 25, 51–52, 110
National Socialism, x–xi
neoplatonism, 150
Newton, Isaac, 106, 17
non-being, 150
non-presence, 102–6
nothing, the, 105–6, 123n11

ontological difference, 9–11, 43–44, 61, 126n12, 144n15
origin (*Ursprung*), 25, 26, 29, 38, 50, 49, 77, 87, 136n47; originary experience, 28, 43, 53, 139n6; originary sources (*ursprüngliche Quellen*), 53, 116; original repetition, 69; in Nietzsche, 134n38, 135n40
ousia, 16, 104; contemporary relevance of Aristotelian substance ontology, 15–17

particular, the, 35–36
passion (*Leidenschaft*), 48–9, 112, 141n15; in philology, 47–48
phenomenology, 3, 18–20, 45–46, 71–78, 108–9; Aristotle as proto-phenomenological vii, 81–83, 146n4, reduction, 73–74, construction, 74–76, destruction, 76–77; post-Heideggerian, 123n9; as practiced already by the ancient Greeks, 146n22. *See also epochê*
philology, 47, 147n5; and passion, 47–48; in Nietzsche, 51
philosophia, 98–99; *philein* as essential to thinking Being, 113
philosophical method, 81–82
phusis, 64, 84–85; in Nietzsche, 23
Plato, 98–99, 146n1; Platonic Idea, 13, 81, 91; versus Aristotle, 81, 93–94, 98–99

Platonic corpus, xi, 40, 99, 113, 149n13; early aporetic dialogues, 121n1; *L*, 108; *Phdr.*, 135n44; *R*, 91; *Soph.*, 6
poetry, 110
pragma, 105
presence-at-hand (*Zuhandenheit*), 107, 126n13
Pre-Socratics, 98–99, 110, 151n4

questioning, xii, 19–20; as retained in thinking itself, 57, 64–65, 66, 113, 114–15; in the Aristotelian text, 67–69, 81–83, 89; as focus of destructive method, 28–29, 46, 63, 64–65, 80, 141n14

radicality, 45, 108, 123n11, 151n3; and *radix*, 60, 67, 125n4
rationalism, 20
readiness-to-hand (*Vorhandenheit*), 126n13, 150n20
Ricoeur, Paul, ix

school of suspicion, ix
scholasticism, 81, 147n5, 149n16
Scotus, Duns, 3
Socrates, 40, 135n44
Spinoza, Baruch, 17, 147
sterêsis, 103
substance. *See ousia*

telos, 100, 104; teleology, 100
temporality, 5, 6, 8, 128n15; tragic temporality vii; ecstatic temporality, 10
Thomas of Erfuhrt, 3
to kath' hekaston, 35–36, 140n7
to katholou, 35–36, 140n7
trace (*Spur*), 117; trace in questioning, 64–65, 78; traces of excess in the Aristotelian text, 69, 80, 85–86, 98, 106, 112, 118
tradition, viii–xi, 4, 11–13, 17, 53, 77, 78–79, 110, 117–18, 125n5, 141n10, 143n7, 146n23; traditionary text (*Überlieferung*), 121n3; versus the "past," 4–5, Werner Marx and tradition, 55–58; and historicality, 128n15
transcendental idealism, 20; versus realism, 126n13, 133n31, 134n

truth, 72–74, 93–95; as *alêtheia* (disclosure), 72–73; as *adequatio*, 72, 95, 133n31

universal, the, 35–36

world, 10; Dasein as being-in-the-world, 10; worldliness, 96–97

zôê, 96–97

zôon logon echon, 93–99, 110

www.ingramcontent.com/pod-product-compliance
Lightning Source LLC
Chambersburg PA
CBHW020857020526
44107CB00076B/1934